MILTON FRIEDMAN

Milton Friedman

A GUIDE TO
HIS ECONOMIC THOUGHT

*

EAMONN BUTLER

UNIVERSE BOOKS
NEW YORK

Published in the United States of America in 1985
by Universe Books
381 Park Avenue South, New York, N.Y. 10016

85 86 87 88 89 / 10 9 8 7 6 5 4 3 2 1

Printed in Great Britain

Library of Congress Cataloging in Publication Data

Butler, Eamonn.
    Milton Friedman.

        Bibliography: p.
        Includes index.
        1. Friedman, Milton, 1912–   —Contributions in economics.
        2. Economics—History.   3. Monetary policy—History.
        I. Title.
HB119.F84B88   1985   330′.092′4   85-9020
ISBN 0-87663-476-5
ISBN 0-87663-878-7 (pbk.)

Contents

Preface   vii

PART 1: FRIEDMAN IN CONTEXT

Chapter 1:   Friedman's place in the history of economic
              thought   3
Chapter 2:   Friedman and the quantity theory of money:
              an overview   25

PART 2: MONEY AND INFLATION

Chapter 3:   Velocity and the demand for money   53
Chapter 4:   The supply of money   67
Chapter 5:   The empirical evidence   91

PART 3: QUESTIONS FOR THEORY AND POLICY

Chapter 6:   The causes and nature of inflation   113
Chapter 7:   Inflation and unemployment   133
Chapter 8:   The lag and business cycles   149
Chapter 9:   Keynesian versus monetarist economic policy   161
Chapter 10: The role of monetary policy   175

PART 4: MARKETS AND METHODS

Chapter 11: Friedman the market economist   197
Chapter 12: Methodological issues   227

Notes   247
Select bibliography   263
Index   267

Preface

MILTON FRIEDMAN, with whom modern 'monetarism' has come to be identified, is a remarkably prolific writer. But, unfortunately for those wishing to gain an overall impression of his work and its importance, his writings are to be found in diverse places and are pitched at every level, from the most technical to the most popular. To attempt to get an overall appreciation of Friedman's theories is therefore difficult, because it requires the reader to skip across different volumes and to adjust to very different levels of difficulty.

Yet a patchy appreciation of Friedman's work, based on only a small portion of his large output, is necessarily misleading, particularly when popularists are prone to caricature his opinions. In consequence, it seemed to me that there was a strong need for a one-volume work which would outline the main points of his theories and the criticisms that have been ranged against them, and which would draw from Friedman's technical as well as popular presentations, distilling them into a coherent whole on a digestible level. I hope that this book will be a useful guide not only to the student of monetary economics, but to the intelligent layman who has been captivated by Friedman's ideas and wants to know more.

Thanks go to those at the Adam Smith Institute who have helped and advised on this work: Mr Warren Bourne, Miss Jennie Hunt and Dr Madsen Pirie.

Eamonn Butler
The Adam Smith Institute
January 1985

PART 1: FRIEDMAN IN CONTEXT

CHAPTER ONE

Friedman's Place in the History of Economic Thought

There is a standard pattern. When anybody threatens
an orthodox position, the first reaction is to ignore
the interloper. The less said about him the better.
But if he begins to win a hearing and gets annoying,
the second reaction is to ridicule him, make fun of
him as an extremist, a foolish fellow who has these
silly ideas. After that stage passes the next, and the
most important, stage is to put on his clothes. You
adopt for your own his views, and then attribute to
him a caricature of those views saying, 'He's an
extremist, one of those fellows who says only money
matters – everybody knows that sort. Of course money
does matter, but . . .'[1]

MILTON FRIEDMAN'S transition from the unknown challenger
of the prevailing economic orthodoxy to the leading outrider
of a new orthodoxy has occurred at breakneck speed. In the
early 1950s, he was still very much the academic economist,
one who as yet had written only a few short items on monetary
theory. By the end of the 1960s, he had become the leading
exponent of the 'Chicago School' of economics, and was known
throughout the world for his indefatigable emphasis on the
importance of monetary factors in inflation.[2] To the academic
world, his restatement of the quantity theory of money, his
books on monetary and international economic policy, and
his titanic work on the history of money, had made his views
the focus of every macroeconomic debate. To the general
public, he had become famous through his regular trenchant
columns in *Newsweek*, his forthright economic advice to (and
criticism of) leading politicians, and his uncompromising
defence of the merits of the free market economic system.

Friedman's rise was due, in part, to the speed with which

the old economic orthodoxy failed after the Second World War. Expansionary policies that had been designed to stimulate a postwar economic recovery led instead to inflation, a result which was difficult to reconcile with the prevailing economic theories. Friedman's revival of an old notion, that rising prices are the almost inevitable result of a large expansion of the quantity of money in circulation, came just at the right time to establish itself as a new theoretical view that was at its strongest when explaining the very problems upon which the existing economics had begun to founder.

However much Friedman's revival of the quantity theory of money had swung the academic debate in his direction during the 1950s and early 1960s, it still held little sway over the politicians or the monetary authorities themselves. Naturally cautious, they contented themselves with a patched-up version of the old ideas. It was perhaps the violence and swiftness with which the inflations of the early 1970s overtook a world without much belief in monetary policy that made the defectors to Friedman's ideas into the majority.

This final development, in particular, was speeded up by Friedman's unquestioned artistry in promoting a cause. His ability to summarize the essentials of the quantity theory in a few short catchphrases, and his direct and engaging way of arguing his case, undoubtedly brought his theories to the widest possible audience. His popular articles and his defence of the market economy, *Capitalism and Freedom*, had already made his name well known; the success of his monetary theory and policy recommendations would certainly have been slower without them. For the few politicians and others who had not yet heard of him and his views, Friedman's 1979 book and worldwide television series, *Free to Choose*, must have made a large impact; it stands as a testament to his formidable persuasive powers.

Although Friedman's interests and expertise have ranged far beyond the academic world and have made his ideas widely known and understood, it may be that these practical gains have been won only at the cost of confusion and some over-simplification of his ideas in the minds of laymen. 'Monetarism', as the new approach has come to be called, is often misinterpreted as a package of *political* judgements and policies as well as *economic* ones, and the confusion of Friedman's economics with the other views of the politicians who have endorsed them (together with Friedman's own support for limited government) is certainly a large part of the cause.

Professional economists are probably much less confused on the matter; but even so, his presence (and, it must be said, his success) as a promoter of ideas on the public stage have led many of Friedman's colleagues to downgrade his contribution as an academic economist. Even in his technical writings, Friedman has always displayed an originality and a flair for attacking orthodox thinking that has generated occasional envy and frequent irritation in the profession. But his undoubted merit eventually prompted his fellows to elect him as President of the American Economic Association in 1967 (an occasion which he characteristically used yet again to castigate the monetary authorities), although he had to wait another nine years before his acceptability to the world's economics establishment was marked by the award of the Nobel Prize. Few people were surprised that the accolade should have gone to so original and influential an economist. Some were surprised that he had to wait for so long; but the wait was undoubtedly due to the fact that Friedman built his career outside the economics establishment, and did so by challenging virtually every major doctrine of mainstream economic theory.[3]

Nevertheless, Friedman's views have been gradually, if grudgingly, absorbed into a new economic orthodoxy, and what began as a one-man critique has now become a general attitude which has spawned countless research projects, with new names developing the themes in macroeconomic theory which he first identified and established. Although today there are 'few governments which would not pay at least lip-service to Friedman's insistence upon the need for monetary control in the fight against inflation',[4] it is remarkable how much of this new thinking has come directly from the mind of one man; and, in particular, how 'the intellectual revival of the quantity theory... has been almost exclusively the work of Milton Friedman'.[5]

That revival alone would probably have been sufficient to ensure the Nobel Prize for Friedman – sooner or later. But to this achievement must be added a number of further developments in macroeconomic theory, some of them quite unrelated to monetary economics. His development of a new theory of consumer behaviour, his analysis of the role of expectations in inflationary episodes, his review of the consumer costs of restricted entry to the professions, his fight for floating exchange rates, and his critique of the commonly accepted 'trade-off' between inflation and unemployment, must all be added to the list. It is plain that, in creating and exploring these ideas, Friedman's fertile mind has given present and future economists a full programme for research: and that his powerful impact on the development of economic thought will ensure Friedman an important place in the history of the subject.

FRIEDMAN'S BACKGROUND AND WORK

It is remarkable how the most effective advocates of the free market come from poor backgrounds: perhaps they are best placed to understand the importance of liberal and competitive institutions in helping individuals to rise to their full potential. Thus, 'Friedman's own origins were lowly. He was born in Brooklyn, New York, in 1912, the son of poor Jewish immigrants. Before he was born, his mother had worked as a seamstress in a New York sweatshop,'[6] a family history which might engender a contempt for capitalism in the minds of most young people. But instead he recognized this menial work for what it was – an essential starting-point on the income ladder for unskilled workers – and it is interesting that he took his *Free to Choose* television audience to just such a sweatshop in Hong Kong, arguing that attempts to outlaw low wages or unpleasant working conditions simply deny employment opportunities to the young and unskilled people who need them most.

Early in life, Friedman was drawn more to mathematics than to economics; but he did come under the influence of two economists, Arthur Burns and Homer Jones, who both

6

became distinguished in their own right, and who introduced Friedman to the thinking of Columbia and Chicago Universities respectively. It was on graduation from Rutgers in 1932 that Friedman decided to go to Chicago to study economics. Given the number of excellent teachers there – Frank Knight, Jacob Viner, Aaron Director, Henry Simons, Henry Schultz and others – and the importance which the School attached to monetary theory, Chicago was certainly a stimulating and exciting place to be at that time. It left an impression on Friedman that determined his future career.

Unfortunately, Friedman's poor financial circumstances made him unable to continue at Chicago, although he was fortunate enough to be able to take up a generous fellowship at Columbia. This institution once again helped mark out the course of Friedman's career, because it was here that he encountered the scientific spirit of Wesley Mitchell, who emphasized the empirical nature of economics – that economic theories must be capable of testing if they are to add to human understanding, and that the refinement of abstract models was insufficient. Not only did Friedman express this strategy in words and adopt it for his own working method, but he was to begin an association with the National Bureau of Economic Research, of which Mitchell was the principal founder, that was to last throughout his professional life.

Early research work

It seems strange to us now that Friedman left the academic world briefly in 1935, to join the Industrial Section of the National Resources Committee, a body which was collecting information for large-scale economic planning. Plainly, his libertarian and free-market attitudes had not yet hardened. But the work he did, on consumer expenditure in the United States, was to give him a powerful expertise which he later developed as part of his own theory of consumer behaviour.

His formal association with the National Bureau of Economic Research began in 1937, when he took up a research project from Simon Kuznets (himself later a Nobel laureate) on the professional structures of lawyers, doctors, accountants

7

and others. This was eventually to become his PhD thesis, which was completed in 1941. In the meantime, he worked on the NBER's studies on income and wealth, married Rose Director (the sister of Aaron Director and a trained economist who would eventually collaborate on *Capitalism and Freedom*, *Free to Choose* and *Tyranny of the Status Quo*), and spent a year on the faculty of the University of Wisconsin.

But Friedman had to wait until 1945 before his work on *Income from Independent Professional Practice* was published, and until 1946 before receiving his doctorate. It was not only that the war years intervened: Friedman's talent for controversy had begun to show itself. For he argued that professional restrictions on entry into occupations (as exemplified particularly in medical practice) served to make the numbers in the restricted professions grow much less quickly than the growth of the population as a whole. For the consumer, the result of this was to drive up the costs of medical services. Such increased profitability, he suggested, was at least as powerful a motive of professional practitioners as the ideal of 'protecting the public'. At a time when educated and professional people banded closely together, it was not a view that was universally popular.

Taxation and inflation

Today it also seems curious that in 1941, after a year at the University of Wisconsin, Friedman took up an appointment in the Division of Tax Research of the US Treasury. His work was aimed at devising the best taxation policy to prevent inflation (although in later life he would deny that taxation has much effect in that regard), using the methods of Keynes's new analysis (of which he would later point out the inadequacies), and it led him to recommend new and more efficient taxation measures (while he would later regard all taxes with suspicion). But precisely because it did deal with macroeconomic policy, with the analysis of Keynes, and with the relative importance of monetary and taxation policy, this research began to get Friedman to grips with the key economic concepts that would become his principal professional interest.

8

The published version of this research, *Taxing to Prevent Inflation*, and his other writings of the time show little inkling of Friedman's later thought, however. They are concerned with the details of Keynes's analysis of the 'inflationary gap', the situation in which the total demand for goods and services by government, investors and consumers is greater than the supply of resources available to meet it, with the result that prices are bid up. Indeed, in a 1942 article on the subject,[7] he scarcely mentioned the role of monetary factors, and felt obliged to insert seven new paragraphs when it was reprinted eleven years later.[8] But however much he accepted Keynes's general equilibrium analysis method, Friedman did, even at this time, detect some of its shortcomings, observing that the size of the 'inflationary gap' was difficult to measure, and that its net impact on prices was particularly uncertain. Later he would argue that the way in which this 'gap' was financed – particuiarly whether the government financed its expenditures by borrowing or by increasing the supply of money – would be of the utmost importance in predicting inflation.

Friedman's career at Chicago

For the remainder of the Second World War, Friedman became Associate Director of the Division of War Research at Columbia University, which made use of his skills as a statistician rather than an economist. After a short spell at the University of Minnesota, he joined the Department of Economics at the University of Chicago in 1948.

Not only did the years around 1948 see Friedman becoming gradually convinced of the importance of money in inflation; they also introduced him to the kind of controversy which he would attract for the rest of his career. For example, in 1946 he published (with George Stigler, who was also to become a Nobel laureate) a stinging critique of rent and other housing market controls, *Roofs or Ceilings?*. It compared the former system of market rents, where housing was allocated smoothly, quickly and impartially through the price system, with the 1946 method of 'rationing by change and favoritism'. The system of rent controls had dried up much of the supply

9

of rentable accommodation – few landlords would rent out property if they could not charge for its full worth – and had thus made it more difficult for everyone to find a place to live. The result of artificially cheap rents was a chronic shortage of available housing.

This essay, coming as it did from two professional economists, and arguing the case against a contemporary dogma so forcefully, was a short classic which has been reprinted many times since.[9] But precisely because it was argued in effective and popular terms, it was greeted with surprise and even shock in the academic community. With the exception of Keynes, it was uncommon for professional economists to become involved in political arguments. But from his work with the US Treasury, and in despair at trying to explain economic principles to those who were predominantly interested only in political affairs, Friedman had come to understand the need for the academic economist to present his findings in an effective manner to the widest possible audience. It was a skill that Friedman would never lack: but the academic criticism of *Roofs or Ceilings?* made him appreciate that such a strategy was unlikely to be endorsed by his colleagues.

The incident clearly disclosed the extent to which postwar economists had lost their faith in free markets and had embraced a new faith in their own power to analyze, redesign and control the economy. It made Friedman return to the question of whether it was possible to proceed in economic enquiries without moral or political judgements getting in the way, and thus whether economics could be classified as properly scientific. His positive answer to these questions led him to expound a new, empirical method that is crucial to an understanding of his later works, as we shall see. But it was in the development of monetary policy, not economic methodology, that Friedman began to establish his reputation during the early years at Chicago.

Again, his conversion was gradual. As late as 1951 he was suggesting[10] that interest rate policy could be used with success, a view that was soon to be a casualty of his developing thought. But he had already argued against discretionary economic policies on the grounds that lags and uncertainties tend to make this 'fine tuning' counterproductive, a view which prepared the way for his famous suggestion that the growth of the quantity of money should be fixed at a set rate and should not be manipulated in an attempt to correct temporary problems.[11] His increasing emphasis on the importance, and the limits, of monetary policy became clear with the publication of his collection of *Essays in Positive Economics* in 1953.

The new quantity theory of money

Friedman's new emphasis on money stemmed in part from his perception of the breakdown of Keynes's analytical vehicle. The 'Keynesian revolution' of the 1930s and 1940s had established the new orthodoxy of a generation, and had left for dead the traditional quantity theory of money, by which it was supposed that an increase in the supply of money would generate increases in prices or output. The new orthodoxy explained that any such changes would probably be offset by demand – that people would simply hold on to the newly created money and would not use it to bid up prices. And there was a widespread belief that monetary expansion during a recession would get the economy moving again and stimulate new employment without being inflationary.

But the victor in this skirmish was in turn set upon by events, and Friedman notes that the postwar 'easy money' policies that were supposed to stimulate investment, growth and employment succeeded only in generating inflation.[12] This strong inflationary pressure

was brought under control only when countries undertook so-called orthodox measures to restrain the growth in the stock of money, as in Italy, beginning in August 1947, in Germany in June 1948, in the United States in March 1951, in Great Britain in November 1951, and in France in January 1960.[13]

It did, of course, take much longer for the Keynesian view to fade, and *ad hoc* additions to the theory were developed to account for each revealed shortcoming. But although this process quickly robbed Keynes's *General Theory* of its simplicity and elegance, few economists of the time contemplated a return to the type of monetary theories that had lain abandoned for so long. If the quantity theory explanation of these postwar events were to be treated seriously, it would need a new and complete reworking, answering the devastating criticisms that Keynes had made of it. This did not appear in print until 1956, and even then it stood alone for many years. It was, in Harry Johnson's words,

... the condensed and rather cryptic restatement of the quantity theory by Friedman ... a restatement that takes the reader at a hard pace from the fundamental theory to the simplifications required for its empirical application.[14]

Despite its difficulty and brevity, however, 'The Quantity Theory of Money – A Restatement'[15] became the classic modern redefinition of the terms, assumptions and empirical predictions of the quantity theory. Far from being a mere restatement of the classical quantity theory, it embarked on an adventurous and very modern departure. Fundamentally, it argued that the quantity theory is not a theory of output, money income or prices; it is *a theory of the demand for money*. Following Keynes's criticism, the modern quantity theorist had to show that monetary increases do indeed work through to higher prices, without being 'trapped' by perverse or fickle changes in the amount of money which people wish to hold. If people suddenly decided for some reason to spend all the money in their pockets, for example, more would come into active circulation to bid up prices, but if they decided to keep more money in hand, then the opposite would occur. Hence the need to determine just what were the conditions that prompt people to hold a larger or smaller quantity of money – that is, the nature of its *demand*.

The stability of the demand for money

The recognition that the quantity theory stands or falls according to the behaviour of the demand for money was a crucial and important insight. But Friedman went on to defend the theory by arguing that the actual behaviour of demand would in practice be highly stable, so that the quantity theory view that monetary expansions would in fact work through to price increases was broadly justified.

Friedman began from the starting-point of Keynesian port-folio analysis. This argues that individuals hold a 'portfolio' or collection of different capital assets, such as goods, bonds, equities and other investments; but each of these have different degrees of riskiness and will yield different returns, so that each individual will have to put together a different combi-nation of assets according to his or her tolerance of risk and desire for returns. Friedman's departure is to note that *money* can be regarded as a capital asset like any other. Although an individual's holdings of idle cash do not provide a money income, they do provide an income in the broad sense: they provide the useful services of being instantly accessible in the event of unforeseen opportunities arising, of being immediately convertible into other assets, and of establishing a buffer against necessary but unanticipated expenditures.

In other words, money is held for very sensible reasons, and the demand for it is no will-o'-the-wisp that makes the effect of monetary changes unpredictable. On the contrary, since money is a capital asset which generates a stream of future services, just as other assets generate a stream of income, it can be analyzed using the familiar tools of capital theory. And hence, using those traditional tools, Friedman was able to show that the demand for money would be fairly stable. The factors which were likely to affect how much of this asset people desired to hold would be, in his view, future price levels, the yields of alternative assets (such as equities and bonds), the total wealth of the individual or household, tastes, income and other real factors. Most of these would be unlikely to vary a great deal; and any variation in the remainder could be easily taken into account when attempting to estimate the effect of a monetary change.

This novel view of money is another of Friedman's most important achievements. In the words of Harry Johnson again,

Friedman's application to monetary theory of the basic principle of capital theory – that income is the yield on capital, and capital the present value of income – is probably the most important development in monetary theory since Keynes' *General Theory*. Its theoretical significance lies in the conceptual integration of wealth and income as influences on behaviour . . .[16]

The Keynesians had tended to stress the importance of interest rates and the demand for financial securities in determining the ultimate level of economic activity: from now on, money itself was asserted to have a direct impact on the economy; it could not be relegated to the sidelines.

The consumption function

In 1957, Friedman published his book on *A Theory of the Consumption Function*, an elegant testing of the 'permanent income' hypothesis. Although the original idea was not Friedman's, his development of it has credited him with the intellectual parentage of the theory; and although it was not seen at the time as being connected with his monetary theory, Friedman was later to use it to reinforce his views about the stability of the demand for money.

The permanent income hypothesis, which we will examine in more detail in Chapter 5, starts by reminding us that people usually receive their income at lengthy intervals – perhaps weekly or monthly – but that they do not behave as if they receive a massive income on one day and nothing the next. They treat their income as a smooth flow over the period between pay packets. In some cases, income fluctuates seasonally; once again, people so affected tend to smooth out their spending patterns over the year, saving in prosperous times and dipping into their savings in others. The same phenomenon might be seen over even longer periods, with people weighting today's expenditures in anticipation of their expected future incomes.

Thus Friedman develops the notion of the smoothed or 'permanent' income upon which people base their spending, saving and investment decisions in preference to their actual, but fluctuating, money income.

The point later became important in the debate about the stability or instability of the demand for money. The Keynesians thought that the evidence showed demand to be greatly altered by changes in income. But Friedman noted that money is held for the consumable services (such as ready convertibility and security) which it yields, and so the demand for it will be adjusted, like all consumption, to *permanent income* rather than to actual money receipts. Upon analysis of the evidence, he concluded that demand was in fact highly stable with respect to permanent income, and that its behaviour tends to reinforce, rather than offset, the effects of monetary changes.[17]

Tests of the theory

By the time this analysis was complete, Friedman had built up a simple but powerful theory that could be subjected to the sort of empirical testing that he considered necessary in any scientific theory. It was simple because it rested on the hypothesis of a stable demand for money, and it was powerful because, if the hypothesis held, it could predict a similarly stable link between changes in the quantity of money and changes in prices or incomes. There was no need to set out a vast and complex general equilibrium theory to explain the workings of the economy, as the Keynesians had attempted to do: the modern restatement of the quantity theory would stand or fall on a comparatively simple proposition that was easy to test, and its usefulness would be decided accordingly.

It was with this methodological approach in mind that Friedman and David Meiselman set out to test the new version of the quantity theory. They compared it with a hypothesis distilled from the Keynesian structure, which linked consumption to governmental and investment expenditures rather than to changes in the money stock. Looking at the historical record, Friedman and Meiselman found that the behaviour of the money stock was a much better guide than the Keynesian 'autonomous expenditures' figure. In their defence, the Keynesians could only argue that individual parts of their own analysis could not be tested in isolation, and embark upon the design of yet further additions and amendments to a theoretical system that had already lost its elegant simplicity.

Friedman's technique of checking the predictions of a simple theory against the historical record was used to devastating effect in *A Monetary History of the United States*, which he co-authored with Anna Schwartz. At this stage, Friedman's interests were turning away from the technical issues of the demand for money towards determination of the best policy for its supply: this empirical work, covering monetary history over nine decades, showed quite conclusively the importance of the supply of money and its relationship to prices and incomes.

This work was a major and effective test of the quantity theory over a lengthy period. But just as important, perhaps, its recapitulation of monetary events revealed that prewar economists had been scared away from the quantity theory by what was, in fact, a phantom. Keynes and most other economists of his generation believed that the Great Depression in the United States occurred despite feverishly expansionary policies from the monetary authorities – an interpretation naturally encouraged by the authorities themselves. Even though Keynes had previously stressed the importance of money,[18] the events of 1929–33 (as he understood them) led him to devise a new analysis in which spending and investment, not the supply of money, was the crucial issue. 'And,' concludes Friedman, 'it was the apparent impossibility of explaining the Great Contraction in monetary terms that, more than anything else, made the economics profession so receptive to Keynes's message.'[19] But on re-examination of the facts, Friedman and Schwartz discovered that the events of the Depression were in fact 'a tragic testament to the effectiveness of monetary policy, not a demonstration of its impotence',[20] because, in spite of the monetary authorities' claims, the record showed clearly that the quantity of money *fell* by a third from 1929 to 1933. Though small at first, the reduction triggered bank runs and closures, so that the failure of the Federal Reserve to provide liquidity when it was needed caused the largest monetary contraction and the gravest depression in US history.

Work on monetary policy

The years following the publication of the *magnum opus* on monetary history found Friedman not only busy with the defence of his findings, but also writing position papers on economic policy for political candidates, and developing further his ideas on correct monetary policy. These thoughts were set down in his 1967 address as President of the American Economic Association, in his 1969 book, *The Optimum Quantity of Money*, and at various places in the 1968 collection, *Dollars and Deficits*.

As far back as 1951, Friedman had pointed out that the attempt to use monetary policy to correct short-term economic fluctuations was not only mistaken but almost certainly desta-bilizing.[21] There would be a lag between a monetary change and its eventual impact on output or prices, and this lag was not only long but variable and unpredictable. A monetary authority trying to offset an upswing or a downswing would almost certainly find its monetary measures biting well after the swing was over. Throughout the 1960s, Friedman reworked this analysis in various ways and used many platforms to broadcast his conclusion that discretionary monetary policy would generally *exaggerate* economic fluctuations rather than dampen them.[22] He argued that the monetary authorities should give up discretionary policy and should opt instead for a monetary *rule* – expanding the quantity of money at a roughly stable rate, regardless of the circumstances of the moment. This new statement of his ideas led to numerous studies on the relative speed and effectiveness of monetary and other types of economic policy.

The monetary authorities in every country are naturally reluctant to abandon the powerful controls that they are in charge of. But, largely as a result of Friedman's effective high-lighting of the importance and limitations of monetary policy, politicians and their advisors have come to use monetary con-trols with more care. His frequent admonitions have at the least ensured that monetary factors cannot be overlooked; indeed, a number of prominent countries have adopted his strategy of aiming for smooth growth of the money supply according to set targets. Friedman's influence has clearly shown itself on the practical as well as academic level.

Expectations and unemployment

Friedman used his 1967 address to the American Economic Association to promote two further ideas: his critique of the orthodox notion that there is a trade-off between inflation and unemployment, and his view of the importance of people's expectations about future prices to the course and severity of an inflation. These themes were taken up again in his 1975 monograph *Unemployment Versus Inflation?* and in his 1976 Nobel lecture, *Inflation and Unemployment*.

Many countries had experienced rising prices associated with rising levels of unemployment during the 1960s and 1970s, yet the Keynesian orthodoxy found this difficult to explain. It was presumed that a rise in total spending for any reason (such as an expansionary programme of government expenditure) would initially induce people to bring more goods onto the market in order to capture some of the new demand, and that this would require them to take on new workers and use their machines to the full. Only after the maximum or 'full employment' output had been reached could the higher spending start to bid up prices and produce inflation.

Some Keynesians had already gone further. Professor A. W. Phillips, in his famous analysis of 1958,[23] built upon Keynes's views to suggest that there existed a trade-off between inflation and unemployment, a trade-off which could be plotted on a 'Phillips curve'. But within a few years this analysis began to break down: inflation and unemployment began rising together. At first, this was thought to be temporary, a slight outward shift in the curve that orthodox measures would resolve. In the 1970s, however, it became all too obvious that increasing doses of inflation were not curing unemployment, and that the two were rising rapidly together. The era of 'stagflation' had begun.

18

Friedman anticipated this problem before many others even saw it: his explanation was that 'full' employment was an unattainable ideal. Even in the smoothest economy, there would always be people moving between jobs: either changing jobs voluntarily or out of work and looking for a suitable new appointment. These changes take time, and so the very best that we can expect to achieve is some 'natural rate' of unemployment that takes these structural problems into account. Any attempt to reduce unemployment below this minimum attainable level will fail, and expansionary spending programmes will only cause inflation once it has been reached.

Although this line of reasoning implied that there could be no long-term trade-off between inflation and unemployment, Friedman suggested that it *may* be possible to get unemployment below its 'natural' rate, but only for a short time, and at the cost of accelerating doses of inflation. As the quantity of money is expanded, it stimulates new output and employment, as Keynes recognized. Initially, businesses enjoy a boom: almost everything succeeds, fewer people find themselves involuntarily out of work, and those who do leave one job can find another quickly, so the recorded level of unemployment dips down. But eventually the new money works through to prices, and as the new rate of inflation becomes more and more widely anticipated, people adjust their expectations and their business activities accordingly. As the initial prosperity is swallowed up by the rising cost of living, people cut back their output and their employment, which falls back to its 'natural' level. Because all of the people cannot be fooled all the time, monetary expansions fail to raise employment beyond this level for very long. To do so would require a bigger and bigger monetary expansion, which would always keep ahead of people's expectations: but that, of course, would produce an *accelerating* inflation.

Friedman has made this *expectations analysis* the centrepiece of his explanation of how people adjust to monetary changes,[24] and has even used it to suggest that inflation might actually generate *rising* unemployment.[25] Over the years, its power has become apparent, and it is difficult today to find research on wage and price determination which does not make use of expectations theory. It is much easier nowadays to find studies which confirm that there is no durable trade-off between inflation and unemployment, and perhaps 'even more surprising is the degree to which this notion has penetrated into official thinking in a large number of industrial countries, despite the understandable aversion of policymakers to the implications'.[26]

International economics

No less effective in persuading officialdom have been Friedman's views on the international economic system. Exchange rates, always a source of contention, caused various difficulties throughout the postwar years, and the attempts to peg exchange rates in some 'orderly' fashion were thwarted by a train of worries, crises and sudden devaluations. The quantity theorists had all recognized that rising or falling price levels in different countries, stemming from their various monetary and other economic policies, would lead to different demands for their exports and imports, and that this in turn would put pressure on exchange rates. Friedman argued for a system of *freely adjusting rates*, rather than one of fixed rates and frequent crises; he made out a strong case for this as far back as 1950.[27] In 1968 he reported:

I have for many years been in favor of setting free the prices of both gold and the dollar and letting them be determined by private trading in open markets. Time and again when I have made these proposals, I have been told that, however much sense they might make on economic grounds, they were not politically feasible. I have been, in effect, advised to stop wasting my time on idle dreams of a fundamental solution...[28]

Within a short time, nevertheless, Friedman's fundamental solution had been widely adopted. The United States set free the price of gold – in effect in 1968 and in official terms in 1971 – and in 1972 the British pound was floated. The succeeding oil crisis made it impossible to return to anything like the old order, and in 1974 the representatives of the main commercial countries accepted a general system of floating exchange rates.

Popular works

John Burton has observed that attempting to capture the essence of such a prolific thinker as Milton Friedman is like trying to catch the Niagara Falls in a pint pot.[29] His writings have ranged from the very technical to the very popular, and this was certainly true of his remaining years at the University of Chicago. A statistical companion volume to *A Monetary History of the United States* was published in 1970, and this collection of *Monetary Statistics of the United States* was joined by another large work on *Monetary Trends in the United States and the United Kingdom* which developed and tested some of the theoretical hypotheses put forward in the earlier book. A tightly argued debate with his critics appeared as *Milton Friedman's Monetary Framework*, and an enlarged version of his textbook on *Price Theory* was published shortly before Friedman retired from the University of Chicago in 1977 to take up a position as Senior Research Fellow of the Hoover Institution at Stanford University.

The technical depth and intricacy of these professional works, however, is in marked contrast to the forceful and combative style of Friedman's more popular writings, notably his 1962 *Capitalism and Freedom*, the collections of his *Newsweek* columns that appeared as *An Economist's Protest* and *There's No Such Thing as a Free Lunch*, his 1979 *Free to Choose* book and television series, and the overtly political *Tyranny of the Status Quo*.

These writings begin by observing the enormous power of the market system to provide for human needs. No man would sell, and no other would buy, unless both derived some benefit from the exchange; and thus the everyday operation of the marketplace is a convenient and voluntary means of increasing human welfare. Following the arguments of another Nobel laureate, Professor F. A. Hayek, Friedman in *Free to Choose* stresses the remarkable power of the price system in showing where there are shortages or surpluses, and in correcting them by inducing people to enter markets where their products command a high price and to leave markets where demand is low.[30] Millions of individual prices, fluctuating every day according to the supply and demand conditions of the moment, form a much more efficient mechanism for allocating resources than any central planning system would be capable of.

The diversity, rapid adjustment, innovation and experimentation found in the market was also one of the themes of *Capitalism and Freedom*. But perhaps more important to Friedman at that time was the fact that the voluntary exchange system, by its very decentralization, extent and diversity, prevented massive concentrations of power and therefore posed much less of a threat to individual freedom than the collectivist alternative. The power of a capitalist is limited: his competitors can quickly undermine his hold over any market by serving the customer better. The power of a government, however, is limited only by its ability to use force. His fear of the concentration of official power makes Friedman into what he calls a 'liberal': he seeks a government that is limited primarily to preserving the legal structure that allows people to co-operate voluntarily in the marketplace, and whose power is dispersed.

Because Friedman sees individuals as free agents who sometimes co-operate voluntarily together, rather than as cogs in a mechanism of collective action, he has opposed the provision by government of health, welfare and education services, which in his opinion only robs them of their diversity and responsiveness. Far better, he suggests, to provide a minimum standard of living for all through a *negative income tax*, so that poorer people would be given the resources they need to compete effectively in the marketplace for services open to everybody. For education, Friedman suggests that poorer families should receive a 'voucher' which could be used to purchase some or all of their children's education at any school; and although the idea is much older, Friedman has been credited deservingly with its modern revival. He has campaigned with success for an all-volunteer army, while his economic recommendations to abandon controls and discretionary monetary policy are consistent with his ideal of limited government.

22

His emphasis on personal liberty means that Friedman does not fit on the conventional 'left-right' political spectrum, for he abhors the concentrations of power that are required to enforce the economic principles of a socialist state and the moral principles of a conservative one. To him, communism and fascism are equally bad examples of coercive collectivism, and he would be far away towards the individualist end of the scale, along with the classical liberals like Adam Smith, and perhaps even near to J. M. Keynes.[31] There is no doubt that by popularizing an attractive and humane alternative to the socialist ideas that were at their height in the decades before and after the Second World War, Friedman has helped classical liberal attitudes to permeate the thinking of a number of leading Western governments.

CONCLUSION: FRIEDMAN'S CONTRIBUTION

It may well be that many of the principles and policies for which Friedman has long argued would eventually have become accepted in any event. Perhaps the repeated and often disastrous discrepancies between orthodox theories and actual events would have generated widespread skepticism about the powers of Keynesian policies. But Friedman's effective presence as a critic certainly made it more difficult for orthodox economists to continue making amendments to an already clumsy theory so that they could always appear wise after the event. He provided instead a point of view which did not claim to be comprehensive in scope, but which predicted the emergence and scale of a particularly damaging phenomenon – inflation – and which spelt out the measures necessary to avoid it.

In a similar manner, Friedman not only produced some timely and effective criticisms of collectivist ideology, but built up a sensible alternative based on voluntary co-operation and a welfare system which operates through the power of the market and not the power of politicians. Once again, although the socialism that was once so prevalent might have revealed its practical weaknesses in any case, Friedman's critique helped to expose those weaknesses, and his alternatives stood ready as a mustering point for those who found themselves drifting away from the old ideas.

Friedman has fulfilled this role with enthusiasm and energy. His powerful and straightforward presentation of new economic and political ideas has helped to build a bridge between the economics profession and the politicians and general public, and to foster an atmosphere of wide debate about economic issues.

For the science of economics itself, Friedman has propounded and tested a cascade of new ideas. His approach has led the research of others in a hundred fruitful new directions, insisting as it does that economic theories should be lauded not for their complexity, but for their ability to predict events, however broad or limited in scope they might be. But this methodological stance, an understanding of which is vital to the appreciation of Friedman's work, is perhaps better considered in the context of some of the key elements of the strategy that has come to be known as 'monetarism' and that has become inextricably linked with the thinking and personality of Milton Friedman.

CHAPTER TWO

Friedman and the Quantity Theory of Money: An Overview

The broad outlines of the quantity theory of money
were fully developed by the eighteenth century.[1]

AT several points in his writings, Friedman refers to the 'classical' quantity theory of money, acknowledging his debt to it,
and in some cases outlining it at length.[2] In his judgement,
his own university, Chicago,

...was one of the few academic centers at which the quantity theory
continued to be a central and vigorous part of the oral tradition
throughout the 1930s and 1940s...[3]

although critics have argued that the versions of the quantity
theory espoused by Friedman and his colleagues have little
connection with the 'classical' approach.[4]

The early quantity theory

Friedman mentions the contribution of David Hume, whose
1752 essay, *Of Money*, can still be read 'with pleasure and
profit'; it outlined the classical quantity theory with 'few if
any errors of commission'.[5] Yet Hume's statement is an elegant
and intelligent rendition of what is an old theme: John Locke
in 1692 had already analyzed the problems of debasement
of the coinage,[6] and the same understanding was undoubtedly
known, less systematically, to the ancients.

The classical approach, whereby (in Hume's words) 'the
prices of commodities are always proportioned to the plenty
of money',[7] grew in repute following the celebrated *Report of
the Bullion Committee* of 1810,[8] which attributed the inflation
of the time to an uncontrolled increase in paper money.

Attempts to give the theory a mathematical base flourished, particularly in Britain, but the modern renaissance in monetary theory began with the American economist Irving Fisher and his famous work of 1911.[9]

Fisher's version of the theory. To Fisher, the volume of payments made in an economy can be considered as the product of a price and a quantity. For example, the total amount of money that an employer spends on labour is the hourly wage rate multiplied by the number of hours worked; the total amount a merchant receives for his goods is the price per unit times the number of units sold; the income of a shareholder is the dividend per share times the number of shares he holds. If we want to express the *total* volume of transactions in the economy, therefore, we can use the same technique, by multiplying the average prices of goods by the total (or 'aggregate') quantities traded in the period under review.

The total volume of transactions can also be viewed from another angle, not in terms of the payments made, but in terms of the money used to effectuate them. The total quantity of money in the economy, multiplied by the number of times each unit of that money is used to make a purchase, will once again give us the total volume of transactions. And thus, if we put the two together, we get the well-known 'Fisher equation':

$$MV = PT$$

where M represents the total quantity of money in the economy, V represents the average number of times each unit of money is used to make a purchase (the 'transactions velocity of money'), P represents a suitably chosen average price, and T represents a suitably chosen aggregate of quantities traded during the period under examination.

As Fisher noted, this result is a vindication of the classical quantity theory, if two assumptions are granted. If T is supposed constant (as is reasonable in a full-employment economy, where the physical volume of transactions it represents will have reached its maximum because no more goods can be produced), and V is supposed constant as well (being determined by traditional practices, habits and banking institutions), the strict quantity theory will hold. In this case, the relationship between the volume of money and the value of money would be straightforward: increases in the quantity of money would produce rising prices, so that each *unit* of money (a pound, dollar, shekel or drachma, for example) would purchase a smaller quantity of goods. The relationship between the volume of money and the value of money would then trace out a rectangular hyperbola, as in Figure 1.[10]

Figure 1
The simple quantity theory of money

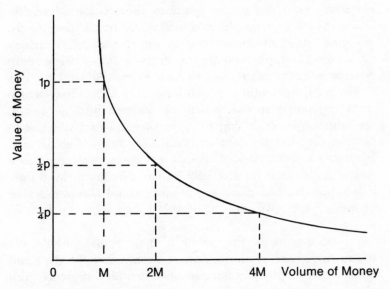

The income version. There are, however, two problems with Fisher's version of the quantity theory. First, it is rather difficult to apply the Fisher equation in empirical work, because the available economic statistics do not measure the total volume of transactions, T, or anything much like it. In Fisher's total, *every* purchase must be included, so that the value of wheat, for example, is included once when it is sold by the farmer, a second time when it is sold as flour by the miller, a third time when baked and sold to the grocer, and a fourth time

27

when sold to the consumer. These are all discrete purchases, all directly observable, but to add them all up would be an impossible task. However, the statistics do give us figures for the *income* of the farmer, the miller and the baker, and the best we can achieve in practical terms is therefore to add up each one's income, which is the total of his receipts *minus* his outlays. The national income statistics accordingly count only the *value added* at each stage, with the value of the intermediate goods (in this case, the wheat) being netted out. So there is a need for a reformulation of Fisher's approach which takes this statistical point into account.

A second problem is more subtle. The Fisher approach is a *transactions version* of the quantity theory. Its underlying assumption is that people hold money in order to buy goods. To some extent, of course, they do, but they also hold money for a variety of other reasons, such as to earn interest or to provide security against unpredictable events. All these motives (and there are undoubtedly others) will affect how people react to changes in the quantity of money: in other words, we cannot guarantee that the transactions velocity V will in fact remain constant when the volume of money M is changed. In Fisher's formulation, 'the most important thing about money is that it is transferred';[11] but to Friedman this is only half the story, and if we are to understand the importance of money fully, we must understand *fully* why people hold it.

In response to the first problem in particular, there arose the *income version* of the quantity theory. Superficially (and hence to the great confusion of economics students) this appears very similar, being expressed at its simplest as

$$MV = Py$$

where M represents the money stock and P the price index as before, but where V now stands for the average number of times each unit of money is used for making *income* transactions and y is the national income (adjusted for inflation).

Confining our attention to *income* transactions means that a number of questionable items, such as the recurring intermediate goods (the wheat in our example), the value of gifts, the purchase of existing assets (houses, land, shares and so on), money-changing transactions and other items which are not counted as part of 'national income', can be ignored. For empirical purposes, the approach is therefore much superior, because we have the appropriate national income statistics available to check it, which is not the case with the transactions approach.

According to Friedman, the underlying assumption about the role of money is also superior: in this version, the important thing about money is not that it discharges debts so much as that it is held as an *asset* that generates a stream of income and other services. This, as we shall see, is very much Friedman's own conception of money: but critics have argued that earlier proponents of the income approach did not recognize this subtle distinction at the time, and that Friedman is attempting to give his own views a longer pedigree than they deserve.[12]

The Cambridge cash-balance approach. The Cambridge version of the quantity theory, engineered by Marshall, Pigou, Robertson and the early Keynes, raises a further question: why people actually *want* to hold their assets in the form of money. Larger incomes are certainly likely to mean that people want to make larger volumes of transactions and that larger cash balances will therefore be demanded; but what of psychological and other factors? Taking these into account, we can write

$$M = kPy$$

where the new variable, k, represents by definition the ratio of the money stock to income – not necessarily the actual ratio, but the 'desired' ratio (taking cognizance of psychological factors), with M representing not the actual but the 'desired' quantity of money.

Although it shared the statistical and empirical advantages of the income version, this approach was, in Pigou's phrase, 'a more effective engine of analysis' because it focused attention on the underlying motivations that determine the amount of money people desire to hold. For example, the transactions approach made it unclear whether to include as 'money' those items, such as time deposits or savings deposits, that are not instantly available to pay debts without first being coverted into currency. The cash-balance approach has no such doubts: an important motive for holding money is that it provides a *temporary abode of purchasing power,* such that we do not have to seek out people with exactly reciprocal needs (like hungry barbers in search of bakers needing haircuts) before transactions can be made. This motive makes it natural to include time and savings deposits and other convertible funds without controversy or debate.[13] Again, the transactions approach suggested that the mechanical aspects of making payments – the banking institutions, the speed of communication, and other things affecting the time required to make payments – are the most important determinants of how much money the economic system requires. The cash-balance approach accepts this routinely, and stresses instead the importance of factors that make money more or less useful, such as the costs of holding it, uncertainty about the future and so on. There is a third point, of special interest to Friedman: the cash-balance approach brings monetary theory firmly back to the traditional supply and demand analysis, with the value of money being determined by the same supply and demand forces as those determining the price of any other commodity. And since the *supply* of money is determined from outside (by the workings of the international gold standard, by governments, or by changes in the banking sector), the main attention is focused on the psychological factors determining *demand.* The quantity theory of money therefore takes on a new form, as 'a theory of the demand for money, not a theory of the price level or of money income'.[14] This is consonant with Friedman's approach.

The Keynesian attack on the quantity theory

Keynes is remembered for his attack on the quantity theory, although he was initially a subscriber to the cash-balance approach: in his *Tract on Monetary Reform,*[15] written at the time of the German inflation, he extended it to show how rapid price rises generate expectations about future price rises that encourage people to spend money more quickly, reducing *k* and pushing prices even higher.

But 'Keynes was unusually quick and flexible – both in his mental reactions and in the policy positions he adopted'.[16] The apparent impotence of monetary policy to stem the depression of 1929–33 (based in Friedman's view on a misinterpretation of the facts)[17] drew attention away from the importance of monetary factors, and Keynes accordingly suggested an alternative analysis in which income was seen as dependent on the behaviour of investment (or 'autonomous') expenditures rather than upon changes in the stock of money. The publication of this new economic model in 1936,[18] says Friedman,

led to a temporary eclipse of the quantity theory of money and to perhaps an all-time low in the amount of economic research and writing devoted to monetary theory and analysis, narrowly interpreted. It became a widely accepted view that money does not matter, or, at any rate, that it does not matter very much . . .'[19]

There are two major developments in the *General Theory* which Friedman designates as the crucial blows in Keynes's attack on the importance of money. The first point is that the velocity of money is suggested to be *unstable* in conditions of less than full employment, which means that it will be unstable for most of the time. This is because the demand for money can be broken down into two segments, according to Keynes: there is a *transactions and precautionary demand,* whereby money is held in order to make purchases and to guard against unforseen needs, and a *speculative demand,* whereby people hold larger or smaller amounts of money to benefit from the future course of interest rates that they anticipate. The latter is highly volatile, depending on the behaviour of interest rates; but the former will also be unstable, particularly if the economy is not at full employment and transactions are therefore less than their practicable maximum, and liable to fluctuate up or down.

The second point is that Keynes foresaw conditions in which speculative demand would be highly or even totally elastic, so that changes in the quantity of money would be absorbed entirely into speculative balances – the so-called 'liquidity trap'. In this case, they could have no effects at all on prices or income, and the traditional quantity theory must be abandoned. According to Keynes, this is likely when interest rates are very low, so that the yields on bonds, equities and other securities will also be low. At some sufficiently low rate, the yield will cease to attract anyone – investors might as well hold cash, which at least has the advantage of being instantly negotiable. Any new money created goes instantly into speculative balances, and is put into bank vaults or cash-boxes instead of being used for invesment, without any effect on income. Equally bad for the quantity theory, income could change without any change in the quantity of money: the larger transactions balances that people would need if incomes rose, for example, could be achieved by dipping into speculative balances with no further effect. Under these conditions of 'absolute liquidity preference', the quantity theory does not hold (Figure 2).

To Keynes, therefore, and particularly to his followers (who, says Friedman, were readier than he was to accept a high or even absolute liquidity preference as the actual state of affairs),[20] monetary changes have a rather feeble effect on economic activity. If they work at all, they work indirectly, through interest rates: a change in the quantity of money may produce a small change in bond prices and interest rates, although most will be absorbed into speculative balances, and 'trapped'. If interest rates do change, they will have an effect on investment, and therefore on future income; but plainly in this model, the route from monetary changes to income changes is a precarious one. To the Keynesians, therefore, money might matter, but it certainly does not matter very much.

Friedman's objections to Keynes. Friedman has many objections to this view, but four stand out prominently as explanations of why Keynes's rejection of the importance of monetary policy cannot be accepted.

Firstly, it must be remembered that Keynes was writing for a depression period, when inflation was not a serious threat.

Figure 2
The Keynesian liquidity trap

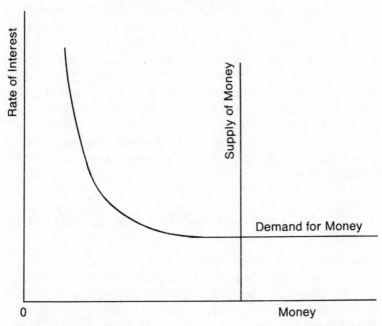

Keynes mistakenly treated prices as being fixed, says Friedman, so that if money had any effect, it would tend to appear in terms of output – in terms of the quantity of goods traded rather than their average price. Hence, Keynes is led on a roundabout route, through bond prices, interest rates and investment, whereas the actual effects of monetary changes are far more direct. Secondly, the belief that monetary policy failed in the Depression led Keynes to conclude that money had little effect on income. In fact, as Friedman shows, a serious monetary contraction precipitated the Depression, contrary to the common assumption at the time that there was no shortage of money. The Depression is therefore a testament to the *strength* of the impact of money on national income, not its weakness. Thirdly, having rejected the notion that monetary changes could have much effect on prices or incomes, Keynes presumed that monetary changes would be largely absorbed by changes in the only factor left in the Cambridge

$M = kPy$ equation, the demand for money. But Friedman, citing his own empirical studies, maintains that demand is in fact highly stable, so that Keynes could not have gone down this route if he had known the facts. The fourth mistake is Keynes's misunderstanding of the nature of money. It can be exchanged for many different kinds of assets, not just the bonds to which Keynes confined his attention. Accordingly it can (and does) have a very direct effect on economic activity, not just a weak impact through the medium of interest rates and the financial markets.

It is these four criticisms of the Keynesian approach that form the cornerstones of Friedman's restatement of the quantity theory.

FRIEDMAN'S RESTATEMENT OF THE QUANTITY THEORY

Whatever the merits of the theoretical case, it was in terms of practical issues that the debate between the Keynesians and the monetarists was concluded. Certainly, Friedman had led the intellectual campaign against Keynes's view with a particularly influential article[21] in *Studies in the Quantity Theory of Money,* which he edited, but it was the practical failure of Keynesian policies that tipped the balance, as he acknowledges. The failure of postwar 'cheap money' policies, the spread of inflation (rather than the unemployment predicted by Keynes) and the better understanding of the true nature of the monetary changes during the depression years were crucial events.

The point at issue between the Chicago School and the Keynesians was therefore 'empirical rather than theoretical':[22] was the *level and pattern of investment spending* a better predictor of income than the *quantity of money and its demand?* To Friedman, there is not much doubt. Keynesian policies designed to improve investment have plainly failed to deliver high and growing national income. The present change in the climate of theoretical opinion has therefore not been produced

by the persuasiveness or lack thereof of the arguments adduced by economic theorists . . . the resurgence of the quantity theory (renamed undescriptively 'monetarism') and the rejection of simple Keynesianism have been a reaction to the emergence of inflation and stagflation.[23]

What, then, are the fundamental principles of this new version of the quantity theory that has come to supplant the Keynesian ideas?

Money and prices are related

The empirical generalization that there is a definite and discernible link between changes in the quantity of money in the economy and changes in the level of prices or output is one on which all monetarists concur. Says Friedman,

the central fact is that inflation is always and everywhere a monetary phenomenon. Historically, substantial changes in prices have always occurred together with substantial changes in the quantity of money relative to output. I know of no exception to this generalization, no occasion in the United States or elsewhere when prices have risen substantially without a substantial rise in the quantity of money relative to output or when the quantity of money has risen substantially relative to output without a substantial rise in prices. And there are numerous confirming examples. Indeed, I doubt that there is any other empirical generalization for which there is as much organized evidence covering so wide a range of space and time.[24]

Although this link is clear, however, Friedman recognizes that it is not as perfect as some commentators suppose. The fact that Friedman confines his remarks to *substantial* changes, and that his empirical work is preoccupied with *major* monetary and income fluctuations, testifies to the point. The level and growth of output, restrictions on the operation of markets, interest rates, expectations and other phenomena are a constant sources of 'looseness' in the link between money and prices. Monetarism is frequently and easily attacked by those who suppose it to argue that *every* change in the quantity of money produces a precisely *proportional* and *instantaneous* change in prices; the real nature of the theory is far more sophisticated.

Yet, whatever the details, the first proposition (accepted by all modern and classical adherents to the quantity theory of money) is that there is a consistent relationship between the rate of growth in the *quantity of money* and the rate of growth in *nominal income*. Income, rather than the price level, is stressed today because it is recognized that monetary changes may be manifested either in price changes or in changes in the quantities of goods traded. Nominal income, which depends on *both* prices and quantities, is therefore the better indicator.

At several points in his writings, Friedman is anxious to bring out the distinction between *real* and *nominal* quantities,[25] arguing that the quantity theory in its modern version in fact rests upon an understanding of this distinction. Nominal income and the nominal quantity of money in the economy are measured in the prevailing units of currency – dollars, francs, pesetas, pounds, lire, shekels, talents and so on. Real income and the real quantity of money are expressed in terms of real goods.

However, real quantities are rather elusive magnitudes because they can be measured in different and conflicting ways. The real amount of money which a family holds as cash, for example, might be measured in terms of the number of weeks of average consumption that these holdings can buy. If its nominal holdings double but prices all double as well, the real value of its holdings is unchanged. On a broader scale, the real quantity of money in the economy can be estimated with reference to the price of some typical basket of commodities bought by some representative group, a routine method of constructing a 'cost of living' index. The measurement problems arise, however, from the fact that prices do not usually move in unison but fluctuate against one another according to market conditions. A drought, say, might greatly affect the price of a basket of commodities that contained fresh food (and hence the real measurements derived from it), while a basket containing only canned food might be unaffected. Friedman himself has discussed these problems in detail.[26]

Whatever the difficulties of measurement, it is clear to

Friedman that *nominal* changes (such as a rise in the quantity of money) produce effects that are also principally *nominal* (such as a rise in money incomes). Although nominal incomes might rise after an expansion in the quantity of money, prices will also rise, so there will be no (or very little) increase in *real* incomes. Only real factors, such as the enterprise and ingenuity of individuals, will produce much change in those.

A stable demand for money

The relationship between the growth of the nominal quantity of money and the growth of nominal income is a generally consistent one, argues Friedman, because (as we shall see in detail in Chapter 3) the demand for money is highly stable. People everywhere are remarkably consistent in the real quantity of money they choose to hold: the amount is very similar over the decades and between countries with very different political and economic institutions. In the United States, people hold a fairly consistent average of about four weeks' income as currency, a figure not much different from that of a century ago, although wars and catastrophes have caused occasional deviations. In countries with less developed financial institutions, the number of weeks' income held in currency might be as high as six or eight, but although different in size, it is still astonishingly stable.[27]

The stability of the demand for money is a crucial part of the link between the quantity of money and nominal income. If all the new money which is created during an expansion is simply added to families' money holdings without being spent, it is hardly in a position to affect prices or output: cash which is stored idly (under the mattress, for example) cannot affect anything, and so there would be no link between the quantity of money and nominal incomes. Similarly, if households were to spend only *some* of the new money and store the rest in an inconsistent manner, then the effects of the monetary expansion on income would naturally be unpredictable, and the quantity theory would not hold.

This feature has led Friedman to say that the quantity theory of money 'is in the first instance a theory of the *demand* for

37

money'.[28] He does not suggest that demand is completely stable and that the way in which newly created money is used is completely predictable; but he argues that it changes very little in general: when it does change, it is the result of comparatively few factors which are easy to allow for in judging the ultimate effects of the monetary change.

The transmission mechanism

The process by which changes in the quantity of money work through to prices and output is open to many different interpretations. Friedman's own views have been amended over the years, and the pattern of his work suggests that he thinks it more important to establish that there *is* a consistent link, rather than to speculate at length about the disputable question of *how* it is effected. While Friedman does give us a sketch of the transmission mechanism, therefore,[29] it is limited to a rough outline only.

The following chapter will examine the transmission process in some depth, but the elements of it can be set out as follows. Suppose that for some reason the amount of money in a community becomes higher than people – with their stable demand for money – wish to hold at that time. The exact source of the new money is not important to this analysis: it could come from the government minting new coins or printing new banknotes, or it may be generated from other immediate sources. However it emerges, people find themselves holding more money than they desire, and so they set about converting their excess money balances into other assets that they think will be more useful. But there is a snag, because one man's expenditures are another man's income, and thus when one person spends some of his excess money holdings, it is simply added to someone else's, who must in turn spend to bring his own money balances down to the desired level. It becomes an endless paper-chase.

This higher level of expenditure and receipts means that nominal incomes rise. But as people vainly attempt to spend more than they receive, it becomes a sellers' market, with the prices of all kinds of goods and services being bid up in the process. The rising prices erode the increased nominal incomes and nominal holdings back down to their former *real* levels. People have succeeded in keeping their real balances stable, but only by raising prices rather than by reducing their nominal holdings.

Prices and output

The transmission mechanism is admittedly more complicated than this outline sketch: for example, there is a tendency to overshoot, and the prices of different goods may not adjust equally rapidly. Another point to bear in mind is that the process takes time, and that (as Chapter 6 explains) the changed rate of growth in nominal income tends to show up in terms of increased output at first, with little or no immediate effect on prices. This is because the increased spending induces sellers to expand the range and number of items they have for sale, rather than to turn customers away or to increase their prices and risk customers going to a competitor. It is in any event easier to order new supplies than to try to pitch prices at exactly the right level to meet a demand that may not last long and might require another price change later on.

This temporary boom is, of course, one of the reasons why monetary authorities like to inflate. An initial increase in the rate of monetary growth prompts an initial increase in business activity, with a rise in output and employment after only a short time. This can be used to give the illusion of prosperity before an election (an illusion which often beguiles the monetary authorities themselves and urges them to increase the monetary growth even more in order to keep the boom mechanism well lubricated), but, unfortunately, after output has expanded to its maximum extent, the new spending will go entirely to bid up prices. And, of course, the greater the monetary growth, the higher those prices are likely to be.

The lag in effect of monetary policy

It is this *lag* between the onset of a monetary change and

its eventual effects that makes the link between the quantity of money and nominal income difficult to see, despite its consistency. One factor which makes the link particularly hard to discern is the *variability of the lag:* a monetary change today will affect nominal income in the future, but how long the process will take is not entirely predictable.

According to Friedman's impressive empirical work on the subject,[30] which is reviewed when the lag is given more in-depth consideration in Chapter 8, a change in the rate of growth of money will, on average, produce a change in the rate of growth of nominal income about six to nine months later. This seems to be roughly true for a number of different countries which Friedman has studied, including Japan, Israel, India, the United States, the United Kingdom and some South American states. He is aware that the lag is sometimes longer, sometimes shorter, but argues that it is remarkably consistent across geographical boundaries and over generations. Failure to allow for this delay, he concludes, is one of the main reasons why people misinterpret the effects of monetary growth or overlook its effects entirely. And the variability of the lag sometimes means that the ultimate effects of *different* monetary changes can become confused.

Naturally, where the changes in monetary growth are largest, the pattern of effects is easiest to see, because they are less likely to be confused or disguised by other factors. In the historical record there are, fortunately, many examples of major fluctuations in the rate of growth of money and many instances of severe inflations or depressions, and Friedman's examination of these incidents forms a powerful defence of his theory. (More recently, however, the very success of Friedman's ideas has caused most monetary authorities to be more careful about their monetary policy, and so there are fewer such incidents to judge from.)

There is, however, a second lag to be considered: the lag between the effect on output and the effect on prices. On average, says Friedman, prices have historically taken another six or nine months to adjust, so that the total lag between a change in monetary growth rates and a change in the rate of price inflation can average twelve to eighteen months. But a lag of two years is not particularly uncommon.[31]

The fact that monetary changes influence output first and prices only later explains the ineptness of much monetary policy up to now. All governments are pleased to take credit for the initial stimulus that an expansion gives to trade and employment, although they are less eager to admit that such a policy will eventually work through remorselessly to higher prices which will absorb all the initial prosperity. Once an inflationary episode has begun, it has proved almost impossible for politicians to steel themselves to overcome it, because the required decline in monetary growth will cause an initial decline in output without much effect, at first, on prices. This is naturally a difficult time for any monetary authority, with all the political pressures tempting them back down the inflationary path. If these temptations and pressures can be resisted, then prices will – eventually – begin to slow down and hold steady. The problem for politicians is that inflation is easy to start, but cannot be stopped overnight nor without some degree of hardship.

Short-term and long-term effects

It is clear from this that we must distinguish the short-term and long-term effects of monetary changes. Friedman accepts that a change in the nominal quantity of money may well have certain effects on *real* quantities such as the level of output, but claims that these effects will be mostly temporary. Over a period of years, the net effect of a monetary change will be largely limited to changes in *nominal* quantities such as money prices and nominal incomes.

The effects of monetary changes are different, therefore, depending on the time horizon which is considered. As Chapter 6 will explain more fully, Friedman suggests that the short term, in which output changes more rapidly than prices, might last anything up to five or ten years, because expectations are often slow to adjust. In a typical inflation starting from zero, he says,[32] people do not at first anticipate any rise in prices. If the increased spending does bid up prices, it is assumed that these rises will be temporary, and people are willing to hold slightly larger real money balances for the time being because they think that prices will soon fall. But if the growth in the quantity of money continues to rise faster than output, prices will go on rising, and eventually the public will come to anticipate that future prices will continue along this upward trend. Cash is now an expensive asset to hold, because it buys less with every day that passes, and so people will make greater efforts to reduce their cash balances. Their attempts to do so will serve only to bid up prices and therefore receipts and nominal incomes. By this time, prices will be rising very fast, possibly at a much faster rate than the quantity of money is growing, because people continue to expect that future prices will be ever higher. Even when the initial monetary stimulus has ended and its effects have worked right through, so that prices are beginning to stabilize once again, people will still be inclined to anticipate continued rises, and hence may overshoot in their efforts to spend their excess cash holdings. It will then take additional time before the genuine level of price changes is fully perceived and real household balances are adjusted back to their desired level.

Unemployment and inflation

Expectations also explain why inflation cannot be traded off against unemployment, in the opinion of Friedman and most of his fellow monetarists. The assumption that unemployment could be cured by a larger dose of inflation was a widespread one until it was falsified by events, and Friedman's application of expectations theory to this so-called 'Phillips curve' trade-off allows us to understand why it should have failed (which is the main subject-matter of Chapter 7 below).

Consider the case of a typical manufacturer. Monetary growth will swell people's money balances, making them willing to pay higher prices for goods. The manufacturer – not being familiar with the prices prevailing in other markets – will not recognize that this effect is global, and will interpret it as being wholly or partly an increase in consumers' preferences for his own product. He thinks that the willingness of customers to pay more indicates that they want more of his product, and he will try to capture this apparent new demand by expanding his output and increasing his workforce. So the initial monetary boost does stimulate employment.

In the longer period, however, people get wise to events. The manufacturer begins to understand that there was no special change in consumer tastes that favoured his own products, and that the higher prices his customers are willing to pay are nullified by the higher prices he has to pay for everything he buys. The upward movement of prices was general, and was not confined to him alone, so his gearing up for higher output was unjustified because there was no real increase in demand to be captured. Even worse, his workers will be demanding higher wages in order to compensate for the general increase in prices, and may even demand extra payments to cover the future price rises they anticipate over the next year. The employer has to reduce his workforce to bring his total wage bill into line, and the level of employment is drawn back to roughly what it was. The only thing which has risen is the level of prices. In the long run, the dose of inflation has done nothing to improve employment.

Monetary policy is therefore powerless, except in the short term, to pull unemployment below its 'natural rate' according to Friedman, but there may be circumstances in which an expansionary policy actually causes *more* unemployment. If people are very uncertain about the future course of prices because economic policies (or previous price fluctuations) have been erratic, workers may try to bid up wages even higher as a precautionary measure, while employers may try to trim employment even more closely. Since, in Friedman's judgement, higher rates of inflation are generally less stable, this effect is likely to be most powerful at the higher rates, so that rising inflation will tend to be associated with higher rates of unemployment.

Inflation is a monetary phenomenon

Many explanations other than monetary growth have been mooted by critics as the true source of price rises. These range from wars to import prices and the upward pressure of wages.

As we shall see in more detail in Chapter 6, Friedman argues that some of these factors may indeed affect the level of individual prices – a rise in the price of oil, for example, will tend to force up the prices of goods which are oil derivatives or which have a high element of transport costs in their price. But *unless there is an expansion in the supply of money*, it is impossible for people to pay these prices without consuming *less* of something or other. They may consume smaller quantities of the oil-related goods; or they may bid down the prices of others. Lower prices elsewhere will keep down the average price index, while a smaller trade in oil-related goods will alter the composition of the typical basket of commodities used to calculate the general price level. In either event, the *general* level of prices of traded goods cannot rise without an influx of new money.

Traditional economic theory distinguishes between 'cost-push' and 'demand-pull' inflation, but Friedman argues that all inflation stems from the increased demand for goods and services that is precipitated by a monetary expansion. Rising costs might lead to rising prices in *some* markets, but they cannot do so overall unless the quantity of money is growing. For example, suppose that a high wage settlement is agreed in a particular industry. If employment is not to be reduced to compensate, the industry must divert more of its receipts into wages. Either its other costs must be cut – bidding down the prices of its suppliers – or it must earn more money by selling more products or raising prices. Its customers will then in turn be faced with the choice of cutting their spending on other products or raising their business receipts. *Their* customers must make the same decision, and so on. At the end of the day, it is only an expansion in the total quantity of money which can sustain this pyramid without somebody cutting down on consumption somewhere. While rising costs can and do lead to higher prices for certain products, they can do so only if prices go down elsewhere or if people buy less, in which case the *general* level of prices is unaffected.

Just as this 'cost-push' mechanism proves to be inflationary only in the presence of a monetary expansion, says Friedman, so does the 'demand-pull' process. Suppose, for example, that there is a sudden new demand for shoes for some reason.[33] Shops will be delighted to sell more shoes, and will order more from the manufacturers, who will have to buy more leather and take on new workers. But to get more leather for themselves, manufacturers will have to bid higher at auctions; and to get new workers they will have to offer more generous wages. The retailers, similarly, will find that the shoes they buy cost more because of the higher leather and manufacturing costs; and to satisfy their customers they may have to take on new sales assistants, which will again raise their costs. Although everyone discovers that their *costs* have risen, the whole process was initiated by a rise not in costs but in *demand*. Unless that demand was diverted from the purchase of other goods – in which case *their* retailers and manufacturers will have to lower their prices and the overall price index will be unchanged – it can only have come from the increased spending created by an increase in the quantity of money.

Friedman's conclusion is that however an inflationary episode may appear to arise, it is everywhere based on an increased demand for goods and services as people try to spend their cash balances. And because the demand for money is fairly stable, this excess spending derives ultimately from a rise in the nominal quantity of money supplied to the economy. Inflation is *always* a monetary phenomenon.

The sources of monetary growth

As Chapter 4 will explain, Friedman sees the government, the ultimate authority over the quantity of money, as the source of long-term inflation and the increased unemployment that it often generates. But government spending is not always inflationary, as some popularizers of monetarism often suggest. Clearly, government spending *will* be inflationary if it is financed by the creation of new money, as when the government spends more than it receives in taxation and finances the deficit by printing new banknotes, minting new coins, creating bank deposits or otherwise extending credit. But if the increased government expenditure is financed by higher taxes or by borrowing from members of the public, it amounts to no more than a transfer of the existing quantity of money out of private hands and into those of the government.

So, according to Friedman, fiscal policy (that concerned with the size and structure of taxation and the level and pattern of government expenditure) obviously determines what share of national income is taken by the government, but does not have much of an impact on inflation. He concedes that large-scale government borrowing might tend to bid up interest rates, which may have a minor impact on the demand for money and thus the bidding up of other prices. But the effect of fiscal policy on prices is weak and indirect (see Chapter 9).

Interest rates

How interest rates behave is an important question in monetary theory, because some of Friedman's critics believe that the demand for money depends very heavily on their level and movement. They argue that a change in interest rates will cause people to run down or add to their money balances on a sizeable scale, since higher interest rates will induce them to use their cash to purchase new investments, while falling interest rates will see them selling other assets for cash. The result, they say, is an instability in the demand for money and therefore a weakening of the link between the quantity of money and its final effect on output and prices. Indeed, some argue that the manipulation of interest rates can be used deliberately to produce these effects.

Friedman sees the relationship between money and interest rates as precisely the other way round. To him, changes in monetary growth can significantly disturb interest rates, and interest rates are therefore a very poor guide to the underlying state of the economy. This is particularly true because the effect of money on interest rates is not uniform: following a monetary expansion, for example, interest rates will initially tend to *decline* because people have more money in hand and less need to borrow, and lenders are unable to charge high rates for loans; but as the new money works through its course and begins to raise prices, it will produce a rise in the demand for loans which will in turn *raise* interest rates. If monetary growth is now retarded, the effects will be mirrored: initially, interest rates will be high and may rise further; only gradually will they fall.

Plainly, this anomalous variation presents a problem for economic policymakers. How can they possibly decide the 'correct' level for interest rates to be set at, when the same rate of interest could mean that a number of different underlying forces are at work? The difficulty of estimating where we are on this interest-rate switchback makes 'money market conditions' a very poor guide to anti-inflation policy, concludes Friedman, despite its postwar popularity.

The poverty of price controls

Just as inflation can be generated only through a monetary expansion, so Friedman and other monetarists agree that only monetary measures can end it. It may be a difficult process, particularly in the short term while output and employment are falling and prices have not yet begun to adjust; but it is the only genuine solution.

Wage and price controls, so commonly used in an effort to curb inflation, are relatively powerless to do so. They may have some useful effect in curbing expectations, according to Friedman, but their most prominent effect is merely to suppress some of the symptoms of inflation, without actually ending it. The inflationary pressure is always there, and only monetary measures will reduce it. To use an analogy, price controls

are like putting a brick on top of a boiling kettle to keep the lid from blowing off. If, simultaneously, the flame under the kettle is turned down, the brick may prevent the lid from blowing off. But if the flame is turned up, the pressure will build until the lid blows off or the kettle explodes.[34]

Likewise, inflation will always burst out, despite attempted controls, unless the monetary heat is turned down.

But wage and price controls are not just ineffective: they are damaging. The result of price controls in Germany immediately after the Second World War, says Friedman, was to reduce output by half, because price controls freeze an economy's adjustment processes and generate shortages and dislocations that require further controls. The sudden removal of controls in Germany heralded the economic 'miracle' that followed.[35]

Inadequacy of exhortation

If statutory price and wage controls can do nothing to reduce an inflation, it is clear that mere exhortations to the public to reduce their spending are likely to be even less effective. This is, however, often advocated as a serious proposition, and it is possible to see the germ of sense behind it. If appeals by politicians did in fact cause people to spend less rapidly, then velocity would drop, tending to offset the price effects of the monetary acceleration responsible for the inflation. In other words, the slowing down of spending would work to reduce the speed with which prices were being bid up.

Friedman does not give us a direct answer to this common proposition, but it is possible to infer what his answer would be from his general writings on the demand for money. Such a policy might well have some hope of succeeding, if people really believed in it, if they were confident that others would also contain their spending, and if they were prepared to make a *permanent* change in the size of the real money balances they consistently like to hold. If they had doubts whether others would co-operate in the spending slowdown, the policy would fail, because it would plainly be against common sense for an individual to hold on to his depreciating cash while others continued to spend and to force prices higher and higher. And to succeed, it would require people to make a *permanent* increase in their desired cash holdings, because as soon as people started to loosen their belts again, velocity would rise and would soon be manifested in the bidding up of prices once more.

Similar reasoning reveals the inadequacy of attempts to cure economic depressions by exhorting the public to spend more rapidly, as President Roosevelt did during the interwar depression in the United States. It cannot work because it goes against human nature: in a depression, cash is a very valuable commodity, and nobody would go on a spending spree at the behest of the government unless he understood the purposes of the policy and was utterly convinced that his fellows would all do the same. Only a monetary stimulus will have the desired effect, gradually filling people's pockets until the point where they feel that they no longer have to conserve every cent in order to ward off even greater disaster. Rises or falls in velocity cannot be legislated, but result from aspects of human psychology which have proved to be remarkably resistant to change.

Other policy prescriptions

Friedman and other monetarists sometimes find themselves in considerable disagreement about the policy prescriptions that follow from the theoretical analysis they share, and to orthodox economic thinkers his prescriptions, summarized in Chapter 10, may seem radical indeed.

An important point is that while monetary policy is undoubtedly powerful, the length and variability of the lag makes it very limited in its usefulness. It certainly cannot be employed for 'fine tuning' to smooth temporary recessions or inflations, because by the time its effects show themselves, conditions may have changed entirely and the policy may be completely inappropriate. The best policy, therefore, is to follow some sort of monetary *rule*, says Friedman.[36] He suggests that the quantity of money should be expanded at a fairly steady rate of growth between three and five per cent per year, so that there is sufficient liquidity available to allow growth without price reductions being necessary, but not sufficient to lead to runaway inflation.

Friedman suggests other policies which would help to remove the pressure on politicians to inflate. Indexation of government securities and tax thresholds would help, he argues,[37] because it would prevent the government fixing its obligations in nominal terms and then inflating so that it did not have to repay so much in real terms, and because it would ensure that taxpayers did not find themselves drifting remorselessly into higher and higher tax brackets just because their *nominal* incomes were rising even though their *real* incomes were not. He goes on to suggest that indexed contracts should be generally encouraged, so that people can distinguish the real effects of an inflation from the nominal effects, and can thus distinguish relative price changes from rises in prices generally.

Other policies recommended by Friedman are designed to make the quantity of money easier to control, so that when the monetary rule is adopted, it will not be undermined by monetary movements that are outside the control of the monetary authorities. One such measure, and a radical one, is the proposal for 100% reserve banking, so that banks will be unable to 'create' new money.[38] At present, since depositors are unlikely to want to withdraw all their deposits at once, a bank need keep in its vaults only a small fraction of its depositors' cash, just enough to meet the day-to-day withdrawals, and can lend out perhaps two or three times what it holds in reserve. Each new dollar printed by the authorities and deposited in someone's bank account can thus produce another two or three dollars in bank lending. This private 'creation' of money makes each new dollar very powerful, and the banks' leeway in deciding exactly how much to keep in reserve and how much to lend out makes its effect unpredictable. Friedman would separate the deposit-managing role of the banks from their lending and investment activities, so that a dollar deposited could not 'create' new money elsewhere.

Also on Friedman's shopping list are freely floating exchange rates: since nearly all of the output of most countries is destined for the home market, it is pointless to aim at fixed parities; it is much more important to prevent inflation or depression at home by ensuring that domestic markets can work smoothly in a stable monetary framework. As a final recommendation, Friedman insists that unemployment and interest rate targets should *not* be aimed for by using monetary measures, which are entirely inappropriate to the task.

PART 2: MONEY AND INFLATION

CHAPTER THREE

Velocity and the Demand
for Money

The quantity theory is in the first instance a theory
of the *demand* for money.[1]

THE *velocity* of money and the *demand for money* are simply two
ways of analyzing the same phenomenon. For various reasons,
people want to hold money: so that they can spend, save
or invest, for instance. Usually, they will want to hold a certain
amount in *real* terms – perhaps an amount equivalent to so
many weeks' consumption or income[2] – and they will not
be attached to specific *nominal* holdings that change their value
as prices change.[3] If people choose to keep larger real balances,
holding on to their income rather than spending it quickly,
the 'turnover' of each dollar, or pound or drachma is obviously
smaller. *Greater demand* means *lower velocity*.

For the community, velocity is therefore simply the reciprocal of some particular expression of the real quantity of money.
The 'income velocity of circulation', for example, is the reciprocal of the proportion of a year's income held as money. Analysis
of the factors that determine the demand for real money
balances also leads to the determination of its reciprocal,
velocity.

Velocity, prices and output. As we have already seen from the
brief summmary of Friedman's monetary economics given in
the last chapter, the behaviour of velocity is absolutely crucial
in determining the extent to which changes in the money
stock produce subsequent changes in prices or output. To
Friedman, it is an empirical fact that the demand for money

is highly stable – that people are remarkably consistent in the number of weeks' income that they choose to keep in the form of cash or easily accessible bank accounts and the other things we call 'money'. This fact can be verified easily enough, and it means that there is a very powerful link between the number of dollars, pounds or pesos the monetary authorities allow to go into circulation one month and the prices of goods in the shops a few months later.

There are all sorts of ways in which this new money can be created (the traditional caricature is of the government simply printing more banknotes so that it can boost the pay of its own workers without having to raise more taxes), but the effect is much the same. The new money pours into the community, swelling people's pockets, filling their tills, and increasing their bank accounts. Assuming that prices are stable, people now find they are holding larger amounts of cash than they really want, since the money in their pockets, their tills and their accounts would cover them for more weeks' spending than they consistently choose to hold. So they set about reducing these cash balances.[4]

Short of burning banknotes, the only way an individual can reduce his cash balances is by spending. But, as we have seen, that simply means that the extra cash is passed on to someone else, who now faces exactly the same problem of excess cash balances.[5] That person, and the next, will also spend, in an attempt to keep their holdings at the traditional level. The net result is that everybody wants to spend: shopkeepers find that they can charge higher prices, people in auctions are prepared to pay more, but still the spending spree continues. The rising prices, of course, erode the value of any nominal unit of money, until at last people find that the *real* value of their cash holdings has been whittled back down to the level they were seeking all along. Thus the spending spree peters out and prices stabilize at their new level.

This, says Friedman, 'in a nutshell and somewhat over-simplified', is the process whereby changes in the stock of money exert their influence on the price level.[6] It is plain from this process that the stability of people's demand for money is crucial to the result. If the public were happy to hold on to the newly created money, leaving it to lie idly in their bank accounts or even in the pockets of their old suits, it would have no effect at all on prices. If they *sometimes* tried to spend the excess and *sometimes* held on to it in an unpredictable and capricious manner, then the resultant effect on prices would also be unpredictable. And thus, to Friedman, the quantity theory stands or falls on what we can discover about the *demand for money*.

A 'theory of the demand for money'?

However much Friedman might like to suppose that the quantity theory has *always* been concerned with discovering the nature of the demand function for money, there is rather little evidence for it. True, David Hume may have noted that increases in the nominal quantity of money would have no effect if they were locked up in chests; the Bullion Committee[7] may have observed the technical improvements in banking that served to raise the speed of transactions; but not even the Chicago School in its prewar days devoted much attention to the psychological factors which determine the shape and stability of the demand function.[8] It was left for Friedman himself, with his collaborator, Anna Schwartz,[9] to demonstrate empirically that demand is stable and that the quantity theory therefore holds.

If few before Keynes had troubled themselves much over the demand function – the mathematical formula showing how people make decisions about their cash holdings – nobody after him could ignore the fact that the quantity theory depended crucially on its shape and stability. It is to Friedman's credit that he, more than anyone else, placed the demand function at the centre of the quantity theory debate and was able to specify it in a few, stable terms that countered the attack by Keynes and his successors such as Tobin.[10] That attack highlighted the different motives – transactions, precautionary and speculative – that coexist in the minds of everyone who holds money, and the numerous, unpredictable and unstable factors acting upon them, such as prices, income, the rate of interest, uncertainties about future interest rates, unemployment and so on, any of which could change their attitudes. With this battery of factors influencing it, how could the demand function be stable and reliable?

FRIEDMAN'S ANALYSIS OF DEMAND

The challenge for Friedman was thus to show that the demand function was stable, for only then could anyone produce accurate predictions of the results of monetary changes. Friedman answered the challenge with both empirical and theoretical responses.

From the empirical point of view, Friedman says that the Keynesian interpretation of velocity is indefensible.[11] Keynes in the *General Theory,* for example, ignores the quantity theory and treats nominal income as if it were determined by forces largely independent of the quantity of money. Carried to its extreme, as it is by Alvin Hansen, this treatment makes velocity (and its reciprocal) merely the ratio of two statistically independent magnitudes, money and spending or income,[12] so it is hardly likely that it would behave in any regular way. Friedman replies that, over more than a century, velocity has been far more stable than either of its components, so plainly there *is* some statistical linkage between the quantity of money and nominal income. Although velocity does indeed vary over short periods, its effect is generally to *reinforce* monetary changes rather than to confound them.

From the theoretical viewpoint, Friedman examines the kinds of factors which are likely to influence the demand for money of individuals and businesses, and concludes that they are few in number and not likely to be inherently unstable. Furthermore, he adopts the (revolutionary) view that two important factors, income and wealth, can be treated identically in terms of their influence on the behaviour of money holders, reducing the potential instability of the demand function even further.

The derivation of the demand function[13]

Friedman's conceptual breakthrough is to treat money as an

asset or capital good, rather than a consumption good. A consumption good is demanded for its immediate utility, and the demand is determined by its various characteristics, its price, the prices of other close substitutes, the tastes of potential consumers and their income constraints. An asset or capital good, however, is not purchased to be consumed immediately: it is *held* for the stream of income or 'consumable' services (such as security or even status) which it renders. The tastes and preferences of individuals, and the character of the asset, will be important factors in the determination of its demand; but so will be the stream of income or consumable services which the asset will generate (or is *expected* to generate) while it is held.

The character of different assets varies enormously, as does the flow of income or services which they render. The yield on bonds or equities, for example, will be principally financial – their rate of return, anticipated capital gain or dividend. But they may bring other benefits in terms of convenience, ease of transfer or durability. Cash holdings, according to Friedman, are just one asset among others, and although they *may* produce financial returns (as, for example, the income on demand deposits), their principal 'yields' to their holders are security, liquidity and convenience.

Tastes and preferences, in other words, will influence people in their decision to hold money or other assets, as will their anticipations about the future value of each asset in their portfolio. If we want to know the factors which are important in the demand for money, therefore, we have to list the various factors which determine the total volume of assets held and discover how people choose to divide that portfolio between various competing assets, including money.

The important factors. The first factor which Friedman thinks it important to list is the *total wealth* which an individual (or any other unit) possesses. This, logically, sets the upper limit on the potential demand for money, but since people will choose to hold some assets other than money, the effective limit is even lower.

Not all wealth is held in physical assets, of course. The

major asset of most people is their earning potential, and the proportion of total wealth that is attributed to this *human wealth* is once again important in setting a limit to the demand for money holdings.

Money is an asset that is held for its *real* 'yield' in terms of convenience, security and liquidity, but obviously the real yield of any given nominal amount is affected by the price level, so that *prices* will be an important determinant of the nominal quantity of money people desire to hold. They must be included in the demand function.

Financial assets that yield a fixed stream of income, such as bonds, are made more or less attractive by changes in interest rates, and so the *bond rate* will influence how people switch their assets between money and bonds. Financial assets such as equities, which yield an income stream that is constant in real terms, are made more or less attractive by the market rate for *equities*. Both are affected by anticipated *capital appreciation or depreciation*, and so all these factors must be included as having an influence on the demand for money.

Physical assets do not usually yield a financial return, but they do provide non-monetary 'yields' in terms of utility. But since the real value of these non-monetary services will be affected by the prices of other goods and services, the *price level* must again be included.

Lastly, there are all kinds of *tastes, preferences and expectations* about the future which are important in deciding how people divide their asset portfolios between money and other things, and which must also go into the function.

Conclusion. Adding these factors together, we find that the demand for money depends upon the level of prices, the expected rate of return and capital appreciation on financial assets, the rate of change of prices, total wealth, human wealth, and general preferences, tastes, and anticipations.

For businesses, the demand function is roughly similar, although the 'total wealth' and 'human wealth' division is not very useful, since a firm can buy and sell capital in the marketplace and can hire and fire its 'human wealth' almost at will. But the other factors are still important.

The significance of Friedman's formulation

Although it may look complicated and dependent upon a large assortment of potentially destabilizing factors, Friedman's version of the demand function for money is in fact relatively free from the sort of unstable factors that cause Keynes's 'speculative demand' to be highly volatile and unstable. Market interest rates, for example, which are regarded as critical in the Keynesian formulation, are downgraded to a comparatively unimportant place in the Friedman formulation. Expectations about other events, such as the future trend of prices, certainly do enter the function, but Friedman's view is that these will be temporary in their effect and will soon drop out of the reckoning once price changes have brought real money balances back to their desired level following any monetary disturbance.

A second point of difference with Keynes is that, in Friedman's view of the demand function, there is no division of money balances into 'active' (transactions and precautionary) and 'idle' (speculative) elements. For Friedman, money is held for a variety of different purposes – indeed, its versatility is one of its greatest attractions – and it would be wrong to try to fragment them in this arbitrary and misleading way. Rather,

each dollar is, as it were, regarded as rendering a variety of services, and the holder of money as altering his money holding until the value to him of the addition to the total flow of services produced by adding a dollar to his money stock is equal to the reduction in the flow of services produced by subtracting a dollar from each of the other forms in which he holds assets.[14]

In practical terms, this is elegant, because it saves us having to deal with two different demand functions, as Keynes has to do. In theoretical terms, it is highly significant, because it takes account of the many and various motives for which money is held and is therefore a significant advance on Keynes's theories about how people decide and adjust their asset portfolios.

Friedman's treatment of money as an asset leads to further

significant differences about how changes in the quantity of money make their effect on economic activity. In the Keynesian model, monetary changes have their effect through bond prices and interest rates. The traditional way by which the authorities augment the money supply is to buy bonds. An effect of this is to raise bond prices and therefore reduce their rate of return. Lower returns on bonds induce people to put their money elsewhere, such as in laying down new productive capital that will boost future output and hence incomes. The monetary increase *does* have some effect on income, therefore, but it is a weak and indirect effect, easily 'trapped' in the financial markets if people decide to hold on to the new cash rather than to invest. In Friedman's model, on the other hand, monetary disturbances will have their effect *directly* on the prices and production of all kinds of goods, since people will buy (or sell) any asset they want to in the process of adjusting their cash holdings back to their preferred level. To him, monetary changes do not have to be mediated through the narrow channel of financial asset interest rates (and their power cannot be halted by attempts to manipulate interest rates in the opposing direction or otherwise to control the money markets, as Keynesians recommend). Put simply,

Keynesians tend to concentrate on a narrow range of marketable assets and recorded interest rates. The monetarists insist that a far wider range of assets and of interest rates must be taken into account. They give importance to such assets as durable and semi-durable consumer goods, structures and other real property. As a result, they regard the market interest rates stressed by the Keynesians as only a small part of the total spectrum of rates that are relevant.[15]

The limits of Friedman's formulation. Friedman's derivation of the demand function for money does not suggest that demand is a numerical constant, but that it is dependent upon a small number of factors that in most cases can be expected to be fairly stable, and that the function itself is therefore fairly predictable. Thus, the effects of monetary disturbances are in turn relatively clear and regular.

But it is important to note that Friedman's version of the

quantity theory says little about the movement of *prices* that will occur after a monetary disturbance, although this is how it is often caricatured. Even if the demand function were perfectly stable, the effects of monetary disturbances would still be predictable only in terms of *income*, not prices. Since a rise in nominal income could come about through rises in prices (and therefore receipts), *or* through a larger volume of goods being traded – or some combination of the two – the theory would tell us nothing about how much of any change in nominal income would be reflected in real output and how much in prices.[16]

Friedman's own view is that, over the decades, monetary disturbances will show themselves predominantly in price movements; but clearly, the effect depends on all kinds of additional factors, such as whether output is already at its feasible maximum or not. So when we come to look at the empirical evidence for Friedman's view, it is important to remember that we are seeking correlations between the quantity of money and the level of *income* rather than prices.

IS DEMAND STABLE?

The first task which Friedman faces in trying to perform empirical tests on his version of the demand function is that it must be pared down to those variables which can in fact be measured. Some of the elements in Friedman's function do indeed pose some difficulties of measurement, and so they must be dropped if they are thought to be relatively unimportant, or estimated by other related variables if they are thought to be necessary and significant.

For example, no figures are available for *expected* rates of return on financial assets, since these are psychological in nature, are all different, and will change as interest rate changes cause different capital gains or losses. For computational ease, it is better simply to use one or two straightforward, actual interest rates to approximate to them. The rate of change of prices, says Friedman, can usually be dropped because it becomes important only in hyperinflation. Total wealth is hard to measure, but the income variable does much the same job; and the balance between human and non-human wealth is generally rather stable in a non-slave society (people *can* improve their earning prospects by adult education and training, but it is a slow process and balances out over the society as a whole), so that the wealth factors too can be dropped for empirical purposes. Income is important, however, and so are the tastes and preferences and other values that make money more or less attractive (though these are almost impossible to measure).[17]

After all these simplifications, we are left with a stripped-down demand function for money: that *the demand for real money balances is a function of interest rates, income and the general utility of holding money.* This simplified version can be used much more easily for empirical testing, says Friedman, and is a good approximation to the actual demand function because all the main variables have been retained. And, he believes, empirical testing will show the stability of the function and therefore the usefulness of the quantity theory.

The theory under test

With the simplified version of the demand function, we can now study empirically the relationship between the quantity of money and other economic magnitudes. Of course, because the stripped-down function is only an approximation, the results will depend considerably on the exact definitions used. Having searched the evidence, Friedman takes *money* to mean currency plus an adjusted figure for bank deposits; *income* to be approximated by the annual estimates of net national product that are in common use; and *interest rates* to be his own mixture of short-term and long-term bond yields.[18] Other data and definitions may fit better, according to some investigators, but Friedman thinks it important to use data that have been available for many decades, so that the nature of the demand function, even if approximate, can be studied and checked over a lengthy period.

Is there a liquidity trap? The first priority for any such study of the nature of the demand function is to check the Keynesian belief that fluctuations in interest rates can have a big effect on the amount of money demanded, and see whether liquidity preference does in fact become absolute, as Keynes supposed it might, at low rates of interest. Friedman's earliest empirical studies caused him to conclude that interest rates in fact had only the most minor effect on demand:

the rate of interest had an effect in the direction to be expected from theoretical considerations but too small to be statistically significant.[19]

Most evidence since then, however, has suggested strongly that interest rates *are* significant, although their impact on the demand for money is quite predictable. Estimates of the strength and stability of this impact, however, vary according to which definitions of interest rates and money are used.[20]

The evidence remains controversial. Friedman himself has concluded that short-term interest rates are more important than long-term interest rates in their impact on the demand for money. But he also thinks it is necessary to include the yield on assets other than money, including the 'yields' or expected 'yields' on physical assets such as land, buildings, machinery and so on. These are naturally difficult to measure, because they are often subjective, but since in Friedman's view they are legitimate alternatives to holding money, they must be considered in some form.[21]

Most studies, however much their differences in definition may produce different results, are united on one broad finding: there is almost no evidence that at low rates of interest the interest elasticity of the demand for money approaches minus infinity. In other words, *there is no liquidity trap*. In fact, there is little indication that the demand curve changes at all as interest rates fall: this is 'one part of extreme Keynesian doctrine that has been decisively rejected by empirical evidence'.[22]

The effect of inflation. The empirical studies of the demand for money do confirm that the expected rate of inflation is an important variable, at least in times of hyperinflation. This evidence, however, is not completely clear, since high rates of inflation tend to be associated with high nominal interest rates, which might confuse our judgement concerning the *relative* importance of prices and interest rates in the demand for money.[23]

Income and wealth. To Friedman, income and wealth are merely different aspects of the same phenomenon: assets are held for the stream of future services or 'income' that they generate, while wealth is just a figure representing the present value of that income stream. Problems of measurement mean that our estimates of the two might not match up, however; indeed, it appears from empirical studies that measured wealth, rather than current income, is a far more reliable factor, although the 'human wealth' element seems to have little importance.[24]

Friedman's examination of the data over many decades shows that the long-term average levels of the real stock of money per capita are highly correlated with those of real income per capita. There is, however, not an equal growth: as real incomes grow, people have tended to hold more of their wealth in money balances. Money, as it were, is treated as something of a 'luxury' good.[25] Over the period 1867–1975, Friedman notes, the computed elasticity was about 1.8, meaning that a 1% increase in real income per capita has, on average, been associated with a 1.8% increase in real cash balances per capita. Hence its status as a 'luxury'.[26]

Implications for the quantity theory

If the demand for money were not a fairly stable function, or if it had some special form like the 'liquidity trap', or could not be estimated at all, the prospects would be bleak for the quantity theory. Critics could then argue, without fear of being contradicted, that the quantity of money was not necessarily linked in any way with nominal income. To put it at its most extreme, it could then be insisted that nominal income is determined by forces that have nothing to do with the quantity of money, and that money and income are two entirely independent magnitudes, as Hansen supposes.

The simple quantity of money equations would therefore

be undermined, since the crucial variable of velocity would simply represent the ratio of two magnitudes that were not linked in any consistent way. It could take any value: and it could easily vary in such a way as to offset any changes in money.

Friedman, however, argues that the evidence reveals a clear covariance between money and income, and that velocity is therefore a relatively steady figure. It is not a numerical constant, as would be required to show that changes in money are reflected equiproportionately in income changes, but that view is nevertheless very near the mark. Velocity does seem to be somewhat variable in the short term, but by and large there is a steady link between money and income over the long term, a link which is not only in one direction but always of roughly the same degree. In other words, the demand for money is fairly predictable, and the quantity theory stands up to testing.

Of course, the data recorded over nine decades is confused by the fact that there is a marked upward trend in both incomes and the nominal quantity of money. But Friedman argues that even if we eliminate this trend mathematically, the crude version of the quantity theory will still take us a long way. He concludes from the data that

a numerically constant velocity does not deserve the sneering condescension that has become the conventional stance of economists. It is an impressive first approximation that by almost any measure accounts for a good deal more than half of the phase-to-phase movements in money or income. Almost certainly, measurement errors aside, it accounts for a far larger part of such movements than the other extreme hypothesis – that velocity is a will-o'-the-wisp reflecting independent changes in money and income.[27]

This finding is particularly important in view of the common rejection of the quantity equations on the grounds that any change in the quantity of money is in fact completely offset by a movement in velocity in the opposite direction. Friedman's empirical research has led him to the conclusion, however, that while this opposite movement does tend to occur over long periods, the long-term variation in velocity is so small that it makes hardly any impact. The movement in velocity might moderate the effects of monetary changes, but it certainly does not stifle them:

Over the nine decades that we have studied, there have been a number of long swings in money income. As a matter of arithmetic, these swings in money income can be attributed to movements in the nominal stock of money and in velocity. If this is done, it turns out that the swings in the stock of money are in the opposite direction from those in velocity and so much larger in amplitude that they dominate the movements in money income. As a result, the long swings in prices mirror faithfully the long swings in the stock of money per unit of output.[28]

Troublesome details. The evidence, however, is not so straight-forward, and there are some nagging details that require some more sophisticated treatment. While velocity is fairly predictable over long periods, it tends to fluctuate over the shorter, cyclical changes, and (paradoxically for the simple quantity theory) 'velocity, as measured, generally rises during economic expansions and falls during economic contractions'.[29]

This pattern, where velocity tends to fall slowly over the very long term, but spurts up and down over cycles, is indeed a confusing position. It seems to suggest that velocity works weakly to offset monetary changes in the long term, but works strongly to reinforce them in the short term (Friedman says that, during these short cycles, a monetary change of one fifth of one per cent produces an entire one per cent change in income).[30] The quantity theory is therefore threatened by this anomalous and erratic behaviour of demand. Fortunately, Friedman has an explanation to hand in the form of his *permanent income hypothesis:* but before explaining this it is perhaps best to consider the wider principles of how money is supplied and the broader lessons contained in the empirical analysis of its effects.

CHAPTER FOUR

The Supply of Money

I do believe that changes in the supply of money have accounted for more than half the variance of money income for reasonably long periods and for changes measured over intervals of a year or more. But they certainly have not done so for all periods and all intervals.[1]

THE PROBLEM OF DEFINITION

According to Friedman, the *real* quantity of money held in the money balances of individuals and business enterprises is ultimately determined by the individuals and businesses themselves. In the wake of any change in the *nominal* quantity of money, which is determined principally by the monetary authorities and institutions, there may be a long period of readjustment: but ultimately, by bidding prices up or down, the public will push the *real* quantity of money back to the level at which they choose to hold it as a community. And since their demand is fairly stable, the behaviour of the *nominal* quantity of money will be of vital importance in the behaviour of prices.

But quite how the 'nominal quantity of money' is defined is a matter of dispute. The obvious qualities which an asset must possess if it is to be called 'money' are that it should be a medium of exchange and that it should act as a temporary store of purchasing power in the interval between receipt and payment; its function as an accounting unit might also be added. Unfortunately, there are many assets which do, or could be argued to, perform these functions, and so the precise definition of 'money' seems to be rather arbitrary. But the choice of definition, say Friedman's critics, could be crucial: the supply of money defined narrowly in terms of currency, for example, might perform entirely differently from the supply defined in terms of currency, plus bank deposits, plus savings deposits, plus savings bonds, and so forth. So a first step must be to review the alternatives.

Narrow and broad definitions of money

For systems like those prevailing today in the United States and the United Kingdom, *notes and coin in circulation* are obviously to be classified as money and, equally obviously, are controlled by the monetary authorities. But this was not always so. When coins were minted from precious metal, their supply was limited by the discovery and extraction of the metal; only dilution could stretch their quantity, but this would obviously dilute their value as well. Or again, under an international commodity standard, where a commodity such as gold was used for international payments, it would be the balance of those payments which determined the amount of coin in circulation. Today, however, the monetary authorities can adjust the quantity of notes and coin in circulation more or less at will.

There is also little doubt today that certain forms of bank deposits can uncontroversially be treated as money, particularly *demand deposits*, so called because the holder can transfer his deposits (by cheque) or withdraw them on demand. Since these can be used immediately for transactions, there seems little question about them. But there *is* doubt about *time deposits* or *savings accounts*, where some period of notice has to be given before a withdrawal can be made. If we accept people's time deposits with the commercial banks in the definition of money, we have also to decide whether building society deposits (in the UK) or savings and loan association deposits (in the US) should be included, since they are superficially very similar.

Deposit ratios. Including deposits with commercial banks makes a large difference to the behaviour of the money stock, because of the fractional reserve banking system. As we saw in Chapter 2, provided a bank can meet its day-to-day demands for withdrawals, there is no need for it to hold all its depositors' money on hand as notes and coin: some of it can be kept in coin to meet immediate daily demands, some can be kept in fairly liquid assets in case of unexpectedly heavy demand, but the rest can be invested in longer-term securities or other assets which might produce a profit for the bank and its depositors, but which would not be instantly accessible in the unlikely event of all depositors demanding their money at once. (This system, which worked unaided for many centuries, has been formalized in modern times, so that banks today are required by the government or monetary authorities to hold a certain proportion of their customers' deposits in liquid or currency form – a proportion known as the *reserve ratio*.)

The effect of this is to give money supply increases greater leverage than otherwise: if new money is created by the authorities and the holders put it into bank deposits, the banks can create overdrafts or undertake long-term investments totalling perhaps more than twice the sum of new deposits they need to keep as cash in their vaults. The amount of money effectively created is therefore much greater than it originally appears. For this reason, the money supply narrowly defined is often called 'high-powered money'. As Friedman says of the United States system:

High-powered money is currency held by the public plus currency held by commercial banks plus deposits liabilities of Federal Reserve Banks. In other words, it is the kind of money that can be used as bank reserves. It is called 'high-powered' because for each dollar held by a bank as reserves, the bank can have a number of dollars of deposit liabilities.[2]

Here, however, is an immediate source of concern for the quantity theorist. Banks are governed by laws setting their minimum reserve requirements; but they might *choose* to remain *more liquid* than the minimum. The economic effects of changes in the money stock are therefore influenced by the *actual* ratio of bank deposits to bank holdings of high-powered money, and to predict the precise impact of a monetary change, we have to predict the probable behaviour of the commercial banking sector. If banks choose to become more liquid, the impact of the change in money stock will, in total, be less.

The same behavioural question hangs over individuals: will they choose to hold their cash as currency in their pockets or will they put it into bank deposits? Once again, if the ratio of the public's deposits to its currency holdings is low, the 'high-powered money' will not be quite so high-powered.[3]

Non-bank institutions. The assets described so far, currency plus certain bank deposits, are those which Friedman treats as 'money' for empirical purposes. But there are many other assets which some critics argue should also be included.

Savings deposits in non-bank institutions are an obvious one. Although these institutions cannot 'create' money as the fractional reserve system enables the banks to do, they hold an increasing portion of total demand deposits, which can be used for making payments just as easily as those in commercial banks.

Time deposits, whether in commercial banks or non-bank institutions, are often in practice available for withdrawal on demand, although the 'notice of withdrawal' rule can obviously apply if necessary. Critics argue that this makes time deposits almost completely on a par with demand deposits and that they should be included in the definition of money stock without qualification. Only *genuine* time deposits would merit special treatment.

Certain other assets might also be included in definitions of money because of their relative ease of transfer, but clearly an asset cannot be considered as money unless it is redeemable at a known face value and is easily disposable. One such asset in common circulation is life insurance policies, which have a set surrender value if they are cashed in. Although most people are reluctant to cash in insurance policies, they nevertheless provide a store of value, and some writers have suggested that they should be added to the money supply definition.[4]

Eurocurrency. Another obvious definitional problem is generated by the existence of 'Eurocurrency' accounts. These are simply accounts which are held in one country, but designated in the currency of another (the term arose originally to describe dollar accounts held with institutions in Europe, but has now been broadened to include all currencies and countries). It may be that these accounts are used chiefly for foreign transactions and have little influence on the domestic economy, but there will probably be some. And it is a two-edged difficulty: we have to decide how to treat not only the balances which foreigners hold in the currency of the home country, but also the balances which residents hold in foreign currencies. At present, this phenomenon has not grown common enough to present undue definitional difficulties,[5] but it may well do so in the future.

Friedman's definition of money

For the empirical study of monetary trends over the decades, Friedman uses a working definition of the money stock which is towards the narrower end of the spectrum of available possibilities. This working definition is 'the sum of currency plus all adjusted deposits in commercial banks'[6]

This 'adjustment' was devised by Friedman and his co-worker Anna Schwartz to take account of the increasing financial sophistication of the commercial banks (and the community). Clearly, a demand deposit, for example, is only equivalent to cash in our definition if cheques written upon it are widely acceptable, and if banks are sufficiently numerous and convenient so that people can turn cheques into cash or add them to their own deposits without delay and difficulty. Similarly, a system of instantaneous electronic transfers between bank accounts might enable even higher velocity of circulation to be achieved. The same kind of bank deposit can therefore have very different effects, depending on the sophistication of the financial sector. Unfortunately, as Friedman admits, it is not possible to establish a single index of this sophistication, so, even with his adjustment, cash and deposit monies are not strictly comparable over long periods.[7]

For empirical purposes, however, it is clear that Friedman thinks the definition of money used is comparatively unimportant. Different definitions will yield different empirical results, particularly because the velocity of circulation of some forms of 'money' is higher than that of others. But provided we understand the nature of the assets we are including under the definition, the results will be clear enough in any event. Hence,

the selection of a specific empirical counterpart to the term money seems to us a matter of convenience for a particular purpose, not a matter of principle... Though the definition we use seems to us clearly the best choice for the period as a whole, its superiority to any of the other totals is slight, and for some specific periods one of the others may be preferable.[8]

Methodological issues. This attitude sometimes causes disquiet among Friedman's supporters and considerable irritation among his critics. There are perhaps two related points of concern, the first of which is Friedman's view that the definition is more a matter of personal choice than sound practice:

Just where the line is drawn between those temporary abodes of purchasing power we choose to term money, and those we term 'near monies' or 'liquid assets' or what not, is largely arbitrary.[9]

The second is the feeling that Friedman is choosing his definition of money in a very selective way so that it best fits the theory:

Our aim is to formulate an empirical definition of money that will facilitate, as far as is possible, the separation and analysis of the forces of demand and supply for the country or countries and period or periods studied... a definition that will enable us most readily and accurately to predict the consequences for important economic variables of a change in the condition of demand for or supply of money.[10]

But Friedman's selection of the best definition of money for the job is in fact a perfectly legitimate exercise, although it is easy to become confused about the methodology involved. It would certainly be illigitimate for Friedman to accept a measure for money and then alter the *theory* at each stage if it did not seem to explain events. That would leave us only with an unhelpful mass of *ad hoc* explanations of the past. But it *is* legitimate for him, having perceived a rough correlation, to investigate whether some more accurate definition of the money magnitude will lead to better results. This is entirely in keeping with his view of economics as a 'positive' science, where the strength of a theory is *what it predicts*, and how well.'' If there is some combination of currency, bank deposits, non-bank deposits and any other group of assets which *does* seem to determine the future level of income, or prices, or any other important quantity, then we have indeed learnt something by isolating it and watching it, since we can then start to make useful predictions about the future.

THE CONTROL OF THE MONEY SUPPLY

Even in this fairly superficial tour of the money supply, we have seen that it is not a completely exogenous policy variable. That is to say, although governments and monetary authorities may be able to determine the total quantity of money to a large extent, other factors such as the behaviour of depositors and banks are clearly of importance in determining the net impact. Even if Friedman is correct and the demand for money is stable, the quantity theory will lose much of its value if monetary *policy* cannot in fact control the total quantity of money in the economy. The forces influencing banks' and the public's behaviour, and wider questions concerning the financial intermediaries' ability to create new deposits, must be essential parts of the quantity theory. It is, unfortunately, a part which has not received Friedman's full attention, although his colleagues have taken up the issue, and its importance has been recognized more and more in recent years. However, Friedman does give *some* views on the subject, and these are interesting.

Is money supply truly exogenous?

Friedman's theoretical statement of the quantity theory of

73

money was subjected to much criticism on the grounds that the supply of money was not a policy variable which could be completely controlled by the monetary authorities, but responded passively to the demand for it. This is a criticism which is the modern equivalent of the traditional 'banking school' argument, but it is nonetheless powerful today.

In its modern form, the criticism would suggest that the stock of money is not determined exclusively by the authorities, but depends largely on the behaviour of banks, financial institutions and the public. Prices, output or interest rate changes can all be expected to change the behaviour of these actors in the drama, and hence the total quantity of money cannot be regarded as exogenous. Friedman's critic James Tobin, for example, has gone so far as to insist that the empirical evidence, including the cyclical patterns of money and money income, could be explained equally well on the assumption that money supply was entirely *endogenous*[12] and not determined by the authorities at all.

Monetary theorists such as Gurley and Shaw[13] have pointed out that banks are profit-making institutions and that they certainly will not always stick at the minimum allowable reserve ratio. On the contrary, they will adjust their portfolios in order to maximize their return from all available assets, with an adjustment to allow for the risk on each asset. The balance of available risks and returns might well be such that falling interest rates would cause banks to sell their interest-bearing assets, thereby raising the cash/deposit ratio above its legal minimum.[14] Money supply is therefore not completely in the control of the monetary authorities; it depends partly upon how banks adjust their portfolios of deposits and investments.

Other factors can influence money supply under this 'new view'. Friedman has noted that the demand for money balances rises disproportionately as national income rises; but critics say that this rise will probably produce an even greater rise in bank deposits, because the rise in real national income will probably be associated with a rise in large transactions, where payment is usually made by cheque. Wider availability of new forms of payment such as credit cards may induce people to hold their money balances in bank deposits yet further. Over a shorter period, changes in the relative prices of commodities normally bought with currency (bus travel, food, etc.) compared with those usually bought by cheque (consumer durables, etc.) will also influence the public's desired ratio of currency to deposits and will therefore affect the total money stock. Philip Cagan has suggested that high taxes may induce people into evasion by conducting transactions in cash.[15] (It is incongruous that Friedman is a campaigner for lower taxes, which would presumably make the control of the money supply that he favours just that bit more difficult.) In summary, the money supply under this view is a function not only of the *monetary base* (the 'high-powered money' determined by the authorities), but of *interest rates, income and other factors* which alter the proportion of money balances that the public holds as cash. It is not the exogenous, controllable item which Friedman supposes it to be.[16] Changes in business activity can change unpredictably the behaviour of banks and the public. And if we cannot foresee changes in the currency/deposit ratios of the public or the deposit/holding ratios of the banks, we cannot predict the net effects of monetary changes on the economy.

Friedman's view. Friedman accepts that these behavioural ratios will influence the supply of money, even in his latest writings; but he tends nevertheless to proceed from the assumption that the money supply is determined exclusively by the monetary authorities, and he states bluntly that the supply of money can be taken as an autonomous variable for empirical work, and that it is influenced little by feedback from cyclical or long-term changes in business activity or any other variables.[17] Only in defensive or more cautious moments does he explicitly state that

changes in the money stock are a consequence as well as an independent cause of changes in income and prices, though once they occur they will in their turn produce still further effects on income and prices. This consideration blurs the relation between money and prices but does not reverse it. For there is much evidence ... that

75

even during business cycles the money stock plays a largely independent role.[18]

Life would be much simpler, of course, without the confusing
round of business cycles: we could then embark on a sudden
monetary expansion and see whether this did indeed stimulate
business activity, and if this in turn produced changes in the
behaviour of individuals and banks which stimulated the
creation of a yet larger stock of money. But the evidence gets
confused in practice because of the constant ups and downs
of business activity and monetary policy. This has led some
critics to stress that it is by no means obvious that the direction
of causation runs solely from monetary change to economic
developments, and that much monetary change is in fact
caused by the ups and downs of business activity.[19]

Friedman's answer is, characteristically, on the empirical
plane, and *A Monetary History of the United States* is in large
part a testament to the autonomous nature of the money stock.
One obvious point, says Friedman, is that monetary changes
generally precede changes in general business activity. Presumably if there were then a feedback from industry, it would
boost the supply of money at a *later stage:* but this process
is difficult to discern.

But suppose that money and business expansion are simply
the outcomes of some third set of forces, which affects money
stock first and then business? Friedman refutes this proposition
by reference to wartime episodes where the supply of money
was clearly determined by factors other than prior business
conditions, but where the effects were nevertheless broadly
similar to other, peacetime changes in the supply. No 'third
set' of factors is needed or can be found to explain the wartime
inflations – government expansion of money is quite sufficient.

A third argument is deployed by Friedman. If causation
runs principally from money to business, then once the money
has been created, the monetary institutions have no further
role to play, and roughly the same results should follow no
matter what institutions exist. If causation runs from business
to money, then different monetary institutions may have very
different effects on the amount of money ultimately created

in response to the business expansion. But, says Friedman, in a long history peppered with very different financial institutions, the results of monetary changes have been broadly similar, suggesting very strongly that it is money which causes changes in business activity and not the other way round.[20] Although Friedman accepts that there might well be some feedback from business activity to monetary expansion, he mentions it rarely and doubts that it will be a major force.

Given a particular quantity of high-powered money, therefore, it seems unlikely that changes in income or wealth will have much effect on the total money supply. Friedman also suggests that interest rates and other variables have comparatively little effect – the rate of interest does not produce a marked shifting in banks' deposit ratios. He is therefore not suggesting that strict independence of the money supply is necessary if the quantity theory is to hold; in fact, as long as the supply conforms fairly predictably to any change in the amount of high-powered money created by the authorities, the theory will still be useful.

Opposing strategies for control

There are two opposing strategies which are sometimes referred to loosely as 'monetary controls'. The first strategy is to establish some kind of direct control of the quantity of money, particularly on the *monetary base*. A restrictive policy based on this strategy, for example, might employ the tools of a reduction in public sector deficits, or lower sales of government securities, savings bonds and the like. The banks would therefore find their asset base shrinking and would have to reduce their liabilities: and so it is believed that the restrictive policy would work through to the various different types of money and near-money which people hold. The opposing strategy seeks to control *interest rates* and to work through the *demand* for money. A restrictive policy would be to fix high interest rates, which would encourage people to hold more financial securities instead of cash, and which would allow the government to finance more of its activities by supplying those securities, i.e., by borrowing instead of creating money.

Clearly, both strategies cannot be used at once. If the monetary base is restricted, interest rates will settle at a new level decided by market forces; if the interest rate is controlled, the pattern of money and securities which people choose to hold will also settle of its own accord.

The confusion of money and credit. Friedman argues that the attempt to control interest rates is always a difficult one, and it is in any case a very poor and indirect way of attempting to control the quantity of money. It is rather like attempting to control the output of the motor industry by controlling the incomes of potential car buyers or by manipulating rail and air fares. Direct controls are likely to be far more reliable, and it is only their *incidental* effects on interest rates that has caused some people to suppose that the two methods are equally effective:

Of course, direct control of the monetary base will affect interest rates . . . but that is a very different thing from controlling monetary growth through interest rates.[21]

Some critics, however, have argued that interest rates are exactly what Friedman and other monetarists *should* be seeking to control. After all, they say, the true index of the scarcity of any commodity, such as tin or copper, is its *price;* similarly, the true index of the scarcity of money is its price – the interest rate – rather than the quantity supplied. It seems an odd heresy for a supporter of the free market economy to overlook prices when trying to gauge the scarcity of a commodity – in this case, money. But that, not the quantity that is actually supplied, must be the best guide to its actual sufficiency.[22]

But Friedman argues that the total *stock* is the correct indicator of the scarcity of money, and that interest rates are misleading. In his words:

The 'price' of money is the quantity of goods and services that must be given up to acquire a unit of money – the inverse of the price level. This is the price that is analogous to the price of land or of copper or of haircuts. The 'price' of money is not the interest rate, which is the 'price' of credit.[23]

The interest rate, in other words, is the cost of borrowing a unit of money which someone else has temporarily given up: it is not what that unit can be exchanged for once it is held.[24]

Money and credit, then, should not be confused. They are entirely different things, and their effects can be completely different:

... money and credit are two different magnitudes or sets of magnitudes; for example, the deposit liabilities of commercial banks are the bulk of the stock of money; their assets in the form of loans and investments are a minor fraction of the total outstanding volume of credit.[25]

Thus, says Friedman, in gauging the scarcity of money, like any commodity, it is important to look at its price as well as the quantity supplied; but in the case of money, it is the *level of prices* at which goods can be exchanged against it, not the *rate of interest*, which is the proper 'price'. There have been periods of liberal monetary policy conjoined with low interest rates as well as high interest rates. The rate of interest, therefore, is a poor indicator of monetary stringency or ease.

Base controls

What instruments are available to the policymaker who would seek to control the money supply? And are they effective? Friedman suggests that the evidence is fairly plain. *Open market operations*, where the monetary authorities alter the supply of money by buying or selling government securities, are in his view the most effective and sensitive tool of policy available. They can be effected speedily and can be as large or small as desired. *Reserve requirement changes* – altering the conditions under which the banks can create new deposits – are, on the other hand, a crude tool whose short-term effects are hard to predict. Other measures of credit control, such as '*moral suasion*' of the banking system by the authorities or 'voluntary' agreements regarding loans, have typically had only temporary effects, according to the data Friedman has collected. They may cause the banks to stay their hand for a while, but economic reality will out. *Changes in the discount rate* (the interest rate which the central bank charges other banks for loans) have been effective in the past, but this has been a discontinuous and crude tool compared to open market operations. *Credit restrictions* on time deposits, hire purchase arrangements and other loan contracts have never worked.[26]

Practical problems of controls. Apart from such brief statements as these, Friedman's major writings offer us little on the difficult question of whether the monetary authorities *can* in fact control the nominal quantity of money. However, he does show at length how the monetary authorities have produced depressions, inflations and other undesirable results by their *mis*management of money, particularly by their use of effective monetary controls at the wrong time or aimed in the wrong direction.[27] This does seem to indicate that Friedman has considerable underlying confidence in the ability of policy instruments to control the money stock.

It is perhaps a compliment to Friedman, however, that it is only in recent years that people have begun to argue much about the practicalities of money supply control at all. Because of the new emphasis on monetary questions – an emphasis stemming largely from his work – there has been a steady increase in the discussion about whether monetary growth should be controlled, and how. That increased attention has led to a number of questions becoming more obvious.

The first problem, which became all too clear as governments attempted to reduce the high rates of inflation that had become common in the 1970s, is that even the base items that are in the government's direct power are nevertheless hard to control *quickly*. To take three principal determinants of the stock of high-powered money in circulation, for example: changes in the *public sector deficit* certainly cannot be engineered overnight, particularly where this implies that some items of government expenditure must be trimmed; the rate at which *government debt* matures is also not within the short-term control of the government, so that to change the balance of the deficit between borrowing and monetary financing is not always easy; and *flows of currency abroad* are only partially controllable, and even this involves an undesirable intrusion into market forces (previous attempts have caused profound difficulties for the controlling authorities, particularly where fluctuating interest rates generate large-scale movements between currencies). These and other difficulties mean that inflation will take time to remove. Friedman would argue that an inflationary economy should be gently coaxed back to stable monetary growth, so that expectations have time to adjust and controls have time to take effect. However much he might like to agree with Hayek and the Austrian School that inflation must be stopped dead, Friedman recognizes that there are severe practical difficulties in such a policy.[28] As he says:

It takes time – measured in years, not months – for inflation to develop; it takes time for inflation to be cured.[29]

Another recent problem has been the *behaviour of idle balances*. Suppose that there is a restrictive monetary policy: interest rates are forced up as potential borrowers bid against each other for credit. The banks will *sell* some of their government securities to the public in order to get the bigger interest payments on new investments. No extra deposits have been created in this process, but deposits held by the public which were once idle have now become very active, being used to purchase the securities that the banks are selling. In other words, velocity has increased and offsets the monetary change.[30] In reply to this, Friedman argues that the actual impact of the change in velocity is small: money is overwhelmingly the dominant factor in this situation and interest rates, in time, will adjust back down again in any case, removing the offsetting effect that occurred in the short term.

The problem of *non-bank financial institutions* has also become much more important in recent years. Restrictive monetary policies have led to a great deal of innovation as financial institutions attempt to free themselves from the web of controls.

But this development again means an increase in velocity that could offset monetary policy. For example, a restrictive monetary policy will cause borrowers to drive up interest rates as they compete for scarce credit. The non-bank institutions will finance such investors, paying more interest to their own depositors to attract a flow of funds. Deposits are attracted away from the banks and into the non-bank institutions – who promptly deposit them back with the banks. Thus bank advances are unchanged, but the non-bank institutions, depending on the size of their reserve ratios, can now extend the total quantity of lending to their clients. So money has been created, or velocity has increased.

Parallel markets also cause problems for the monetary authorities. For example, local government institutions may issue their own debt which is outside the controls of the central authorities. There is a good deal of borrowing between banks and discount houses, which might again cause some looseness in the effects of monetary policy. Eurocurrency deposits are also important, although their total effect on the domestic economy is still a matter of debate.[31]

Empirical observations. Of all the assaults upon the idea that the money supply can be largely controlled, it is perhaps that of the so-called 'new view' of money that has been the most persuasive, the view that reminds us that banks are profit-making institutions, and that they do not always stick to their reserve requirements, often being in excess of the legal minima. Thus it is quite a simple matter for them to adjust their asset structure in order to change their lending patterns, thus offsetting or confusing the effects of monetary policy.

Of course, this view can be reconciled with Friedman's, if the legal reserve ratios imposed on the banks are in fact higher than those they would have chosen for themselves at any time, so that the banks always stick to the minima, and monetary changes thus have a predictable effect.[32] But, in any case, Friedman finds no reason to be very concerned about the 'new view' analysis, because it has not performed well in the past: in the United States and the United Kingdom over a century or more, it appears that while financial institutions have been very various and changed often, this made little impact on the velocity of money or its eventual effects.[33] The exact nature of the financial institutions, in other words, makes very little difference when it comes to monetary control: and this is not a theoretical guess but an empirical fact.

Certainly, agrees Friedman, the obvious factors such as changes in real income and in interest rates will affect the reserve ratios desired by banks and the capital-to-currency ratios desired by the public; international capital flows may be affected; the behaviour of the monetary authorities themselves may be changed. But, he continues, it is plain that many of these effects will run in opposite directions and will often offset each other. Likewise, major changes in the banking and financial structure have occurred over the last century – with changes from a commodity standard (gold) to a fiduciary standard, for example. But the supply of money still seems to be largely independent of anything other than the behaviour of the monetary authorities. Consequently, Friedman concludes that the *supply* of money is not dependent on the same variables which shape the demand function for money and does not respond passively to demand: it *can* be treated as an *exogenous* variable.

MONEY IN AN OPEN ECONOMY

Even if monetary control is possible domestically, some critics have objected that the movement of money across international boundaries makes it at best unpredictable in its results. Friedman began work on questions of international payments and international commodity standards almost before he began to expound his views on the quantity theory in any systematic way, and he has had much to contribute on this subject. His writings have been crucial in convincing politicians that a system of free exchange in currencies is better than the unworkable pseudo-gold standard that applied for much of this century, and in explaining how domestic monetary policy is actually made easier by floating currencies, not more difficult as some critics suppose.

The gold standard[34]

According to Friedman, the gold standard provided an automatic adjustment mechanism for international payments, and although gold was a costly form of currency to produce and an inconvenient one to use at times, nevertheless it worked well.

If a currency is fully backed by gold – if notes or coins can always be exchanged for the appropriate weight of gold (or other precious commodity) – then a true gold standard is in operation. If all countries are on the gold standard, then the different currency names – dollar, franc, pound and so on – are simply names for different amounts of gold. The government's role would then be limited to certifying the fineness of the metal used in transactions, coining it on demand, and issuing notes – in reality warehouse certificates – backed by gold. This system, or something very like it, operated until the early years of the twentieth century.

International payments, notes Friedman, were automatic under this system. If the market price of gold deviated between countries, then speculators would ship gold from one country to the next in order to take advantage of the differential, just as today's traders ship commodities from one country to another to take advantage of price differentials. So the market price of gold would stay fairly even. Exchange rates, in other words, were kept within narrow limits by market movements.

Another effect made the gold flows self-limiting. A country shipping out gold would experience a decline in the quantity of its money, since gold *is* money in this system; a country receiving gold would experience an increase. These changes would in turn influence prices and incomes, and thereby the demand for gold, limiting the temporary imbalance. For example, a country shipping out gold because the same weight of gold could command more purchasing power abroad would find that its money supply was reduced, and prices and incomes would fall shortly afterwards: this in turn would reduce the demand for imported goods in that country and thus reduce demand for the money (gold) necessary to pay for them. Thus, gold provided a completely automatic means of keeping international payments in harmony.

Domestically, gold-backed currencies did work well but had a number of drawbacks. In Friedman's view, these drawbacks were sufficient for the system to be discarded without too many tears being shed – although the rapid inflations which have followed the introduction of unbacked fiduciary notes might cause us to wonder.

The main *dis*advantage of a gold standard is the cost of producing the currency. A banknote costs almost nothing to produce, so that new currency can be quickly and effortlessly produced (or withdrawn) as required. But gold is costly to produce: it requires a significant investment of time and effort in order to mine a commodity which is used almost entirely for money (although artists and manufacturers do have alternative uses for it). This investment of manpower consumes a significant portion of the national income, and seems hard to justify for a commodity whose principal use is merely as a medium of exchange.

Changes in technological conditions of production will tend to produce permanent changes in the price level under any commodity reserve standard. If gold becomes cheaper to mine for some reason, its output will be stepped up, increasing the prices of other commodities relative to it. Because the present production of a currency commodity like gold will probably be small with respect to its existing stock, however, changes such as an increased demand for money, a change in velocity or higher prices for other commodities can cause a departure from equilibrium that might take a very long time to correct. Periods of increasing prices as well as periods of decreasing prices are both quite possible under a strict commodity standard.

These problems, and perhaps particularly the cost of production – Friedman calculates that it would require about $1\frac{1}{2}\%$ of the national income to sustain sufficient production of a commodity currency in order to keep prices roughly stable

– are the main reasons why the gold standard and other commodity currencies have tended to disappear. Unfortunately, the devices which have replaced them have usually turned out to have severe defects of their own.

Pseudo gold standards

To Friedman, the pseudo gold standard which began in the 1930s was the worst possible international monetary arrangement. Instead of a unit of currency representing a certain weight of gold, the price of gold was now pegged against national currencies. Gold became a commodity whose price was supported by the US and other governments, just as a government might support the price of wheat or butter. Thus, with a large number of different currencies being pegged to gold, currencies were effectively pegged to each other. If there was pressure on one currency (which would formerly have been equalized easily by gold shipments), there was no automatic balance: rather, the country in question had to buy some of its own currency with its reserves of foreign currencies in order to try to keep the price up.

Pseudo gold standards of this sort have proved damaging in countless historical episodes, some very severe:

either a real gold standard throughout the 1920s and 1930s or a consistent adherence to a fiduciary standard would have been vastly preferable to the actual pseudo gold standard under which gold inflows and minor gold outflows were offset and substantial actual or threatened gold outflows were over-reacted to. And this pattern is no outmoded historical curiosity . . .[35]

This is a far from satisfactory procedure. Reserves have to be substantial to provide the necessary breathing space, and even so, countries are not prepared to accumulate foreign currencies indefinitely. The only real adjustment mechanism is to do deliberately what the gold standard did automatically – to reduce the domestic money supply and let prices and incomes fall, so reducing the demand for foreign exchange. Such a policy, however, was not always popular, and a more common method of controlling exchange rates was direct control – limiting the amount of foreign currency that could be bought and thus allowing supply to outstrip demand and bringing rates back into the pegged alignment. Friedman's verdict is unequivocal:

With all this we have not succeeded. The experience of countless price-fixing schemes has been repeated. Let the fixed price differ from the price that would clear the market, and it will take Herculean efforts to hold it.[36]

Floating exchange rates

Friedman has long argued that the only lasting solution to these problems is to let the market price of currencies prevail, under a system of floating exchange rates. Although few of his colleagues thought that free exchange rates would ever be 'politically possible', events have forced them upon a number of the most important countries in recent years.

Friedman says that completely flexible exchange rates have many advantages; one of the greatest, as far as he is concerned, is that such a system allows the monetary authorities to concentrate much more fully on their monetary policy, without fear of its effect on the foreign exchange markets. In a floating exchange rate system, there is no need for domestic prices to rise or fall just in order to keep the exchange rate at some preconceived level or within some prearranged limits. The exchange rate will adjust automatically to reflect differences in prices between countries and the balance of their trade.

Since most transactions in a country's currency are likely to be domestic – overwhelmingly so in nearly all cases – Friedman considers it much more important to create the proper conditions for domestic trade to prosper than to construct the entire edifice of economic policy around the comparatively unimportant exchange rate. Freeing the exchange rate completely removes one policy target that is often in conflict with the monetary policies necessary to cure domestic problems.

Another advantage of completely flexible exchange rates is that they eliminate the need for the authorities to hold official reserves of the currencies of other nations. Private individuals will buy and hold all the reserves needed, and different currencies can be bought or sold at any time at the prevailing market price.

Lastly, because of the separation of internal and external policies which they make possible, floating exchange rates prevent inflation being exported. The routes by which the inflationary policies of one country are transmitted to the economies of others are many;[37] but, in essence, the problem is that rapid monetary expansion in one country will, under a fixed rate system, lead to balance of payments deficits as its goods become uncompetitively priced. Other countries will experience corresponding balance of payments surpluses, which cause an increase in their domestic monetary growth. Thus, inflation is transmitted. The advantage of a floating system is that inflationary policies at home cannot be exported: all that happens is that the exchange rate depreciates and acts as a buffer.

Objections to flexible rates. Some critics point out that it is unlikely that exchanges rates will ever be determined fully by market forces, however. The state of the exchange rate is not only important in terms of international prestige, but large changes in export or import prices could spell ruin to some industries at home. Thus, governments will always see it as their duty to interfere by resorting to controls or quotas. Secondly, even if the exchange rate did float 'cleanly', it might often be out of equilibrium because of the lags and adjustment problems that are evident in all markets, but are particularly severe in international transactions. Thirdly, even if the adjustment were smooth, floating exchange rates might still cause the authorities some problems in stabilization policy: a falling exchange rate would lead to rising import costs, which might still lead to inflationary pressure being 'imported'.

On the first point, Friedman believes that the advantages of freeing the exchange rate completely outweigh any temporary advantages of a 'dirty' float. Inflation can be overcome more rapidly, and the economy can adjust back to its noninflationary pattern of activity more smoothly, if the temptation to interfere with the exchange rate is resisted. Governments with floating exchange rates will eventually come to recognize this, and so 'clean' floating *is* an available option. As for the second problem, Friedman would argue that the essential test of the floating rate system is whether it is *better* than a fixed one in settling at the desirable equilibrium level: and his answer to that question is unreservedly affirmative. The third objection again comes back to government policy; if it has expanded the quantity of money, it must expect rising prices, including rising prices for inputs from abroad, and it must expect some reduction in international competitiveness. In fact, the floating exchange system puts a marked pressure on governments to *solve* their domestic inflation, so that they can achieve a competitive edge over those who do not.

Friedman had considered other objections to floating exchange rates as far back as 1953, but concluded then that they are all insubstantial.[38] In the first instance, he says, it is not true that flexible exchange rates must necessarily mean greater uncertainty and instability in international transactions. The very opposite is much more likely, in fact, but instability tends to be feared because of a confusion with the instability that affected pegged rates in the past, where a worsening balance of payments generally precipitated a run on the currency and added to existing problems. Under flexible rates, on the other hand, the price would automatically adjust to a new equilibrium position. Secondly, the problem faced by importers and exporters regarding the estimation of future exchange rates is insubstantial; futures markets would (and now do) take care of any uncertainty about the future by allowing importers and exporters to contract to buy currency in the future at an agreed rate.

The uncertainty might extend to speculation on the exchange market, however: since moving exchange rates are available for all to see, some critics argued that any hint of inflation or deficit problems in one country could rapidly have everyone, knowledgeable or not, selling the currency in order to be on the safe side. Friedman's answer is characteristically blunt. A fear of inflation has almost no chance of *causing* an inflation: only an expansion of the money supply will be guaranteed to do that. Consequently, even if there was an uninformed selling of currency following a rumour of future inflation, people would immediately buy back when it failed to materialize.

It is rather the rigid exchange rate which causes most difficulty in these times: it gives governments a symbol to fight for, and any devaluation is a mark of shame. Governments tend to hold out for as long as possible before making the inevitable devaluation, and meanwhile the speculators have been anticipating the change and selling in such a way as to accelerate it.

Of the ideas which Friedman conceived or championed, that of flexible exchange rates was most of all the one whose time had come, and come it did. The pegged rate system broke down, in effect, when a two-tier system for gold was adopted by the United States, and the United States officially suspended its commitment to buy and sell gold at a fixed price from and to foreign governments. The British pound was floated on 23 June 1972, and shortly afterwards twenty of the world's major nations formally agreed to continue with the new system of floating rates that had been forced upon them by international developments, particularly the oil crisis of the early 1970s. They hoped that it would be possible to return to a system of fixed exchange rates later on: but the attractions of floating rates became clearer each day.

CHAPTER FIVE

The Empirical Evidence

Throughout the near-century examined in detail we have found that:

1. Changes in the behavior of the money stock have been closely associated with changes in economic activity, money income, and prices.
2. The interrelation between monetary and economic change has been highly stable.
3. Monetary changes have often had an independent origin; they have not been simply a reflection of changes in economic activity.[1]

WITH his collaborator, Anna Schwartz, Friedman has completed two major reviews of the historical evidence on money, business cycles, interest rates, the demand for money and other factors bearing on the quantity theory. *A Monetary History of the United States* appeared in 1963, although many of its main findings had previously been summarized in articles; *Monetary Trends in the United States and the United Kingdom* appeared in 1982. These were supplemented by a volume of statistical data, *Monetary Statistics of the United States,* making the entire project by far the most weighty investigation of its kind ever attempted. In collaboration with David Meiselman, Friedman undertook another sizeable and significant study to test simple versions of the monetarist and Keynesian models against the historical evidence, a study which was published in 1963 (although it was finished a few years earlier). All subsequent research on monetary policy in the United States and in the United Kingdom has been greatly facilitated by these various publications.[2]

METHOD AND MAIN FINDINGS

The scale of this empirical research is so daunting that it

is difficult to outline briefly. Any short synopsis tends to understate the frequency and regularity of the correlations between money and other economic factors which were discovered. Nor is it possible to evaluate and discuss the numerous methodological issues which were raised in the course of the research. But the painstaking nature of the work of Friedman and Schwartz is clear, involving as it does a derivation of quarterly figures for M2 (roughly equivalent in United Kingdom terms to Sterling M3) from 1867 to 1907, after which monthly figures become available. Indeed, Friedman and Schwartz also make estimates, naturally much more tentative, of the money stock as far back as 1775.

As we have seen, the exact definition of money is not the important point, provided that it is consistent,[3] and Friedman and Schwartz compare various definitions of money from time to time in order to check which definition achieves the highest predictive power and which factors within the definition are of particular importance. They examine in great detail three main indicators of the state of the stock of money: the quantity of high-powered money, sometimes known as the *monetary base;* the *reserve ratio* maintained by the commercial banks (which may be more generous than the minimum reserve ratios laid down by law, as we have seen); and the *ratio of currency to bank deposits* maintained by members of the public. Thus, the behaviour of the monetary authorities, the commercial banks and the public can all be examined and summarized in the results.

To Friedman, there is no doubt that the historical record generally supports his faith in the income version of the quantity theory of money, and that the research makes a very strong case for the strength of the impact of the quantity of money on nominal and real factors. Of the various elements comprising the total supply of money, the behaviour of high-powered money is unquestionably the most significant, confirming Friedman's speculation that the control of the monetary base is the surest way of influencing the total money stock and the other economic magnitudes that are related to it.

The main correlations. The most significant points of the analysis may be summarized as follows:

1. The *rate of change in the quantity of money* is closely related to the rates of change in nominal income, in real income and in prices, the highest correlation being that between the rates of change of money and nominal income. This relationship holds good for cycles and for longer periods. Price and real income changes, although related to monetary changes, are somewhat less predictable, because of the difficulty of forecasting whether monetary changes are likely to be manifested principally in price or output changes.

2. *Interest rates* prove to be important in determining the quantity of money which people desire to hold and the total quantity of money available from a given stock of high-powered money. But there seems to be little relation between changes in interest rates and changes in prices, income or output; nor between the *level* of interest rates and prices, income or output. The quantity of money is a much more certain guide. Friedman concludes that this presumably indicates the looseness of the relationship between interest rates and the monetary sector, which would be expected if the channel for the transmission of monetary changes were wider than in the traditional Keynesian models.

3. Movements in *velocity* have been small over the period as a whole. As incomes have risen over the century, the income velocity of money has fallen slightly – hence Friedman's suggestion that money is a 'luxury' good which people like to hold in greater amounts when their incomes are higher.

4. However, velocity does change over shorter periods, and usually rises in cyclical expansions and falls in cyclical contractions. Thus, velocity changes *reinforce* the effects of changes in the money stock on prices and income. (The presumed explanation is that continued price rises come to be anticipated, and that when prices are rising, people reduce their cash balances, so that velocity rises.)

5. *Expectations are important.* Prior experience of price rises is important in determining how quickly people will respond to the signs of a developing inflation.

6. *Interest rates follow price movements.* Rising prices induce lenders to charge higher nominal rates in order to maintain their real returns, and make borrowers willing to pay more in nominal terms. This finding is hard to justify in empirical terms from the United States data alone, but it does show up on international evidence.

7. The balance between *prices and output* in which monetary changes are manifested is also influenced by expectations. If past price increases have been rapid, future monetary changes tend to produce price rises rather than improvements in output.

8. In the decades after the Second World War, expectations of inflation following monetary policy changes seem to play an increasingly important role in deciding the course of an inflation.

SEVERE INFLATIONS AND DEPRESSIONS

Friedman is not in any doubt that the strength of the relationships he discerns in the historical record may be more evident in some periods than others. Mild monetary movements may have effects which are also mild, and which are therefore swamped by the monetary conditions of other important variables. However, the historical record does give us several clear instances when the monetary 'signal' was so strong that it could not be swamped by the 'noise' of other factors. These are the wartime periods, typified by large monetary expansions and consequent inflation, and several instances of major depressions of which the 1929–33 period was the most significant.

Wartime inflations

Study of the major movements over the last century is particularly revealing. These movements include wartime inflations, hyperinflations after the first and second world wars, and major contractions such as the Great Depression.

Friedman recognizes that the curious movements of money during wartime incidents are to a certain extent abnormal and must be treated cautiously. On the other hand, he says,[4] wartime periods are particularly valuable because of the often violent changes in the economic magnitudes, sometimes for brief periods, which make it possible for the economist to get some crucial insights into the relative importance of different factors.

In the United States data with which Friedman is most familiar, there have been five major wartime periods; the revolution; the war of 1812; the civil war; and two world wars. All of them were associated with sizeable expansions in the quantity of money and a rapid increase in prices. Low interest rate policy after the two world wars caused the inflation to persist long afterwards.

The evidence makes it clear that changes in the stock of money are the principal factor behind the rapid price increases typical of wartime periods. Fiscal indicators (i.e. tax policies)[5] seem powerless to explain the rises in prices or in incomes, as some have suggested they do: Federal tax receipts were about a fifth of total expenditures during the civil war, and about two-fifths during the First World War, yet despite this large divergence, the rise in prices was roughly the same. Again, the pre-year deficit was almost twice as large a fraction of national income in the civil war as in the First World War, which on the Keynesian income-expenditure model – placing heavy reliance as it does on government spending – should have foretold large differences in results. The evidence of other fiscal measures would lead the income-expenditure model to predict a much larger increase in incomes during the Second World War than actually occurred, all of which forces Friedman to conclude that the orthodox theory is not consistent with price and income patterns in the three wars.[6]

There is no denying, of course, that fiscal magnitudes themselves might have a 'knock-on' effect on monetary magnitudes, and in wartime periods this might be very significant. But Friedman reminds us that it is only *through the monetary channel* that they have any inflationary effect:

The level of expenditures and of taxation, the extent of increases in real output, are all important for the problem of inflation primarily because of their effects on the stock of money per unit of output, and they are only important insofar as they have such effects.[7]

One final point is worth noting about the wartime experiences. The rise of the banking sector over the period in question made the impact of high-powered money increasingly great. In the civil war, the total supply of money increased about $1.50 for each dollar of money created by the government, but in the First World War it increased nearly $8.00. If there had been a 100% reserve banking rule as proposed by Friedman, and no private 'creation' of money, prices would probably have risen much less than they did.

Other inflationary episodes

To Friedman, other inflationary episodes are equally clear in demonstrating the impact of the supply of money on nominal income. The only peacetime periods showing anything like comparable price rises were the early 1850s and the period 1896–1913. Friedman argues that these can be attributed to the California gold rush and to worldwide price rises following gold discoveries in Australia and the improved techniques for the extraction of gold through the cyanide process.

These episodes again spell disaster for the Keynesian income-expenditure model, which supposes a rise of investment spending to be the root cause of inflation. In 1896–1913 particularly, there was no obvious large independent shift in spending propensities, and the only immediate factor which is apparent is the increased gold production. The increase over that period was large compared to the gold stock at the start, and therefore produced large effects in itself, but the effect was multiplied through other forms of money. Hence, the gold production represented only a small portion of the increased money supply, but other forms of money expanded along with it. A spending-multiplier explanation, on the other hand, does not seem to fit the facts.[8]

Friedman draws on the work of his student Philip Cagan when it comes to examining hyperinflations. The most obvious examples are those after the First World War in Germany,

Austria and Russia, those after the Second War in Hungary and Greece, and the rapid rises in prices in many South American countries. The evidence shows that these inflations often have their origins in a wartime expansion, where governments use inflation in order to help finance the war effort. Prices begin to rise, but expectations of price rises are minor at first. If the monetary expansion continues, however, prices continue to rise and now become anticipated. People begin to spend very rapidly in an attempt to reduce their *real* balances, because they see no point in holding their normal number of weeks' spending power in the form of cash that loses more of its value every day. This bids up prices even more rapidly. How far the process continues depends on the subsequent rate of growth of the stock of money.

The evidence from deep depressions

The historical evidence of the importance of monetary changes is equally clear, says Friedman, when we examine *depression* phases rather than inflationary ones. Put simply:

Every severe contraction has been accompanied by an absolute decline in the stock of money, and the severity of the contraction has been in roughly the same order as the decline in the stock of money.[9]

There have been six major depressions in United States economic history, and Friedman shows that each was heralded by major reductions in the *growth* of money, and in one case by a substantial fall in the *absolute quantity* of money itself.[10]

1875–8. Political pressure for a resumption of the gold standard led to a decline in high-powered money and the banking crisis in 1873. Banks attempted to become more liquid and the public attempted to convert deposits to currency, thus limiting the amount of money that could be 'created' by the banks on the strength of their deposits.

1892–4. Agitation for silver and destabilizing Treasury actions led to fears that the gold standard might be abandoned, and

97

so foreign investors moved gold out of the United States. This again put pressure on liquidity, and a banking panic in 1893 produced sharp declines in the deposit/currency ratio and the deposit/reserve ratios of the banks.

1906–8. This is a particularly interesting case to Friedman. The banking panic produced a sharp decline in the deposit-currency ratio and banks attempted to raise their own reserve balances, so that there was a substantial fall in the deposit-reserve ratio. The failure of the Knickerbocker Trust Company in 1907 converted what had been a mild decline, as a result of gold exports, into a severe decline as the panicking public attempted to withdraw its bank deposits. The accompanying sharp rise in interest rates put a premium on currency, however, and gold started to flow back; the decline in business also limited the demand for foreign exchange. The banks in concert suspended the convertability of their deposits into cash, and these feedback effects quickly reversed the money decline, with a subsequent recovery in business.

1920–21. Sharp rises in Federal Reserve discount rates produced a sharp contraction in Federal Reserve credit outstanding, and therefore reduced the available high-powered money and the total money stock.

1929–33. This was by far the worst of the contractions.[11] Friedman argues that, like the 1907 crisis, it would have passed without much of a decline, had it not been for the perverse actions of the monetary authorities which turned a mild contraction into a depression. Friedman himself can claim most of the credit for exposing the monetary origins of this depression, which was not thought to be monetary at all when Keynes wrote the crucial *General Theory* in 1936.

Friedman explains that, beginning in mid-1928, the Federal Reserve System, concerned about stock market speculation, imposed a monetary policy of continuous restraint, despite its ambitions to foster business expansion. The resulting policy was insufficient to prevent speculation, but sufficient to restrict business expansion! The stock of money even *fell* slightly during most of the period of business expansion from 1927–9, an unprecedented event.

The cyclical contraction began in late 1929, before the stock market crash. The downward pressure on velocity which this induced was strongly reinforced by the behaviour of the money stock, which fell by 2.6% from August 1929 to October 1930. Although this seems a small decline, it was large given the background of experience, because of the long-term growth in the quantity of money. There were only four earlier contractions in which the quantity of money declined so fast, all of them unusually severe.

Remarkably, says Friedman, the decline in the quantity of money was brought about by the Federal Reserve, the very agency which was supposed to stabilize it. The banks held firm, there was no panic or rush into liquidity, and indeed the public's willingness to hold more deposits relative to currency actually offset much of the contraction. But a series of scattered bank failures continued until the dramatic failure of the Bank of the United States – not an official bank, but a large one and one which had considerable prestige. Now, further runs on banks produced pressure for them to go liquid. This lowered the market value of their assets and made them even more vulnerable. The Fed helped to some extent, but after the immediate crisis was over, its deflationary actions continued. In March 1931 there was a second banking panic, which the Fed did nothing to stem. When Britain left the gold standard in September, the Reserve System made its *passive* deflationary policy into an *active* one, taking the most extreme deflationary measures in its history. 'The result,' says Friedman 'was to turn a crisis into a catastrophe.'[12] The quantity of money had fallen at an annual rate of 13% from March 1931 to August 1931. It fell at the astonishing annual rate of 31% in the next five months:

It fell because the Federal Reserve System forced or permitted a sharp reduction in the monetary base, because it failed to exercise the responsibilities assigned to it in the Federal Reserve Act to provide liquidity to the banking system. The Great Contraction is tragic testimony to the power of monetary policy – not, as Keynes and so many of his contemporaries believed, evidence of its impotence.[13]

1937–8. This depression stemmed from the doubling of legal reserve requirements through 1936 and 1937, accompanied by Treasury 'sterilization' of gold purchases so that they did not enter the active supply of money. This led to a halt in the growth of high-powered money and the attempt by banks to bring their reserves up to the new requirements. The decline in the money stock largely reflected the resultant decline in the ratios.

Friedman's conclusions

Certainly, shifts in the deposit/currency ratio and bank crises played an important role in four of these six depressions. Bank ratios, says Friedman, tend to follow a cyclical pattern, feeding back from business, but in each of these cases there was a shift from the typical pattern. A fractional reserve banking system susceptible to runs is a feature which renders the stock of money highly sensitive to autonomous deflationary changes, and this is what happened in each of the periods under review.

Friedman recognizes that other events may also contribute to the recessions. Silver agitation at the end of last century was intensified by declining agricultural prices, and the financial boom in the early 1900s generated financial activities that laid the basis for subsequent collapses. But the message is clear: changes in the quantity of money were the root cause of every contraction, whether they were reinforced by subsequent patterns of business activity or not. Appreciable changes in the rate of growth of the stock of money are, then, a necessary and sufficient condition for appreciable changes in the rate of growth of income.

Once again it seems difficult to explain these major depressions in terms of income-expenditure theory. In all of them, of course, the incentive to invest, and thus investment itself, declined: but Friedman insists that this was the *result* of the monetary changes and not the *cause* of the economic collapse.

Sudden *upswings* in investment do not, on the other hand, explain rising worldwide incomes between 1897 and 1913, for example. And again, of all the leading countries, China was the only one to escape the Great Depression. Friedman says this is because it was on a silver standard, and did not suffer a contraction until the United States silver purchase programme of 1933 started draining silver from China and caused a sharp decline in its money stock.

Friedman concludes that the policy implications are clear:

we must distinguish between minor recessions and major depressions . . . it takes a monetary contraction or collapse – a monetary mistake – to convert a minor recession into a major depression.[14]

Other explanations

There have been other explanations of these contractions, and of the Great Contraction in particular. Friedman lists five common major mistakes:[15] (1) that the depression was a reaction to prior inflationary excesses, (2) that it was imported from abroad, (3) that it reflected the supreme weight attached to the gold standard as opposed to internal stability, (4) that the Federal Reserve made reserves available but the banks were unwilling to use them, and (5) that the deflationary policy was enforced by a shortage of available gold.

Friedman's monetary history disposes of the free gold theory, as it does of the unwillingness of the banks to use reserves. In the latter case, excess reserves did not materialize until mid-1932, and so were hardly a cause of the problem. As to the gold standard, Friedman says that there was no threat to it up to August 1931, and that it did not appear to feature – until Britain's sudden action – as a goal of policy. As to importing depression, in fact the United States was importing gold from 1929 to 1931: but this was 'sterilized', and so the US money stock continued to fall. The US was an *exporter*, and not an importer, of depression.

The idea that the depression was a reaction to prior inflationary excesses is a more interesting one, and has been frequently cited by Austrian School economists such as Hans Sennholz[16] and Murray Rothbard.[17] The view here is that every credit expansion causes changes in the structure of production which cannot be sustained: only larger and larger doses of inflation will have the stimulating effect required to make them endure. In 1924, the United States Federal Reserve System created $500m in new credit, which led to a bank credit expansion of some $4,000 million within a year. Another burst was launched in 1927 (lasting through to 1928), when another $400 million of Reserve credit was created, discount rates were reduced and bank credit expanded. Total currency outside the banks increased from under $45 billion in June 1924 to over $57 billion in October 1929. According to this theory, the paper-chase had to end sometime.

Friedman replies that the expansion prior to the crash (that is, during 1927–9) was not rapid enough to be inflationary. The quantity of money (including commercial bank time deposits) grew less during that expansion than in any other since 1869, and currency plus demand deposits showed almost no increase at all. And this is true to a lesser extent of the whole decade of the 1920s after recovery from the 1920–21 contraction. Furthermore, says Friedman, there is no correlation between the amplitude of an expansion and the severity of the succeeding contraction (although there is some between depressions and succeeding expansions). This would tend to undermine the Austrian case.

Nevertheless, it is clear that these two explanations are both monetary in origin and to some extent form different ways of explaining the same phenomenon. In any event, Friedman maintains that the long-term record shows the role and importance of money just as clearly as do these remarkable contractions and inflations, whatever might be said about particular periods:

My own belief in the greater importance of monetary policy does not rest on these dramatic episodes. It rests on the experience of hundreds of years and of many countries.[18]

CYCLICAL DISCREPANCIES

As we have seen, the nature of velocity is different over the long and short periods. Over a century or more, velocity recorded a steady fall (according to Friedman's research) which correlates very strongly with income growth, making Friedman conclude that money is a luxury which is in greater demand as real incomes rise. The simple correlation between the real stock of money per capita and the logarithm of real income per capita is 0.99, and the computed elasticity is 1.8. Thus (as noted in Chapter 3), a 1% rise in real income per capita has, on average, been associated with a 1.8% increase in real cash balances per capita and hence with a decrease in income velocity. Because of the strong upward trend in the money stock and real incomes per capita over the century, this view could be challenged, but Friedman maintains that the results hold good even if the trend is allowed for.

Over *cycles*, paradoxically, velocity tends to *rise* along with income and the quantity of money.[19] Allowing for secular trends, a one per cent change in real income during a cycle is accompanied by a change in the real stock of money in the same direction of about one fifth of one per cent, so the reinforcing nature of velocity is strong over cycles.

Friedman is well aware of the difficulties that this enigmatic behaviour of velocity poses for the quantity theory. Indeed, he says:

One factor that has doubtless contributed to skepticism about a monetary theory is the fact . . . that fluctuations in income are wider in relative amplitude than fluctuations in the stock of money . . . income velocity varies positively over the cycle, which means that income varies more widely than money.[20]

Velocity rising strongly with money over cycles but falling weakly over the long term, is indeed a confusing position and would explode Friedman's belief that monetary changes were useful predictors of changes in income or prices, unless he could explain it: which is exactly what his permanent income hypothesis attempts to do.

The permanent income explanation of velocity

Friedman was fortunate that he had already developed the essential explanation of this apparent contradiction, albeit in a different field of study. While examining movements in consumer spending, he developed the hypothesis that measured income, as recorded by the statisticians, was not the same as the longer-term concept of income to which consumers actually adjust their programme of purchases – a concept which Friedman called *permanent income*.[21] It was a stroke of good fortune that the problems of consumer behaviour and of the behaviour of the demand for money are similar, and that the measured/permanent income distinction, when

applied to prices as well as to income, can reconcile the apparent contradiction between the cyclical and secular behaviour of the money-income ratio.[22]

The hypothesis

It is not easy to find a simple exposition of the permanent income hypothesis in Friedman's writings.[23] Although there are many complicating issues, however, its fundamental principle is simple.

Friedman says that we would get a very bizarre view of consumers' behaviour if we measured their income each day. We would find that on one day of the week they received a large income and spent very little of it; and then on the next six days they would not earn anything but would continue to spend. Life would seem to be an endless cycle of excessive thrift followed by reckless expenditure. But, of course, people do *not* think of their income like that: they think of it as being spread over the week or the month. If we measure income in this more spread-out way, we will get a much closer idea of how household spending patterns are determined.

To get a really good idea of consumers' behaviour, however, we have to think in even longer terms, says Friedman. People recognize that their income fluctuates. It might fluctuate over the months with bonuses and overtime rates; over a year it might fluctuate seasonally; over longer periods it might fluctuate depending on illness, unemployment or a host of other factors. People allow for these ups and downs, says Friedman, and have a long-term conception of what their income will be when they have been taken into account. People have an awareness of their *permanent income*, which might be subject to *transitional* increases and decreases as time goes on. And it is this permanent income, and not their income as measured by their paycheques, to which people adjust their consumption patterns.

Measured income therefore comprises *permanent* and *transitional* parts. The transitional element will be completely saved if it is positive, and will come out of savings if it is negative: so the transitional deviations between measured income and permanent income will show up primarily in the consumer's assets and liabilities (that is, measured savings) rather than in changes in the pattern of consumption.

A consumer's determination of his permanent income may not be made consciously, but it will reflect the pattern of his income in the past. The magnitude of the *measured* income received in the recent past will be weighted more than that received long ago, and so the estimate of permanent income will depend upon a set of weighted incomes stretching back into the past. By and large, however, we can say that people have a time horizon of roughly three years when estimating their permanent income.[24]

In passing, it should be noted that this approach has shown its power in explaining a number of observations about how different consumers behave. Indeed, Friedman's analysis in *A Theory of the Consumption Function* is in large part an empirical testing of the theory against observed differences in the spending patterns of farm and non-farm households, employed and self-employed people, and so on; and the explanations do seem to have a ring of sense to them. But, for our purposes, the main question is whether this approach helps to explain the perceived movements in velocity over cycles.

Application of the theory to cycles

Nowadays it is generally assumed that the permanent income

hypothesis should be used when attempting to explain the curious and apparently contradictory movements of velocity in the long term and over cycles and, indeed, that permanent income is one of the best indicators of wealth when Friedman's demand for money function is being subjected to empirical tests. The permanent income hypothesis not only explains these questions well, but it suggests some very revealing points about the nature of money itself.

Friedman's own analysis is complex,[25] but it can be simplified easily enough for illustrative purposes. The general message of the observed evidence is that cyclical movements in business activity are associated with small rises in the growth of the nominal quantity of money during the upswing and small falls in the downswing, while income rises substantially during the upswing and falls substantially in the downswing. Thus, in the upswing, velocity as usually measured (i.e., the ratio of money supply to national income) will be rising as income growth outstrips the growth of money, while in the downswing it will be falling as income shrinks faster than the money stock.

But let us now suppose, along with Friedman, that consumer behaviour is not much influenced by changes in *measured* income, but by *permanent* income. This permanent income might fluctuate a little over the cycle, but is, broadly speaking, steady. And if so, the ratio of *permanent* income to money now conforms *negatively* over the cycle: what we might call *permanent velocity* (i.e. the ratio of money supply to permanent income) falls in the upswing and rises in the downswing, behaving just as it does over the longer period. The anomalous behaviour of velocity evaporates, then, provided that we consider permanent and not measured income in our calculations.

Real balances. Movements in real balances are also enigmatic. In the empirical results, we find only a very slight positive variation in the real balances people hold over the cycle. In theory, we should expect large variations, since in upswings, people would be adding to their cash savings (measured income is rising fast), and in downswings, they would be dipping into them. An explanation is needed.

The explanation is to take Friedman's method even further. Just as people recognize that cyclical fluctuations of income will not persist, and adjust their behaviour to permanent rather than measured income, so (says Friedman) they realize that cyclical price rises and falls will not be permanent. People therefore decide the size of the real money balances they choose to hold in terms of the quantity of goods they can purchase over a *period of time*, not according to the measured prices of the instant. Variations in real balances are therefore small because people are adjusting to what might be called the 'permanent' price level, not to the rapidly changing prices that characterize cycles.

The sensitivity of the economy to money. The permanent income approach makes us aware that the economy is far more sensitive to monetary changes than most people suppose. The fact that money changes are small over cycles when compared to the reinforcing swings in measured velocity has led many to the conclusion that the quantity of money supplied is of little consequence, and that changes in *demand*, and related factors, are the prime determinants of income. But, says Friedman, this belief is, of course, based upon the movements of velocity *as measured*, and on *measured* income, neither of which are good guides to consumer behaviour. If we worked instead with *permanent* velocity and *permanent* income, we would find that monetary changes are dampened, not reinforced, by changes in demand over the cycle: if circumstances arose where velocity came truly to reinforce monetary changes, therefore, their observed impact could be considerable indeed.

Without going into the details, Friedman raises another point which shows just how sensitive the economy is to monetary changes if we look at it from the point of view of permanent magnitudes. Given that permanent magnitudes are important in the determination of the demand for money, and that they are calculated from a weighted average of past measured values, it can be shown that measured income will be highly sensitive in short periods to changes in the nominal stock of money. This is because an increase in the money stock means an increase in the cash balances that people hold

– somebody has to hold the new money – and if cash balances are determined by reference to permanent incomes, a large increase in permanent income will be required if all the new cash is to be absorbed. But because it is pulled down by the weighting of past events, such an increase in permanent income would require *measured* income to rise very much more. Next year, the same problem would arise, and so on. Under the permanent income hypothesis, therefore, measured incomes are highly sensitive to monetary changes.

While able to explain these and many other points, however, the permanent income hypothesis has been criticized because of the implausibility of these wildly fluctuating measured incomes and other apparent problems.[26] But the hypothesis remains a useful and powerful approach to the problem of the cyclical behaviour of money and income.

CONCLUSIONS ABOUT VELOCITY

In summary, it must be concluded that the demand for money is stable in practice as well as in theory. We can therefore be confident that changes in the quantity of money will be fairly predictable in their long-term effects on nominal income. Although velocity is not a numerical constant over time, neither is it 'simply or even mainly a will-o'-the-wisp, over either periods measured in decades or periods measured in phases'.[27] The quantity theory survives, with impunity, the empirical study.

Yet the study of velocity, according to Friedman, tells us something else that is subtle yet all-important. It tells us that money is held as an *asset*, for the diverse stream of useful services that it confers upon the holder, and that holders' motives cannot be pigeonholed as the Keynesians suppose.[28] Keynes's transactions motive, for example, does not explain why the demand for money does not in fact change as rapidly as changes in the volume of transactions; nor does it conveniently explain why velocity has declined secularly over a century or so (particularly since new forms of payment are lessening the need for people to hold cash). The speculative motive is also cast in doubt by the empirical evidence. One would expect wide cyclical fluctuations in cash balances if it were a dominant motive, but this hardly occurs.

The permanent income analysis of velocity also strikes directly at Keynesian views about, and prescriptions for, economic growth. Changes in investment are seen in the Keynesian model as the heralds of subsequent income changes; but in fact, *permanent* income and consumption are unlikely to vary much over the cycle, so the effects of changes in investment expenditure are likely to be weak. The *money multiplier,* on the other hand, can have considerable effects: money is a powerful force in the economy, and potentially destabilizing.

It is to these policy implications of the theory that we must now turn.

PART 3: QUESTIONS FOR THEORY AND POLICY

CHAPTER SIX

The Causes and Nature of Inflation

> ... the quantity of money is extremely important for
> nominal magnitudes, for nominal income, for the level
> of income in dollars – important for what happens
> to prices. It is not important at all, or, if that's perhaps
> an exaggeration, not very important, for what happens
> to real output over the long period.[1]

NOT everyone shares Friedman's faith that all inflation is due
ultimately to monetary movements. Common explanations of
rising prices have included the incidence of wars, the activity
of profiteers and other special circumstances. On a more sophisticated level, economists have argued that there are different
kinds of inflation and that one single factor is insufficient to
explain them. The most usual division is the familiar 'cost-
push' and 'demand-pull' distinction; thus, Sir John Hicks
complains:

Monetarists cannot deny that there is at least one distinction, the
familiar distinction between demand inflation and cost inflation –
'demand-pull and cost-push'. For this is a distinction which, on
the most casual survey of inflationary experience, simply leaps to
the eye. In an inflation where demand-pull is dominant, the receipts
of business rise faster, or more quickly, than their costs; so a demand
inflation is a condition of high profits, high activity and high employment. In an inflation where cost-push is dominant, costs rise faster
than receipts; so profits are low, activity is low and there is at least
a danger of abnormal unemployment. When one considers the history
of the major industrial countries during the last thirty years, examples
of 'boom' inflation (the one sort) and 'slump' inflation (the other)
are very easy to find.

Yet, say the monetarists, they are all the same. How can they
say that?[2]

The answer, of course, is that both phenomena occur only

through the operation of the same cause – a monetary expansion – and that each of them has the same result. Although to individuals they may *appear* to be different phenomena, in fact they are simply part of the same inflationary process.

Rising costs such as wage payments, says Friedman, can be sustained only if money is created to finance them. If the quantity of money is stable and there are no unusual swings in the velocity of circulation, then the firms granting the wage increases or facing higher costs are presented with a different decision. They can either reduce their costs, including their total employment bills, or they can charge more for their produce. If they reduce their costs, those who supply them will in turn have to economize; if they increase their prices, those who buy from them will have to economize. The suppliers and buyers face just the same problems as the initial firms: and so the effect spreads through the economy. Plainly, someone somewhere must be worse off if others are to enjoy higher wages or charge higher prices at the start of the chain.

The cost-push approach forgets the essential distinction between the individual and the community.[3] It may be that an *individual* can sell his products at higher prices, or can charge more for his working hours, than he used to. His products or work might well be worth the new high prices. But *all* suppliers together cannot do this: customers will simply be unable to afford to purchase the same amounts as before, *unless* there is an expansion in the quantity of money. If the quantity of money is unchanged, in other words, there may be changes in *relative* prices: some goods may cost more than before because of a change in their availability or the costs of their manufacture, while others may cost less. But this is not a general inflationary trend. Only an increase in the quantity of money would cause it to become so.

Exactly the same is true of the process known as 'demand-pull', which turns out to be just another way of looking at the same phenomenon. A rise in demand will cause retailers to order larger stocks to keep their customers supplied, wholesalers will order more, and manufacturers will gear up for greater output. But, in so doing, they will find that there is more competition for their factor inputs and that they will have to pay more for their raw materials, and raise wages if they are to expand their workforces. These higher costs are passed on to wholesalers, to retailers and to the public. So although it *seems* to everyone in the chain that this is an example of rising costs pushing up prices, the initial impetus is once more a rise in *demand*.[4] Again, a rise in consumers' demand for one product can be maintained by only two routes: a reduction in expenditure on other products (which will lead to falling prices in those sectors and leave the general price level undisturbed) or an inflationary increase in the quantity of money. As Friedman says:

Short-run changes in both particular prices and in the general level of prices may have many sources. But long-continued inflation is always and everywhere a monetary phenomenon that arises from a more rapid expansion in the quantity of money than in total output – though I hasten to add that the exact rate of inflation is not precisely or mechanically linked to the exact rate of monetary growth . . .[5]

However, it must be said that, depending on his mood and his audience, Friedman does not appear to be convinced that inflation is, in the long term, *always* and *everywhere* a monetary phenomenon. For example:

Inflation is primarily a *monetary phenomenon*, produced by a more rapid increase in the quantity of money than in output.[6]

Note the word 'primarily'. Or again, where, the hypothesis is limited to 'substantial' changes:

. . . substantial changes in prices or nominal income are almost invariably the result of changes in the nominal supply of money.[7]

But the general point is plain: although inflations may *appear* to have very different causes and possess very different natures, they stem from only one cause and have, broadly speaking, only one set of effects.

DOES MONEY AFFECT OUTPUT OR PRICES?

Even with this explanation from Friedman, it is still not clear that the inflation precipitated by a monetary expansion will work its way uniformly through the economy. The trend towards rising prices seems to appear sometimes as rising wages and costs, sometimes as higher consumer spending. Then again, will the method by which the monetary expansion is set in motion have an impact on the way the inflationary pressure is distributed through the economy? Will some prices rise faster than others and cause a dislocation and switching of resources from one sector into another – that is to say, is the effect of a monetary expansion strictly *neutral* or does it have *real* effects on output? Does it work uniformly through to the nominal levels of *all* prices or does it sometimes cause important changes in *relative* prices? These are the kinds of questions which Friedman's quantity theory has had to face.

But we do not necessarily need to consider relative prices to pose problems for the quantity theory: there are macroeconomic problems as well. Friedman's monetarism argues that changes in the quantity of money will, sooner or later and to a larger or smaller degree, work through to cause changes in nominal income. The crucial question to which practical men in particular need an answer is whether this rise in nominal income is generated by an increase in *prices* or an increase in the *amount traded* at the existing prices. Will monetary changes be manifested in changes in prices or changes in output?

The Keynesian mechanism. According to Friedman, neither the Keynesian nor the quantity theory actually has very much to say about how a change in nominal income is divided into prices or output. This, he notes, is true not only in their simple versions but even in their more sophisticated ones. The Keynesian theory, says Friedman, was based on a short-term analysis which assumed prices to be fixed, or at least determined by non-monetary forces; output was assumed to be much more variable, determined largely by changes in investment spending.[8] So the most we can say is that Keynes expected prices to be highly rigid relative to output, such that a short-term change in demand, including consumer spending, would be reflected almost entirely in output and very little in prices. After output has reached its feasible maximum, then prices will indeed be bid up, but this point was of little concern to Keynes, who wrote in a depression period. Thus the Keynesian view, in Friedman's words, is that

all the change income is in output, so long as there is unemployment, and all in prices, once there is full employment . . .[9]

The monetarist mechanism. The quantity theory approach has even less of value to say on the question of whether an expansion will go into output or prices. But Friedman's general and fundamental attitude is that in the *short term*, which may last for some years, there may be some changes in *output* following a monetary disturbance; but in the *long term*, the effects will be principally *nominal* rather than real.

It is essential to remember that the nominal quantity of money will, in Friedman's judgement, affect nominal quantities for the most part, although he accepts that the adjustment to monetary changes may take time and have some real effects on the way. But, in the long term, real magnitudes cannot be much altered by monetary policy:

the monetary authority controls nominal quantities . . . the price level, the nominal level of national income, the quantity of money by one or another definition . . . the rate of inflation or deflation, the rate of growth or decline in nominal national income, the rate of growth of the quantity of money. It cannot use its control over nominal quantities to peg a real quantity – the real rate of interest, the rate of unemployment, the level of real national income, the real quantity of money, the rate of growth of real national income, or the rate of growth of the real quantity of money.[10]

Certainly, we might perceive some immediate changes in real factors such as the structure and level of production when a monetary disturbance occurs. All of the real variables in the quantity equations *could* be influenced by a change in the quantity of money; but the quantity approach looks to the final results and has little to say about short-term adjustment. If the level of output is altered, then, it is more likely to be the result of a change in *real* circumstances, although monetary disturbances may have a temporary effect. But in the long term:

The real wealth of a society depends much more on the kind of institutional structure it has, on the abilities, initiative, driving force of its people, on investment potentialities, on technology – on all of those things. That's what really matters from the point of view of the level of output. But, how many dollars will that be valued at? When you ask that question, that's where money matters."

Adjustment and expectations

In harmony with his views on method, Friedman is much more interested in the long-term relationship between money and nominal income, because this is a link which can be established empirically and which has useful predictive consequences. He is less interested in the question of how monetary disturbances may be divided into prices and output, since the output effects will be temporary and will in any event depend on a host of other factors prevailing in the economy at any time. However, he is prepared to make some guesses, although he believes the question will remain largely open.

Initial rigidities. Friedman's analysis on the question of how money will make its way through output and prices goes back to Fisher. Suppose that there is a monetary expansion. People now have more money in their pockets and are willing to pay higher prices for goods. Because a manufacturer who is operating in one market is not likely to notice that the same is happening in others, he will assume that this willingness to pay more stems wholly or partly from a change in consumer tastes in favour of his own product. His immediate reaction will be to step up his output to take advantage of what he sees as a durable increase in the public's demand for it. Employment will be stepped up, supply increased. It will be some time before wages start to be bid up: wages are usually decided on long-term contracts and it will take time for new rates to be negotiated; but when they are, workers will settle only for higher rates because of the increased demand for the product and for their labour. Profit margins will narrow and the price of the product will be put up in response. Thus is it that output expands first, and *then* prices, in response to the monetary change.[12]

The adjustment to a higher quantity of money, therefore, is not a perfect adjustment through prices alone. Entrepreneurs may prefer to expand output rather than raise prices, but eventually the bidding-up effect will work through into their wage bills and input costs. Relative prices between products will change, because some prices can be adjusted quickly, as can some production schedules, while other commodities take longer to produce; so that the main adjustment must be to the price.

Changes in expections. But the adjustment of prices and output does not depend solely on wage contract rigidities, the production schedules of manufacturers and the entrepreneurship of suppliers. Anticipations about future price movements can be a very important determinant of whether changes in output levels or prices will be more dominant.

Initially, says Friedman, the monetary expansion does not show up in prices; so people continue to plan their behaviour, structure their output, settle their wage negotiations, in the anticipation that prices will continue much as they always have done. If there is a rise in prices, it will probably be regarded as temporary, and people will hold back wage claims in anticipation of it soon passing. But eventually people will perceive the general and persistent rise in prices and will adjust their behaviour to it: wages will be settled at rates which anticipate further rises, and product prices will be set at higher levels. As Friedman describes the process:

Generally, when inflation has started after a period of roughly stable prices, people initially do not expect prices to continue rising. They regard the price rise as temporary and expect prices to fall later on. In consequence, they tend to increase their monetary holdings and the price rise is less than the rise in the stock of money. Then, as people gradually become wise to what is going on, they tend to readjust their holdings. Prices then rise more than in proportion to the stock of money. Eventually people come to expect roughly what is happening and prices rise in proportion to the stock of money.[13]

Although this analysis goes back to Fisher, Friedman introduces some important refinements to it. Fisher, after all, took stable prices to be the norm, whereas today we might take rising prices as the norm. But past price movements, their trend and amplitude, can make a large difference, says Friedman, on whether it will be prices or output which rise first:

The precise rate at which prices rise for a given rate of rise in the quantity of money depends on such factors as past price behavior, current changes in the structure of labor and product markets, and fiscal policy.[14]

The point being made here is that an initial burst of inflation may well have a stimulating effect. Where rising prices are a novelty and it is assumed that they will soon pass, money works through into output before prices. But in a country which has come to anticipate inflation, further monetary expansions will simply lead to even more rapid price rises, with output being hardly touched.

It is an important feature of expectations that the entire course of an inflation can turn on them, since people will alter their money balances according to their expectations of future inflation, and this itself will tend to bid prices higher or lower. Thus we must always remain aware that:

A rise in prices can have diametrically opposite effects ... depending on its effect on expectations. If it is interpreted as the harbinger of further rises, it raises the anticipated cost of holding money and leads people to desire lower balances ... On the other hand, if a rise in prices is interpreted as a temporary rise due to be reversed, as a harbinger of a likely subsequent decline, it lowers the anticipated cost of holding money and leads people to desire higher balances relative to income than they otherwise would.[15]

The cyclical adjustment of prices and output. The presence of lags and expectations has an important bearing on the pattern of adjustment of prices, output and nominal income after a monetary disturbance. The adjustment path of nominal income overall, says Friedman, is likely to be cyclical rather than smooth. And within the overall income figure, increasing or decreasing proportions may be accounted for by prices and by output, since each of these is likely to fluctuate cyclically as well.[16]

The point can be seen by taking the results of a typical monetary expansion, although Friedman realizes that any description of the adjustment process must necessarily be tentative and a matter of speculation. As we have seen, a monetary expansion will tend in the first instance to have a stimulating effect on output. The quantities traded are likely to increase as retailers attempt to satisfy the larger demands of their customers, as wholesalers order more stocks, and as manufacturers begin to employ more people to produce the required goods. At this point, then, the main effect of the expansion is to raise *output* rather than prices.

Unfortunately this cannot last. As prices begin to be bid up in the wake of the expansion, people start to recognize that cash is losing its purchasing power. They attempt to reduce their cash balances, so that the velocity of circulation increases. This reinforces the effects of the monetary change and produces a rise in nominal income that is actually more rapid than the monetary expansion. But now the output portion of that rise may suffer: as cash becomes more expensive to hold, manufacturers spend it with more speed and less discrimination, so their productive efficiency will decline; and there will generally be a reduction in the services that cash is used to generate because it is used less efficiently. During this phase, therefore, prices will rise faster than the growth in nominal income, while output will be lower in real terms.

Although expectations of continuing growth in nominal income will make prices rise faster than the monetary expansion that precipitated them, taking them some way beyond their optimal settling point, this cannot go on for ever. Eventually they will ease and must begin a downward path towards the optimal position. But this again might start its own train of expectations about future price *reductions*, with people prefer-ring now to hold *more* money because they think it is becoming worth more, which can lead to overshooting in the opposite direction.

Figure 3
Hypothetical adjustment path of the rate of change
in nominal income

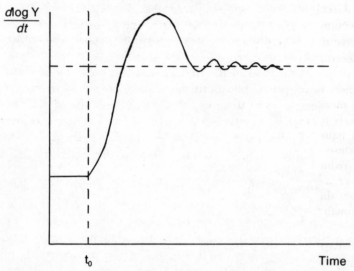

Source: *Monetary Trends in the United States and the United Kingdom,* page 71.

So, clearly, the effect of a monetary change is to set up a cyclical process which – hopefully – converges on the new equilibrium level of nominal income, as illustrated in Figure 3. But within this cyclical adjustment there will also be a fluctuating division into output and prices.

Curbing inflation. From this analysis, it can be seen that Fried-man's view of the effect of monetary changes is in fact much more subtle than he sometimes suggests and his critics suppose. There *will* be some effects on total output following a monetary disturbance, although it is not easy to predict exactly what they will be. What *is* important is that the stimulating effect of inflation carries with it the seeds of an inevitable downturn.

The initial boost to output cannot be sustained, and it will shrink back, perhaps to lower levels than before. Nominal income will similarly go through an unpleasant period of fluctuating adjustments. The only way to sustain the initial boost is to continue the stimulus with an accelerating growth of money. But that, unfortunately, is again fraught with difficulties. The conclusion is that once inflation has started, curing it or continuing it will each have very unpleasant consequences.

Given the objective of reducing prices, a policy which has become attractive in recent years as the problems of inflation have made themselves apparent, we must accept some degree of economic downturn as the inevitable price:

There is no way of getting rid of the after-effects of the high rate of monetary growth of the recent past . . . these delayed effects are likely to mean a decline in the rate a growth of output – a recession or pause or slowdown or tapering off or whatever word one wants to use – even if the present rate of monetary growth continues. A reduced rate of monetary growth will intensify this effect. Moreover, a larger fraction of monetary growth will be absorbed in price rises than would have been the case if that lower rate of monetary growth had prevailed all along.[17]

As expectations of inflation continue, even in the face of the monetary contraction, prices and wages will continue to march upward. The reduced demand caused by the contraction will nevertheless be made obvious in lower sales figures, and unemployment and cutbacks must occur. Thus, the reduction in monetary growth is

almost certain to produce, after some delay, an economic recession evidenced in a growth in unemployment and a decline in the rate of growth of output. That recession will be accompanied . . . by rising prices.[18]

THE DISTRIBUTIVE EFFECTS OF INFLATION

Unless we are familiar with the refinements, it is all too easy to misinterpret Friedman's position. In particular, if we presume that he is interested only in the empirical correspondence of monetary changes and long-term movements in nominal income, we might be inclined to ask what all the fuss is about regarding inflation: if price changes are the only ultimate effect, why worry about monetary policy?[19] Again, we might ask why governments seem to wish to expand the quantity of money at all. We might wonder whether the means by which the monetary changes are made will have any effect on the outcome; and we may go on to enquire whether an expansion may produce changes in *relative* prices that might have a larger effect on the economy than any changes in the *general* price level.

By concentrating on the long-term movements of a few aggregates, Friedman has certainly left himself open to this kind of attack. His strategy may be a wise one from the point of view of the positive scientist: he wishes to establish empirically the existence of an overall pattern which may prove useful, but believes that it would be hard or impossible to investigate and predict with certainty the movements of the individual elements which go to produce and make up that pattern. We could speculate on such things for ever, he might say, but the economy is never in the same place twice and we would find it hard to derive general principles that operated in every case. Short-term effects may indeed be important, but if they eventually cancel out and leave the overall pattern undisturbed, we should, of course, be concentrating on the long-term picture.

The sources of distributional change

There are two principal arguments which cause Friedman's critics to conclude that he systematically underestimates the importance that money can have in generating *real* changes within the structure of the economy. The first is that monetary expansions or diminutions can proceed using different policy instruments, and that these in turn might have different effects on financial markets and therefore the course of an inflation. The second argument is that, however new money is injected into the economy, it will bid up prices in a non-uniform way and will generate major errors in investment and production.

Effects of different policy instruments. Critics using the first strategy point out that different ways of adjusting the quantity of money have different immediate effects. For example, they say a restrictive policy based on an increase in the required bank reserve ratios will require a clampdown by the banks on new lending, although existing borrowers may be comparatively unaffected. Clearly, the control causes marked distributional distortions away from those seeking new loans. Again, Keynesian economists such as Meltzer, Brunner, Tobin and others have argued that there will be differences in the effects of an expansion through increased government borrowing and those of an issuance of new fiat currency.[20] There are various kinds of debt in the financial markets, they say, all with different risk, duration and yield: to a large extent, the immediate impact of open market operations by the government depends upon the proportion in which these kinds of securities are held and exchanged. When they are *sold*, the time deposits and demand deposits used by the public to purchase securities are likely to have different elasticities, so that velocity may be different depending upon which is used. Again, if government bills are issued, taxes will have to be levied to pay the interest on them, and that will imply another distributional change from wage earners to investors. And other similar problems mount up, all revealing *real* side-effects of *nominal* charges.

Friedman's defence. In defence, Friedman argues that some of this criticism is based on a misconception. Inflation has indeed become widely associated with public sector deficits, and deservedly so, because governments often seek to solve their short-term financing problems by a resort to new money creation. But it is also possible to finance a public sector deficit by borrowing: this might cause a shift in resources from the private sector to the government sector, and may even bid up interest rates slightly, but it is not inflationary because no new money has been created. This elementary distinction has been understood for over a century,[21] but the Keynesian tendency to overlook the importance of money has led them into confusion.

Furthermore, the behaviour of the banks helps to keep uniform the effects of monetary expansions of different kinds.

Their methods are similar and their practices largely uniform at any time. While

there will be some difference in detail depending on the source of the increase, whether from gold discoveries, or central bank open-market purchases, or government expenditures financed by fiat money, or a rise in the deposit-currency ratio, or a rise in the deposit–reserve ratio[22]

this uniformity of structure will ensure that

whatever the initial impulse, commercial banks will play a key role in transforming it into an increased rate of growth in the money stock, and this will impose a large measure of uniformity on the outcome.[23]

In summary, then, Friedman's position is that, while it is undoubtedly true that different kinds of monetary expansion have different effects in the financial markets, these will have been largely cancelled out by the time they work through to prices and output. There may be some initial effects spilling over into the economy as a whole, but Friedman dismisses these as 'first-round' effects. Whether they are important is, of course, an empirical question, and the empirical evidence suggests to him that they are not. Thus, he says:

the way the quantity of money is increased will affect the outcome in some measure ... The empirical question is how important the first-round effects are compared with the ultimate effects. Theory cannot answer that question.[24]

Hence his preference for avoiding casual speculation when attempting to understand exactly how the economy readjusts after a monetary disturbance.

Investment errors. Economists of the Austrian School have always gone further in their criticism. To them, the different sources of an expansion (an increase in fiat currency, an expansion of bank credit or some other) not only produce different initial effects: these effects are transmitted right through the economic system, causing systematic errors in the adjustment of every market they work through. The distributional effects of inflation are certainly not limited to the 'first round'.

According to Hayek[25] and the other Austrian economists who developed this argument, money is not neutral in its impact even in the long term. Money is not dropped from helicopters (to use the illustration conjured up by Friedman), uniformly across the whole economy, affecting everybody equally. It enters at some specific point. Just as honey poured onto a plate forms a mound in the middle, so the growth in money and credit bids up prices at the point at which it enters the economy. But prices in other markets will be unchanged at first: there is a *relative* change in prices, which causes resources and enterprise to be attracted away from other markets and to those into which the monetary growth is pouring.

The problem is that investment will proceed apace in the areas which the money stimulates first. More capital will be ordered, longer and more sophisticated production processes will become profitable, and the entire structure of the industries affected may change. But, inevitably, as the change works through to other markets, and the relative price benefit shrinks, resources will be pulled away once again. Capital goods will be abandoned as the temporary boom subsides. And the same cycle of temporary boom and then slump will be transmitted from market to market, right through the economic system. This is no 'first-round' problem: it is a *systematic dislocation of all markets*.

Friedman's defence. Friedman has given increasing consideration to the problems posed by the Keynesians and the Austrians. The account of his own general theoretical framework which appears in the 1982 *Monetary Trends in the United States and the United Kingdon* contains ten pages on the transmission mechanism and 'first-round' effects that are not found in the otherwise largely similar account in *Milton Friedman's Monetary Framework,* published more than a decade earlier.[26]

In his defence, Friedman agrees that there will indeed be

some differences in the way that newly-created money is spent, depending on the particular tastes and spending patterns of the groups that receive it first. But its ultimate effects will depend upon how quickly it spreads from one group to the next: if the new money is mixed quickly with the old, the initial distortions will soon be dissipated. And Friedman can point out to the Austrians and the Keynesians alike that the velocity of money is generally high: it can turn over thirty or more times per year, so that any initial effects will wear off in a period as short as two weeks. Sadly, Friedman is not more specific, but presumably he would like to say that there will in consequence be little malinvestment in the markets that are first affected by the monetary expansion, since the new money very quickly washes through them. But even if this is so, a *sustained* expansion might well keep relative prices in those markets high for a lengthy period, and thus lead to the malinvestment the Austrians fear. Unfortunately, there is little direct answer to this problem in Friedman's major writings, yet it remains a vital issue, because such malinvestment could prove disastrous to the industrialists concerned and very costly to the economy as a whole.

But Friedman does give an indirect answer, in the form of a challenge to his critics to demonstrate that the distributional effects of monetary disturbances *are* important.[27] This is, he says, not a subject which will ever be settled by idle speculation or casual empiricism. The fact is that, despite all the assertions that the nature of a monetary expansion will have important subsequent effects, there is very little evidence available to prove it. The few studies which have been attempted tend to show the opposite. The evidence suggests that the level of output is comparatively unaffected by monetary disturbances: excluding wars (and, in the case of the United States, the idiosyncratic interwar period), the simple quantity theory fits the US and UK data very well, and measurement errors alone would account for any perceived changes in the pattern of output. So while money *may* generate output effects, in practice they are small. Friedman, however, still leaves his Austrian colleagues with the disturbing feeling that the evidence on the macroeconomic measurements of output and prices may conceal a great many important effects in particular markets.

THE SOURCE AND FUTILITY OF INFLATIONARY POLICIES

Bearing in mind the short-term effects of monetary changes, Friedman can suggest several reasons why governments should want to embark on a course of monetary expansion. Each of them, however, is undermined by the adverse side-effects of inflation and the adjustment problems that are inevitable when governments try to contain it.

Redistribution of wealth. Some economists have argued for expansionary policies because inflation is alleged to redistribute income and wealth away from wage earners and towards those who receive profits and therefore invest more; such a redistribution ultimately improves the standard of living of the whole community.

Friedman is by no means convinced. It might work in some cases, but cannot be guaranteed to work in all. If the new money is created in order to cover spending, say on the public sector payroll, it might go to wage-earners rather than entrepreneurs. Furthermore, if the idea of expanding the money supply to help profit-earners were announced, people would simply adjust to the implied inflation rate, and so its distributional effect would be immediately absorbed. And, however successful the policy happens to be at first, the distributional effect will be lost once the new money percolates into the hands of wage-earners, and so it requires larger and larger doses of inflation to sustain.[28]

Indeed, one of Friedman's most heartfelt objections to inflation is that it does *not* redistribute wealth and income to the most efficient producers or to the most deserving consumers, but has precisely the *opposite* effect. Lenders are penalized by inflation, while borrowers gain,[29] but there is no guarantee at all that those who borrow are in any way more productive than those who lend, or that the loans will be used on new investment that will benefit the community. And as regards consumers, it is those on fixed incomes, including deserving people on government pensions and welfare benefits, who see their standard of living most quickly eroded by even a small percentage rate of inflation that is compounded over the years.

Wage flexibility. Another common idea is that a controlled and moderate rate of inflation is necessary to allow for flexibility in wages and prices. Wages are notoriously resistant to downward movement, and if a certain sector of the economy or industry is in decline, this stickiness can mean that sizeable unemployment is the only means of adjustment. With inflation, however, provided that the wages in such an industry rise less quickly than others (it is argued), employment in the industry will grow steadily less attractive and the decline will be managed quite naturally. Once again, however, Friedman can argue in response that people adjust their expectations to the going rate of price increases, and wages are likely to be just as sticky with respect to this rate of increase as they would be to falling in a non-inflationary economy. If there is an effect from this sort of policy, it is probably to trap men and machines in old industries where they are used less efficiently than in new ones.

Hidden tax. A highly plausible explanation of why governments expand the quantity of money is that it benefits their own receipts. This is because of

the effect of the price rise on the real value of those net obligations of government that are expressed in nominal monetary units. The price rise imposes, as it were, a tax on the holdings of such obligations.[30]

Indeed, the tax may be much more direct than that, as people find their earnings sliding into higher tax brackets through the phenomenon known as 'fiscal drag', despite the fact that their *real* incomes are unchanged. It is because of the benefits to a government whose tax thresholds are not indexed and whose debts are payable in nominal units that monetary expansion, with the inflation it brings, is so popular, says Friedman:

Inflation has been irresistibly attractive to sovereigns because it is a hidden tax that at first appears painless or even pleasant, and above all, because it is a tax that can be imposed without specific legislation. It is truly taxation without representation.[31]

Keynes, interestingly enough, would have agreed with this view that inflation is a tax, redirecting resources from individuals to the government:

The public discover that it is the holders of notes who suffer taxation... and they begin to change their habits and to economize in their holding of notes.[32]

Reduction in unemployment. The fact that inflationary policies can produce an initial reduction in unemployment and a temporary boost to industry has long been known. Hume, for example – after anticipating the Austrian economists' point that money spreads gradually from one market and from one industry to another, causing a boost that ripples through the whole economy – concludes that trade will be stimulated. But he observes also that the stimulus is temporary:

In my opinion, it is only in this interval or immediate situation, between the acquisition of money and rise in prices, that the increasing quantity of gold and silver is favourable to industry.[33]

In past experience, it may well be the case that the desire to boost employment has been the principal force pulling governments towards the inflationary path. This has been abetted by the Keynesian arguments that unemployment could be traded off against inflation. But, to Friedman, the stimulus is temporary and there must be an adjustment back down once the monetary expansion works its way through into price changes. The debate between Friedman and the Keynesians on this point has assumed major importance; for it is a dispute about the selection and achievement of fundamental political targets. Accordingly, it is this question that we must consider next.

CHAPTER SEVEN

Inflation and Unemployment

> In my opinion, there is no perpetual trade off between
> inflation and unemployment. The trade off is between
> *acceleration* of inflation and unemployment, which
> means that the real trade off is between unemployment
> now and unemployment later.[1]

ONE strand of the Keynesian orthodoxy that became particularly strong in the 1960s was the view that there exists a
trade-off between unemployment and inflation. Doses of inflation can therefore be used by the authorities as a convenient
(and comparatively harmless) instrument to achieve the high
levels of employment that all countries desire. This view was
formalized in the celebrated analysis of Professor A.W. Phillips,
who plotted unemployment against the rate of change of wages
– the later being a rough guide to inflation, given steady
levels of productivity and roughly constant price mark-ups.
The analysis seemed to show that there was a stable, negative
relation between the level of employment and the rate of
change of wages. Politicians did indeed seem to have the opportunity to boost employment, almost at will, by the simple
expedient of expansionary policies such as increased public
sector deficits. The only cost would be some modest rise in
prices and wages.

The failure of the Phillips curve

To Friedman, such a trade-off is an illusion. Certainly, a dose
of inflation may produce some boost to output in the short
term; but the trade-off cannot be sustained, because as soon
as people come to *anticipate* the rising prices, inflation loses
its power to stimulate economic activity.[2]

Empirical research proved the point. On inspection, the
level of inflation that went with any given unemployment

Figure 4
The simple Phillips curve

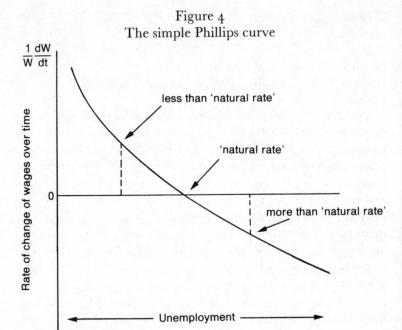

Source: *Unemployment Versus Inflation?*, page 15.

rate did not seem to be very constant and varied widely between countries. Worse still, high inflation came to be coupled with high rates of unemployment: 'stagflation' had arrived; the supposed trade-off just simply refused to appear. Many attempts were made to patch up the hypothesis by allowing for the special features of each time and place, such as the power of trade unions at the time, but it was clear that something was very wrong.

Friedman's explanation. Friedman's explanation of this problem follows from Fisher's analysis. There is no need to assume a stable Phillips curve to explain the *apparent* tendency for an acceleration of inflation to reduce unemployment in the short term. That can be explained by the impact of *unanticipated* changes in nominal demand (particularly in the labour market where contractual arrangements tend to be long-term), because only *surprises* matter. If everyone anticipated that prices would rise by the level they do in fact rise, and was able to renegotiate wages and prices accordingly, there would be no stimulus to employment or output at all from inflation. Everyone would simply adjust their nominal calculations to the new level of prices.

The fallacy in Phillips is therefore to overlook the distinction between anticipated and unanticipated changes. After a monetary expansion, workers may be slow to recognize that prices are creeping up, and that they are in fact receiving lower *real* wages because of it. They might be on fixed contracts and unable to negotiate higher wages even when they *do* perceive the price rises. All of this benefits employers and induces them to take on more workers: but workers cannot be fooled for long, and as soon as they succeed in negotiating their wages back up to the former real rate, the employment stimulus is lost forever.[3]

Short and long-run curves. Friedman says that the magnitude being plotted on the vertical scale of the Phillips curve is in fact the wrong one. Employers and employees usually work on fairly long contracts, which means that they both have to guess what the future trend of prices will be. The real wage rate which matters is not the *current* real wage rate but the *anticipated* real wage rate. If we suppose that anticipations are slow to change, then Phillips's original formulation might hold for a short time, except that the equilibrium position will not be a constant nominal wage, but a changing nominal wage.

If, however, we build in expectations and plot on the vertical axis anticipated change in nominal wages *minus* the anticipated change in nominal prices, then the Phillips curve becomes much more generally useful. Suppose that something such as a monetary expansion starts aggregate demand growing, which in turn produces a rise in prices and wages. Workers, still anticipating constant prices, will take this as a rise in real wages and will offer more labour – unemployment falls. Employers, similarly, will take the rise in the price and demand for their own product as enabling them to hire more workers.

But as time passes, both sides come to recognize that the price rises are general. As a result, they raise their estimate of future price rises, and employment is reduced once again as they slide back down the curve. There has been a short-run trade-off between inflation and unemployment; but there can be no long-run trade-off.

Another way to look at the process (Figure 5) is in terms of an upward shift in the Phillips curve over time. A given rate of inflation will lead to employers and employees settling at a point on the curve with an unemployment rate lower than its natural level. As anticipations change, however, the curve *moves outward*, because at least part of the general increase in prices is now allowed for. A new level of unemployment will emerge. The loci of these eventual settling points trace what might be called a long-run Phillips curve. The question to Friedman is whether it is steeper but still negatively sloping, or whether it is vertical or even positive.

The natural rate hypothesis

To Friedman, there is no 'money illusion', at least in the long run, that will make changes in nominal magnitudes – the nominal quantity of money in this case – generate changes in what is a real magnitude, the level of unemployment. Unemployment is a function of *real* forces, such as the operation of markets, employment policy, and the supply and demand for labour. A dose of monetary expansion, by fooling people temporarily, might cause a temporary boost; but as soon as they get wise to events, employment will drift back to the 'natural' rate that is determined by the real, institutional forces. It would take larger and larger doses of inflation to fool people for any length of time. The attempt to peg employment below what Friedman calls its 'natural' rate, therefore, demands constantly accelerating doses of inflation. Given the obvious disasters of hyperinflation, that is not an appealing prospect.

The natural rate of unemployment is a much misunderstood concept, however. It is meant only to represent the rate of unemployment at which the economy normally settles because

Figure 5
Expectations-augmented Phillips curve

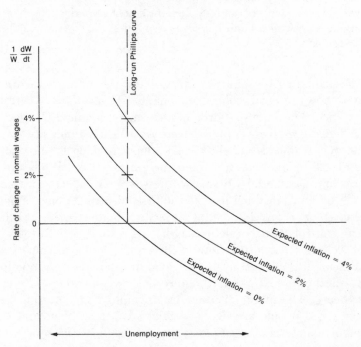

Source: *Unemployment Versus Inflation?*

of its structural imperfections. People cannot change jobs instantaneously; it takes time for workers to recognize where the new opportunities are and to train for them; it takes time also for people to realize that their old skills may no longer be in demand. There are seasonal and other fluctuations in demand and supply conditions which cause occasional surpluses or shortages in the employment market; and there are many more structural sources of unemployment. We are not necessarily stuck with unemployment at a single and unalterable rate, however; we might be able to raise or lower the natural rate of unemployment by making markets less or more efficient. But there will always be some unemployment which we cannot hope to eliminate because there are many causes which it is impossible to eradicate:

the natural rate is dependent upon the structural characteristics of the commodity markets, including market imperfections, stochastic variability in demands and supplies, the cost of gathering information about job vacancies and labour availabilities, the costs of mobility, and so on.[4]

Friedman gives some examples of how the natural rate arises and how political policy can change its level (to a certain extent). The largest source of this unemployment, however, will probably be people *changing jobs*. When times are prosperous, people are likely to take longer looking for new jobs and will be more choosy about the job they take. When times are hard, potential workers will lower their expectations and will be more inclined to take the first job which comes along. *Unemployment insurance* is another factor, obviously within political control, which might lengthen the time people take in searching for a job. It lowers the cost of being unemployed, and might even attract people who are moving from one job to another to take a short 'holiday' in between at the taxpayer's expense. The more generous the unemployment insurance is, the more people are likely to take advantage of it, and the higher the level of unemployment generated by this source.

The extent to which *women and younger workers* enter the ranks of available workers may also have an effect. Many of them are not the principal breadwinners of their families, and so they tend to be more mobile, shifting between jobs and not facing such real pressure to be employed. Consequently, they sometimes stay on the unemployment tallies for lengthy periods and drive up the overall figures.

The *method by which wages are settled* might also make a sizeable difference to the natural rate of unemployment. As we have seen, wages are notoriously sticky downwards: even if prices are falling, people do not like taking wage cuts. An employer who is facing declining receipts may have to shed some of his workforce in such a situation if he cannot get them to accept reduced wages. At the other extreme, when prices are rising, the fact that wage contracts are generally negotiated at annual intervals imposes costs on employers: the more time they have to spend attempting to predict the level of future inflation, the more of a burden it is to reach a settlement, and the more likely they are to make mistakes. Large mistakes mean that there is a risk of employers having to reduce their workforce to bring their total wage bill down to affordable levels. Shorter-term contracts, or wage settlements that are indexed to the cost of living, could reduce this source of friction and therefore reduce the natural rate of unemployment.

Practicalities and policies. A number of economists have pursued empirical research on these sources of unemployment in order to attempt an estimate of what the 'natural rate' is. One measure that is commonly used is the 'benefit ratio' of the welfare statistics – broadly speaking, the level of average unemployment compensation divided by average take-home pay. This ratio has shown a very sizeable increase over the years, and in the last years of the 1960s roughly *doubled*, so it is quite likely that the natural rate of unemployment also rose substantially at this time, and perhaps that explains why politicians were forced to resort to such massive levels of inflation in the attempt to keep the unemployment rate at a low level. Empirical studies have suggested that the natural rate for the United Kingdon is about two per cent: for the United States, which uses a different counting method, it would be perhaps five or six per cent.[5] When governments attempt to reduce unemployment much below these levels by monetary boosts rather than by improving structural inefficiencies, the immobility of the workforce and the other real factors which cause it, then inflation of the scale of the 1960s and 1970s is the probable outcome.

So the natural rate hypothesis should be understood for what it is. The natural rate of unemployment is not an inflexible constant: it varies in response to public policy, and in recent years it has tended to rise as people spend more time (on average) between jobs. It will be influenced by changes in the real structure of markets, but not, in general, by changes in nominal magnitudes. And we must remember, says Friedman, that unemployment is not always a bad sign and therefore not always a fitting target for policy instruments. High unemployment may in fact signify a highly mobile economy, or one with sufficient wealth and security for people not to feel pressured into taking the first job which comes along. A very high employment rate, on the other hand, could signify a forced-draft economy or one where times were hard and people took the first job they could get.[6]

These real forces, then, are ultimately the ones which will decide the level of employment and unemployment. Changes in the quantity of money may have some short-term impact and produce a temporary boom which may stimulate employment for a while. But as expectations adjust, economic reality will assert itself again, and unemployment settles at its natural rate once more. The policymakers who have assumed that a dose of inflation will cure unemployment are sadly mistaken, says Friedman, since a high rate of inflation, although it might have some real effects,

need not alter the efficiency of labor markets, or the length or terms of labor contracts, and hence it need not change the natural rate of employment.[7]

And unless *that* magnitude is changed, economic policy will be misguided as it attempts other ways of reducing unemployment.

Expectations and evidence

Friedman is not content with the empirical attempts that have been made to check the natural rate hypothesis, however.[8] The evidence is highly confusing, and its interpretation depends, he says, upon *how* expectations about future price changes are arrived at. Certainly, people are likely to expect future price rises if prices are already climbing today.[9] But more than this, they learn from their past mistakes, incorporate their views about economic policy and events, and try to anticipate the rate of increase of prices in the future. Workers, for example, negotiate for new wage rates that reflect not only what they have lost through inflation in the past year, but what they expect to lose in the next. If they come to the conclusion that inflation will accelerate because of economic policy, they will build this into their negotiating stance.

This sophisticiation makes it very likely that the long-run Phillips curve will be vertical, or nearly so. But Friedman complains that existing theories about how expectations are formed are inadequate, and contain biases that assume the long-run curve to be negatively sloped, although steeply so. In his judgement, it is much more likely that it would be vertical (confirming the natural rate hypothesis) or perhaps even positive (meaning that increasing doses of inflation tend to generate even *higher* rates of unemployment than before.

Unfortunately, Friedman does not give us a new theory of how expectations are formed that would satisfy him as being free from theoretical or statistical bias. This is a misfortune, and makes his own position somewhat unclear. He seems to suggest that people form expectations about future price rises that are in fact satisfied, because he argues that, after an initial surprise, people come completely to anticipate future inflation, and it is that which makes them adjust back to the natural rate of unemployment. But that is certainly a curious theoretical position. It suggests not only that Friedman's own theories about money and prices are correct, but that everyone accepts them and applies them in everyday life – and does so correctly, thus anticipating fully the extent of future price rises! This is not a very convincing posture: people may well form their own theories about the future, but it is unlikely that they wil ever fully or correctly anticipate future inflation, and so critics argue that there is no *necessary* tendency for unemployment to settle back to any particular rate.[10]

The evidence, however, is certainly not all in, and as more empirical work is done, the nature of the expectations-determination process will be more closely understood. Yet there are some points which do present themselves strongly, says Friedman. For example, in countries with a history of high and variable inflation, expectations seem to adjust much more rapidly than in those where prices have previously been stable. The short-run Phillips curve is steeper in the inflation-bound country than in the one with a history of price stability. This comparison does seem consistent with the belief that people cannot be fooled for long, and that people quickly form theories about the impact of public policy on future prices. The more skill people have at forming expectations of this sort, the more difficult it apparently becomes for the authorities to take them by surprise.

A positively sloped Phillips curve?

The notion that the Phillips curve is vertical, as we have seen, suffers from the criticism that it implies that all expectations are satisfied, and that people *correctly* anticipate the future of prices, respond only to *real* magnitudes and therefore settle at the natural rate of unemployment that is determined by the real workings of markets. This seems very unlikely, however. Critics from the Austrian School would argue that it is highly probable that people do not anticipate price increases correctly, particularly when some prices are almost certain to be rising faster than others. There are bound to be mismatches between supply and demand caused by uncertainty about the future, and that is bound to increase the rate of unemployment. Far from curing unemployment, a dose of inflation is likely to make it worse.

In his most recent writings,[11] Friedman too has been more inclined to accept the possibility that the long-run Phillips curve might not just be vertical, but could be *positively* sloped, with increasing doses of inflation leading to increasing unemployment. As recently as 1975, he plainly doubted this possibility, and was sticking to the notion that the curve is vertical in the long run, as he had proposed in his 1967 address to the American Economic Association. Within a short time, though, he came to accept the likelihood of a positively sloped curve.

Once again, however, Friedman's judgement is based on empirical findings[12] rather than mere theorizing about how the phenomenon might arise – a view consistent with his methodological approach. There are many disputes about how the findings should be interpreted, but there certainly does seem to be some evidence that the long-run Phillips curve is at least vertical and may be positive.[13] Friedman goes further, indeed, and says that the data strongly suggest that while the curve was negative for most of the leading industrial countries between about 1956 and 1965, it became strongly positive thereafter. In other words, as the medicine of inflation has been tried, expectations have become resistant to it and employment has declined accordingly. There are naturally doubts and qualifications, but Friedman concludes that the data strongly suggest that in at least some major countries, rising inflation and rising unemployment have gone hand in hand. He regards this as surprising, but nevertheless,

so far as it exists at all, the Phillips curve – at least for the units of time as long as our cycle phases (averaging two years for the United States, 2.8 years for the United Kingdon) – is positively, not negatively, sloping, except only for the idiosyncratic United States interwar period.[14]

Volatility. The volatility of the rate of inflation is a very prominent reason, says Friedman, why high rates of inflation will tend to be associated with high unemployment. The higher the rate of inflation, the more variable it tends to be: governments tend to produce high inflation as a *consequence* of their other policies, not as a deliberate aim, so its exact level is dependent upon the adoption and working of those other political measures. A burst of inflation, however, is matched by attempts to contain it; then the unpleasant consequences of the contraction show up and require yet more inflation to remove them. Policy goes in fits and starts, and the inflation turns out to be volatile as well as high. There is, in consequence, considerable uncertainty about what the rate is likely to be, and employment suffers.

Friedman recognizes two different ways in which this uncertainty may raise the natural rate of unemployment. First, increased volatility shortens the optimum length of labour contracts, although it is by no means clear that the effect on the natural rate is all in one direction. Shorter contracts may make the labour market more responsive to movements and changes in demand: on the other hand, the delay in adjustment may lead to higher unemployment. The latter is more likely because price indexes usually lag behind price changes because of the length of time it takes to collect the data, which delays the adjustment process.

The second effect has been documented at length by Hayek. Prices convey information, and during an inflation in which there is much uncertainty about the future, and where prices are volatile, it is difficult to separate out the price signals from the confusing noise of rapidly moving prices.[15] Consequently, volatile inflation leads to errors and inefficiency in productive arrangements.[16] At the extreme, the system of prices becomes useless, and people adopt some other unit of currency, or barter, in order to exchange commodities. The effect on productivity and efficiency is disastrous.

Friedman believes that in circumstances of high and volatile inflation, however, methods of adjusting automatically to the inflation will develop. Contracts and wages will be indexed, that is, stated in terms of real prices rather than nominal ones. Methods of avoiding government price and wage controls will envolve. In these circumstances, the long-run Phillips curve would tend to fall back to its vertical position.[17]

Suppressed inflation. Another reason why high inflation is often associated with higher unemployment is the effect of price controls. Higher rates of inflation bring forth appeals for prices to be held or reduced, and this is often done through the medium of price restrictions and controls. Governments themselves, says Friedman, are often producers and sellers of a wide range of commodities, and naturally they will be under pressure to keep their own prices low. The price system, however, starts to break down when this kind of shackle is put on it: it fails to convey the information which it did when free. Markets are plagued by increased frictions, and the natural rate of unemployment rises. Only with the sudden removal of price controls did the German economic miracle begin: it was not a testament to German ingenuity, but the obvious result of allowing the price system to function properly once again.[18]

Another deficiency of price controls is that they tend to

require increasing controls over other things: if the price system is not able to organize resources, then rationing or other physical controls must be resorted to. Foreign trade has always been a favourite target, and attempts to reduce foreign trade by tariffs, import restrictions, tourist allowances, limits on foreign loans and 'voluntary' import agreements have all been resorted to by important countries in an effort to keep up domestic production and stifle import demand.

Suppressed inflation therefore not only leaves the economy without a co-ordinating mechanism: because official prices do not appear to rise, it reduces the prospect of anti-inflation policy being tried at all; it introduces distortions systematically into the allocation and distribution of resources; and it invites extralegal powers of control.

Trade unions

Friedman has little to say about trade unions. The ultimate cause of inflation is government action, and whether or not trade unions coerce goverments into inflationary measures, it is still the government which has the ultimate responsibility. Friedman believes that once we start to look at the political pressures on government decision-making, a sensible theory of inflation becomes almost impossible:

One thing is very clear from the historical record. The actual sources of monetary expansion have been very different at different times and in different places. Hence, if a theory of inflation is going to deal not with the expansion of the stock of money but with what brought it about, it will be a very pluralistic theory which will have many possible sources of inflation.[19]

In any event, says Friedman, for the community as a whole, with a stable level of prices, higher wages without unemployment can be sustained for one group only if some other group is pressured to accept unemployment or lower wages. If there is not some lowering of wages or some unemployment, there will not be sufficient demand in the economy for the higher wages to be sustained. Certainly, strong trade unions may win improvements in wages for their own members, but in the long run this can only be at the cost of lower employment levels or a reduction in wages and employment in other industries. Thus, he says:

> Trade unions play a very important role in determining the position of the natural level of unemployment . . . They play a very important role in the structure of the labour force and the structure of *relative* wages. But, despite appearances to the contrary, a *given* amount of trade union power does not play any role in exacerbating inflation.[20]

But he also admits that, in the process of acquiring increased power, trade unions may influence the government to maintain a 'full employment' policy and therefore generate inflation.

Policy implications

All this makes us understand that employment cannot be plucked out of thin air: it takes appropriate monetary policies if a depressed economy is to get more jobs and if an inflating economy is to keep them. But the most important lesson must be that the alleged trade-off between inflation and unemployment does not exist and never has existed. Inflation today might prevent unemployment rising in the immediate future, but it will surely lead to higher unemployment later on. However rapid the inflation, unemployment will always tend to fall back to its natural rate, a term which

> does not refer to some *irreducible minimum* of unemployment. It refers rather to that rate of unemployment which is consistent with the *existing real conditions* in the labor market. It can be lowered by removing obstacles in the labour market, by reducing friction.[21]

The first implication for public policy is therefore to *improve the institutional structures* to make the labour market as responsive as possible to changing patterns of demand. In addition, some level of unemployment must be accepted as natural in the light of large numbers of part-time workers, unemployment compensation, and other institutional factors.

The second implication is that *unemployment policy is not a fitting aim for monetary expansion.* In the long term, monetary measures affect only nominal quantities, while the levels of unemployment and other real magnitudes are influenced only by real events. Thus the monetary authority cannot use its control over nominal quantities to peg a real quantity such as the level of unemployment, or even real income.[22] The *exchange implications* of employment policy should also be noted. Domestic full-employment policy, coupled with fixed exchange rates, led to inevitable crises in foreign exchange.[23] While floating rates avoid the worst crises, countries using inflation in the attempt to cure unemployment also face depreciating currencies and a steadily worsening competitive position.

But the *costs of an inflationary policy* are not limited to this. In an inflation, people have to spend time and energy distinguishing real from nominal changes, estimating future prices, attending to the paperwork of wage and price increases, and so on.

The conclusion from all this is that, if the error-learning hypothesis is correct, and the Phillips curve is vertical or almost so, then most postwar economic policy, aimed at 'full employment', was a mistake. Employment above the natural rate can be reached only at the cost of potentially runaway inflation. Unfortunately for the policymaker, there is no precise and indisputable measure of what the 'natural rate' of unemployment is. Demand management policies are therefore often aimed at too optimistic an employment target, bringing accelerating inflation in their wake.

According to Friedman, the runaway inflations of the 1960s and 1970s were a manifestation of this attempt to secure a level of unemployment below the natural rate and show the dangers of monetary incontinence:

A little inflation will provide a boost at first – like a small dose of a drug for a new addict – but then it takes more and more inflation to provide the boost, just as it takes a bigger and bigger dose of a drug to give a hardened addict a high.[24]

The message from this empirical experience, therefore, is that if we want genuine full employment – that is, to have unemployment settling at around its natural rate as determined by real factors and institutions – we must give up any thought of using monetary policy for the purpose. Monetary policy cannot alter the long-term level of nominal income. The best policy to secure higher employment is to remove institutional restraints, restrictive practices, barriers to mobility, trade union coercion, discrimination and similar obstacles to those who offer and seek employment.

CHAPTER EIGHT

The Lag and Business Cycles

... changes in the stock of money exert an independent
influence on cyclical fluctuations in economic activity
with a lag that is both long and variable relative to
the average length of such fluctuations.[1]

IT is an essential part of Milton Friedman's version of the
quantity theory of money that changes in the quantity of
money reveal themselves in terms of changes in income. Most
of the misunderstandings which people have about the effects
of monetary changes are due to their failure to allow for this
temporal looseness in the monetary mechanism: when the
quantity of money changes, there is a temptation to consider
the immediate results, which can be totally misleading, rather
than the true effects which show themselves months or years
afterwards.

The notion of the lag is also bound up with the familiar
concept of the business cycle, the up-and-down fluctuations
in business activity which can be discerned so easily in the
historical record. Friedman argues that these cycles are themselves mostly monetary in origin, and that one of their principal
causes is the length of time which different economic magnitudes take to adjust to monetary changes. A monetary change
affects many things, some of which adjust faster than others,
causing a measure of discord in the final result, and giving
rise to the business cycle.

The connexion between lags and cycles is not original to
Friedman, of course. The British economist Ralph Hawtrey
drew up a fairly persuasive version of it in 1939,[2] and even
before then Hayek and other Austrian School economists had
been devising their own version.[3] All these early writers suggested that expanding bank credit would cause businessmen
to expand their inventories, step up production and boost

incomes and spending. According to Hayek, however, that would represent only a temporary boom; eventually, output, inventories, spending and all the other indicators of economic activity would have to contract, thus completing a cyclical movement. To Hawtrey, increased spending would mean an increased demand for new currency as people required more money to make transactions: under a gold or other commodity standard, it would take time for this new demand to be satisfied, so that monetary movements would lag behind the expansion of credit, again setting off the cyclical pattern of economic activity.

The cyclical movement of money

It is not just business activity which, according to Friedman, runs in cycles. The *money stock itself* shows a marked cyclical variation, and this is certainly an obvious starting point in any investigation of business cycles. It led Friedman, together with Anna Schwartz, to conduct extensive research on the historical evidence for the cyclical interpretation of both monetary movements and economic activity.[4]

Empirical evidence. There can be no doubt, according to Friedman and Schwartz, that the stock of money has displayed a systematic cyclical pattern over the decades.[5] There is, of course, a strong long-term upward trend in the volume of the money stock, but when this is allowed for, it is discovered that there is a clear cyclical pattern, with the movement in the money stock closely associated with business cycles. The amplitude of the money stock movements is roughly equal to the amplitude of the business cycles identified by the National Bureau of Economic Research for reference purposes: but the money stock generally reaches its peak before the 'reference' peak of the cycles, and similarly reaches its trough before the 'reference' trough. On *average*, during the eighteen non-war cycles since 1870, peaks in the rate of change of the stock of money precede 'reference' peaks in business activity by about sixteen months, and troughs in the rate of change of the stock of money precede 'reference' troughs by twelve months.[6]

The strong secular rise in the money stock over the decades makes it important to talk in terms of *changes* rather than the *level* of the money stock. In deep depression cycles, the money stock does indeed tend to fall, but in mild depression cycles, the general upward trend swamps the effect, and all that can be discerned is a reduction in the *rate of growth* of the stock of money, rather than any actual *fall*. Hence, the *rate of change* of the stock of money is the most useful point of reference in attempting to calculate the effects of money on the economy.

Doubts about direction. Since the patterns of business activity and of rates of change in the stock of money are both cyclical, it could be suggested that the direction of causation is the *opposite* to that which Friedman has proposed. As we saw in Chapter 4, some critics argue that, instead of monetary changes causing subsequent movements in business activity, changes in the level of business activity in fact call forth subsequent changes in the rate of growth of the money stock.

Friedman, however, has replied that empirical tests 'rather decisively support' treating the rate of change of the stock of money 'as conforming to the reference cycle positively with a long lead, rather than inversely with a somewhat shorter lag', which would be the alternative explanation.[7] There are in addition a number of simple cases which can be used to illustrate the direction of causality: wartime inflations and some unanticipated large depressions make it clear that business activity changes have followed monetary changes, not the other way round. Furthermore, observations of the timing and amplitudes of cyclical variations in money and activity, when applied to the two opposing explanations, make it plain, to Friedman, that monetary changes lead to changes in business activity, not the other way around.[8] Work by Friedman and Meiselman on the influence of the monetary factor on business activity also tended to confirm this view.[9]

Some critics have argued that the perceived 'lag' however, is due simply to errors in the statistical calculations,[10] although Friedman has successfully defended himself against this challenge.[11] And some Keynesians such as Tobin[12] have noted that, even if the lag between changes in money and in other magnitudes does exist, it does not necessarily mean that money is the *cause* of the disturbance: there may be some third factor which disturbs both. But Friedman thinks that the evidence admits no doubt on the issue, and when other factors are considered (such as the large extent to which the quantity of money is in practice consciously determined by the authorities rather than being a magnitude that simply responds endogenously to business conditions), the direction of causation from money to business activity is clear enough.

THE NATURE AND VARIABILITY OF THE LAG

Having established, then, that some sort of lag does seem to exist in the effect of monetary changes, we must now consider the source and nature of the lag and explain why it should be long and variable.

The nature of the lag

To Friedman, it is incorrect to talk of 'the' lag. There are in fact several lags in the effect of monetary policy, all of them stemming from different sources. Moreover, if the effects of a single monetary change could be isolated, it would not have all its impact suddenly at a distance of several months from the change itself: rather, its effects would be mild at first, rising to a crescendo and then subsiding. With the effects of the change being distributed over a lengthy period of time, 'the' lag is not a very useful description. It is more like a *distributed* lag, and is therefore difficult to pin down: to achieve any measure of it at all, techniques such as the use of a weighted average of the effects, compiled over several peaks and troughs, are required.

Even this is not sophisticated enough, says Friedman, since as we have seen, a monetary change might actually produce some overshooting on the road to adjustment, causing a *negative* effect after a while, so that just taking averages is bound to be confusing and to lose essential information. And there is also the practical problem that monetary changes rarely occur in isolation: they tend to be manifested as a series of movements over time, rather than large isolated changes. The effects of different lags therefore become confused, and their study becomes that much more difficult.

On the other hand, there are some factors which help the statistician. The more monetary changes and effects are averaged, the more will irrelevant and stray factors drop out of our assessments. We are also aided by the fact that various measures of the money stock tend to move together, so that the precise definition is not critical. Thus, in practice, it *is* possible to formulate fairly useful measures of the lag; looking at the evidence, Friedman concludes that peaks in the rate of change of the money stock itself precede National Bureau reference cycle peaks by sixteen months on average; peaks in the deviation of the money stock from its long-term trend precede cycle peaks by five months on average; peaks in the absolute level of the money stock precede reference cycle peaks by less than five months, and might even lag behind; and peaks in income, although partly concealed by the strong upward trend, probably follow peaks in the rate of change of the money stock.

Why the lag is long. Given Friedman's explanation of the transmission process from monetary changes to business activity,[13] it becomes clear that there are many places at which delays might introduce themselves. Take, for example, the adjustments following an increase in the stock of money by government open market security purchases. The first effect will be that the community will move to alter its assset and liability structure. Having been offered a good price, they sell their securities, but they will naturally want to shift their assets around to restore their chosen blend of risk, security and income services to much the original position. There will be a demand for other bonds and financial assets, and the price of these will be bid up; then the price of other sorts of assets will be bid up as people move to acquire those; and so on with still other assets as prices rise and people have to look further afield.

There is already a series of delays evident in this process:

people are unlikely to be able to restore their portfolios overnight. And the looseness widens as the effects spread further.
The range of assets sought after will widen: houses and other
assets will become more desirable, raising the cost of these
things relative to the services they provide (indicated by rental
income in the case of housing). This will in turn encourage
people to 'create' more assets, and there will be housebuilding
and general investment as people continue to acquire more
of them. A wider and wider spread of assets is affected. With
capital assets being bid up in price, people will tend to consume
more *services* (such as renting rather than purchasing accommodation), which will then tend to bid up service prices and
interest rates. The result of all this is that expenditures rise
in all directions, but that it takes variable times for the effects
to show in different markets.

The Keynesian transmission mechanism, which is supposed
to work through a fairly narrow range of financial securities
and interest rates, does not conveniently explain the existence
of a long lag: but Friedman's version, in which the prices
and yields of a wide range of different assets are important,
does give us a good indication of how delays could arise and
why they would not be uniform in their effects. The adjustment
of portfolios after a monetary disturbance involves the substitu-
tion of a large number of assets, so it is likely to take much
longer than if the change was confined to the financial markets,
and the ultimate effects will plainly be spread out. The rising
prices of capital assets will not induce producers of capital
to leap in immediately: they will wait until they are certain
that the demand is genuine, and then they will enter the
market at different rates, having taken time to decide, to draw
up their plans, to tool up and to bring their goods onto the
market. Even then, it would take time for the benefits of the
new assets to spread to the earnings of the manufacturer, the
wholesaler and the retailer. Hence the lag is long and spread
out.

Fit with cyclical events. It is interesting, says Friedman, how
well this explanation of the transmission mechanism fits with
empirical observations of cyclical phenomena. In his explana-

tion, first bonds, then equities, then payments for real resources, will be affected: the financial markets will show a boom long before the rest of the economy. And historically, says Friedman, this is exactly what has happened, with bonds, equities and other financial assets recovering before order books start to lengthen and incomes start to rise.

The variability of the lag

It is clear, then, that the lag in the effect of monetary disturbances is long, and that there is a good reason why it should be so. The next issue which must be addressed is the extent to which the lag is variable, and why.

Empirical findings. The work of Friedman and Schwartz reveals that the lag is in fact highly variable. For example:

In the National Bureau study on which I have been collaborating with Mrs Schwartz we found that, on the average of 18 cycles, peaks in the rate of change in the stock of money tend to precede peaks in general business by about 16 months and troughs in the rate of change in the stock of money to precede troughs in general business by about 12 months ... For individual cycles, the recorded lag has varied between 6 and 29 months at peaks and between 4 and 22 months at troughs.[14]

These are plainly wide variations. To some extent, they may be due to measurement errors, since the determination of peaks and troughs and the general measurement of the magnitudes under observation are difficult at the best of times. In looking at individual cycles, these measurement errors could be very great, although they will of course tend to cancel out when averaged over a number of cycles. But even so, the size of the disparity between the shortest and longest observed lags makes it hard to accept as the result of measurement errors alone.

The point is crucial because the variability of the lag adds greatly to the confusion about the true effects of monetary policy. And it is also a difficult point for Friedman because, in theory, a long lag might be expected to be more regular in its impact, since each part of the transmission process will have a 'variable reaction time', and so their combined effect would be to spread the ultimate effects[15] and perhaps to 'average out' any particular anomalies, making the length of the lag predictable. But the lag remains highly variable.

Some critics have therefore claimed that other factors in economic life, such as the prevailing tax rates, have a profound bearing on monetary policy and impinge greatly on the length of the lag. The analogy would be a road vehicle: pressing the brake might stop it, but how long it takes to stop (and whether it does indeed stop) depends greatly on the nature of the road surface and the prevailing weather conditions.[16] Likewise, it would be a gross oversimplification to insist that economic factors other than money are not important in explaining levels of business activity, and the variability of the lag demonstrates emphatically to Friedman's critics how important these other factors really are. Tax levels and government expenditure, they say, are probably just as important if business cycles are to be explained: fiscal policy must be brought into Friedman's calculations, whether he likes it or not.

Certainly, Friedman and Schwartz are happy enough to concede that factors other than monetary changes are likely to be important:

Clearly, the view that monetary change is important does not preclude the existence of other factors that affect the course of business or that account for the quasi-rhythmical character of business fluctuations. We have no doubt that other factors play a role.[17]

If fiscal factors are important, then Friedman would have no doubt that they could explain much of the variability: from his earliest writings through to more recent times, he has always insisted that every tax change or expenditure variation *does* have effects on business, although with different lags, different strengths and different duration.[18] But to admit this too readily is to devalue the strictly monetary explanation of events: so there are problems here for Friedman, and his model would certainly benefit from further refinement on the point.

However, the importance of measurement errors should not be underestimated. The rate of change in the quantity of money is often very fickle, and it is hard to give an exact turning-point for peaks and troughs. This alone could explain a large portion of the apparent variability of the lag. Any single statistical measure, such as the peak rate of change, the peak deviation from the trend, or the absolute peak in money supply and business activity, is a summary number only, and by no means a full description of events, says Friedman, just as a person's face is more than a collection of one or two features. The relationship between monetary indicators and economic activity is clear because there *is* an underlying link, but the link is not rigid; hence the variability of the exact outcome.

THE IMPLICATIONS FOR STABILIZATION POLICY

It has long been supposed by orthodox economists that temporary fluctuations in business activity can be smoothed out by the speedy application of fiscal measures or even monetary policy. There is no need for an economy to go through large swings in its fortunes: traditional Keynesian 'fine tuning', it is alleged, can keep activity on a more even path.

This is a view which Friedman has never had any urge to share. One thing the variability of the lag makes plain is that, whatever its source, it is impossible to predict with certainty, which rules out discretionary economic policy. Indeed, it demonstrates that a discretionary policy, aimed at economic stabilization, may well *add* to the swings in business activity that it is attempting to cure: it would be very easy for the economic authorities to find that by the time their policy began to work, it was actually adding to the severity of the next swing rather than smoothing the one before.

The statistics of destabilization. Using mathematical techniques, Friedman shows elegantly how countercyclical economic policy would be likely to worsen the swings in economic activity rather than cure them. Even if the policy happened to be in the wrong direction as often as the right direction, its impact would still not be neutral, and on occasions it would still add to the variations in income over the cycles and lead to more pronounced fluctuations than before. It can be shown mathematically that, to reduce the cyclical variations by half, an economic policy would have to work in the right direction something like seventy per cent of the time. This seems unlikely, given the variability of the lag.[19]

But the picture is even bleaker for the policymaker, since it may not be possible to isolate the policy instruments that could ease a depression and check a runaway boom. As Friedman notes, the common viewpoint is that government expenditure or lower taxation can achieve the first, and that a tax increase is very effective in achieving the second: but, in fact, their effects depend almost entirely on their impact on monetary matters. This confusion in the selection of policy measures makes it even less likely that the effects of economic policy will be in the right direction at the right time.

Even if the correct kinds of policy are put into effect at the right time (improbable though that would be), they might still be of the wrong strength. It is easy for the effects of a policy change to be stronger or weaker than expected, which might again add to the variation in incomes and activity over the cycles. More importantly, if an anti-cyclical policy were strong, the destabilization which it could produce would be that much more profound, leading to the confusing position that the more *determined* the policy is, the more it is likely to produce results opposite to those intended. All this stems from the doubt and uncertainty in the lag.

The source of the problem. As already noted, in assessing the effects of monetary policy, we are not dealing with just one lag, but with a whole family of them. This means that the ultimate effects of economic policy are that much more variable, and it means that the delays are likely to be long. Any stabilization policy is in consequence very unlikely to have its desired impact at the right time.

Friedman identifies three sources from which lags in the

effect of monetary policy are likely to arise. Firstly, there is a delay in the *recognition* that some policy change is required. It takes time for the onset of, say, a depression to be noticed: they are hard enough to date adequately as a historical matter, but almost impossible to pinpoint at the time. Indexes which indicate the onset of a depression, or a boom, take time to compile, and therefore tend to lag behind the event itself. Once collected, there may be doubt whether the results are temporary, or whether the fluctuations will be mild or profound, or even whether the figures are due merely to measurement errors. In view of the record of economic forecasters, says Friedman, it might be better to shun the 'leading indicators' which are supposed to herald economic changes and rely solely upon some measurement of current activity as our guide. But this inevitably means some delay before the course of a fluctuation in business activity can be fully recognized.[20]

The second source of the policy lag will be the time between the recognition that action is required and the *taking of action.* Institutional arrangements can make this stretch into months or years, particularly where public expenditure and taxation are thought to be the right policy instruments to use. For example, taxes are often collected annually, so it can be up to a year before tax money can be taken out of the economy or transfer payments can be boosted. Printing of new tax schedules and forms following a tax change, and many other kinds of delay, can be expected with fiscal policy. Even if monetary measures are proposed to counter the cycles, they still take time. Whatever is done, therefore, by the time the new policy is prepared and put into effect, it may already be too late.

The third source of delay is the *lag in the effect of the policy* once it has been initiated, which, as we have seen, can be long and variable. What effect there is will tend to be spread out, rather than concentrated at one time. Consequently, some part of the effect might turn out to be in the right direction, while other parts might come too late and be completely wrong: given the length of the delay from the onset of the cycle, through to it being recognized, to policy being initiated and then at last taking effect, Friedman thinks that it will be rare for any policy to be remotely stabilizing.

Conclusion on stabilization policy. The inevitable conclusion is that attempts at stabilization through fiscal or monetary measures are almost certain to be a mistake. Variations and delays in the effects of policy measures mean that they are likely to have a destabilizing effect rather than a smoothing one. Indeed, policy can be destabilizing, even if it is of the right strength and in the right direction, if it comes just too early or too late.

That is why the more robust the initial policy action, the more harm is likely to be done. If the effects of the policy do not occur at the right time, they will add to the amplitude of the original business cycle and produce an even greater series of fluctuations. To expect to get 'fine tuning' policy right every time is foolhardly: but it would have to be right with unprecedented accuracy and consistency if it were not if fact to *worsen* the situation.

Regarding the policy instrument that Friedman considers by far the most potent, monetary policy, the warning is thus clear. It cannot and should not be used in an attempt to correct economic cycles: the best policy is to keep the money supply growing at a moderate and stable rate sufficient to allow liquidity for economic growth. Although this would not, of course, eliminate all fluctuations in business activity, it would at least prevent policymakers from inflating into a boom or deflating into a slump, which has happened so often before.

The Keynesian partiality for 'fine tuning' the economy is, then, an early casualty of Friedman's empirical work on the lag. It is by no means the only victim of monetarist thinking, however, and Friedman's broader analysis strikes at the very heart of conventional Keynesian wisdom about the range of policy instruments that are effective in managing the economy.

CHAPTER NINE

Keynesian versus Monetarist Economic Policy

I know of no empirical student of the demand for money who denies that interest rates affect the real quantity of money demanded – although others have misinterpreted me as so asserting.[1]

WHILE Friedman doubts that discretionary changes in the quantity of money are likely to get the economy moving in the right direction, to the right degree, at the right time, he has no doubt that they do have a pronounced effect. The results of monetary policy are powerful, even if their power cannot be precisely controlled.

Economic policy analysts brought up in the Keynesian orthodoxy tend to be less squeamish about using economic policy as a stabilization measure. They agree that the quantity of money is difficult to control with great accuracy – indeed, it is hard enough to define and measure – but argue that the problem is not very serious anyway because monetary factors do not have all that much impact on the economy. Far more important, in their judgement, is the weapon of *fiscal policy:* that is, making changes in the balance or volume of taxation and government spending. Tax or spending changes are seen as quite sufficient to slow down an inflation and to speed up a sluggish, recessionary economy: there may be a few undesirable effects of such a policy, but monetary measures can be used to help overcome them. Tax changes can also be made fairly quickly (especially where income tax is deducted at source), and with a good deal of accuracy, which makes them useful for a stabilization strategy. Monetary policy is a useful adjunct to fiscal measures, but not much more.

Needless to say, Friedman disagrees with every line of this

analysis, common though it remains in much economic policy debate. To see why he objects, it is necessary to outline the orthodox approach in a little more detail.

Traditional stabilization policy

Changes in government spending and taxation are the building-blocks of fiscal policy, and those blocks come in three different shapes. Suppose that the economy is in recession and the authorities want to stimulate production. The first fiscal policy measure available is that of increasing *public works* programmes, such as the building of new roads or airports. These schemes all require men, machinery and materials, and so the labour market and the production of materials and machines are all stimulated. While this might be useful in a protracted recession, however, public works programmes are unpopular for stabilization policy because they tend to take a long time to set in motion. A second measure is to alter government *transfer payments*. Larger pensions or welfare benefits stimulate spending by the recipients, and that in turn stimulates production. This policy, while easy to start, is often difficult to stop, because beneficiaries would complain loudly, so it too is not popular as a short-term stabilization measure. The third possibility, the one advocated most widely for stabilization, is to change the *volume of taxation* which the government takes. A tax cut, for example, leaves people more to spend and so their increased demand for goods and services will stimulate production and get the economy back in the right direction again.

Whether fiscal policy is effected through tax cuts or changes in the pattern of government spending will, of course, produce some distributional differences: welfare recipients are likely to buy different sorts of commodities from high-rate taxpayers, and so changes in taxes and transfer payments are likely to stimulate different parts of the economy at first. This is a detail, however, and the overall effect of either measure is to stimulate the whole economy. Since taxation policy is more flexible, it is generally preferred, and most discussion of fiscal stabilization strategies centres around it.

Fiscal blueprints. How, then, do fiscal measures produce their effect? How do the building-blocks form a barrier against inflation and a road out of depression? The answer is fairly straightforward.

Let us take the depressed economy first. The fiscal policy for getting the economy out of recession is to cut taxes (or to raise the volume of government expenditures). This means that people now have more money in their pockets because they are paying less tax (or are receiving more in benefits and salaries from the government). They are able to buy more, which they do, and they may even have enough left over to save a little more. If they save, the savings institutions have more funds available to lend to businesses; if they spend, trade is stimulated and manufacturers enjoy larger receipts and thus again have more available to invest. When the business investors take on more labour, the boost to salaries sparks off another round of spending and investment. When they buy machinery and materials, their supppliers in turn hire more labour, boosting spending and investment yet again, and so on right through the economy. Everyone is better off: indeed, they are *much* better off, because every time people invest, it raises incomes, and every time incomes are raised, there is more investment. This *multiplier* effect will very powerfully correct an economic downturn, according to the fiscal theorists.

The situation is completely reversed in an inflation. According to the fiscal orthodoxy, inflation is caused by *too much* spending, where an overabundance of 'demand' serves to bid up prices. The cure is to reduce total 'demand', either by reducing government expenditure or by raising taxes and leaving people in the private sector with less to spend. This time, the multiplier works in reverse: lower disposable incomes mean less spending, less investment, lower incomes, and so on. The fiscal contraction very effectively reduces the inflationary spending spree.

Minor snags. The fiscal policy position recognizes that there might be some adverse side-effects along the way, however. For example, a rise in government expenditures or a reduction

163

in taxes might leave the government with a budget deficit that it has to meet somehow. If it borrows to meet the deficit, this has the unfortunate effect of bidding up interest rates, and that makes loanable funds more expensive and so tends to pull down the investment rise that the fiscal expansion was designed to promote. Most fiscal policy adherents, however, would say that this is where monetary measures can usefully come in. A monetary expansion will increase the funds available to investors, especially since monetary policy is usually conducted through the sale or purchase of government securities directly in the capital markets. This takes the pressure off interest rates and therefore allows the fiscal stimulus to do its work on investment.

In an inflationary period, the problem is that the fiscal tactics of increasing taxes or reducing government expeditures can leave the government with a surplus, in which case it has to borrow less to make ends meet. Once again, however, the downward pressure on the interest rate and the consequent stimulus to investment spending can be checked by a contractionary monetary policy.

Friedman's critique of fiscal policy

Friedman's objections to the belief that fiscal policy can have a significant effect on inflation turn on this point about the public sector deficit.[2] How the budget gap is closed, he says, is of the utmost consequence in determining the future course of inflation, and to skip over the issue, as the advocates of fiscal policy do, is to ignore the fundamental question.

Let us take anti-inflation policy as an example, although similar reasoning would apply for expansionary measures. It certainly sounds convincing that tax rises leave people with less to spend, so reducing spending and bidding down prices. At first sight, it looks as if this fiscal measure is obviously anti-inflationary. However, he continues, that is only half of the story, and what happens to the public sector budget is no mere detail to be glossed over. If the government raises taxes and does *not* alter its spending, then it does not have to borrow so much to balance its books. For each dollar it receives through extra taxation, it has to borrow a dollar less. The taxpayers certainly have less to spend, but the people who would have loaned the government the funds with which to finance its spending have more. There is, consequently, a trade-off: taxpayers have less, but investors have more, so the total volume of spending power in the economy is undiminished: in other words, the purpose of the tax rise is not achieved.

One effect which the fiscal policy will have, of course, is to depress market rates of interest. With government no longer borrowing so much, lenders have more funds than the market will clear unless they accept a lower return. Such a reduction in the cost of credit will encourage other people to come in and borrow the funds that would otherwise have gone to the government, and so opens up the possiblity of private investment replacing government programmes. But it is difficult to see what effect that would have on inflation. If fiscal policy has any effect on inflation, says Friedman, it can only be on a subtle plane, if the falling rate of interest, for example, affected the demand for money and caused people to hold larger nominal balances, which would, in turn, work through to prices in the way already outlined in Chapter 3. While Friedman thinks this might occur in practice, he believes that the effect would be unpredictable and would be swamped by monetary events.

The recession economy poses quite opposite problems. If the government reduces taxes or increases its spending in order to stimulate demand, it will face a larger public sector deficit than before. To Friedman, it is of the utmost consequence whether that deficit is financed by borrowing or by the creation of new money. If it is financed by *borrowing,* then we can expect the interest rate to be bid up as the government and private borrowers compete for the prevailing supply of loanable funds. The higher interest rates will cause people to lend funds to the government that they would otherwise have spent on themselves: again, we have a trade-off, with taxpayers having more to spend but lenders having less. Once more, only the pattern has been changed, not the *volume* of spending power: if the expansionary fiscal policy has any effect, therefore, it must be in a more subtle way, such as by depressing the demand for cash with a highly favourable interest rate. Again, the effect will be unpredictable and of minor importance for inflation.

The story is very different, however, when the government makes up its budget shortfall by a *monetary expansion*. Then, the impact on inflation is direct and powerful. New money entering the economy is soon spent, bidding up the prices of all kinds of goods and services in the process. A monetary expansion has its impact directly on prices and output, not through the unreliable medium of interest rate changes.[3]

Money and interest rates

From this, it is plain that the disagreement between Friedman and those who share the 'widespread faith in the potency of fiscal policy'[4] is a fundamental one that stems from the adoption of two entirely different economic models. In one, fiscal policy changes demand through the income-expenditure multiplier, which in turn has a stabilizing effect on rising prices or falling output. In the other, monetary policy acts immediately on the demand for goods and services, which is then manifested in income terms – the money multipler.

The differences go further, however, because adherents of fiscal policy also argue that monetary measures can be useful in some respects, notably in controlling interest rates. On this point, says Friedman, they are completely mixed up.

Anomalous movement of interest rates. We can highlight the confusion if we look at the curious way that interest rates in fact move following a monetary change. According to the orthodox view, a monetary expansion (for example) will make money less 'tight' and produce a decline in interest rates. That might in turn promote other things, such as a rise in investment spending because the cost of borrowing has fallen; but whatever the results, the point is that interest rates will stay down for as long as the monetary expansion continues.

Once again, says Friedman, that is only half the story. Consider a typical monetary expansion, effected through open market purchases of securities by the authorities. This does indeed bid down interest rates, by adding to the reserves of the commercial banks and enabling them to expand their loans, and thus generating an increase in the flow of loanable funds coming onto the market. As time passes, however, these initial effects will be superceded by more fundamental ones. The initially lower interest rates will certainly boost investment in new capital formation, inventory accumulation, building construction, and so on. But, says Friedman, the effects will be much more widespread than these orthodox 'investment' items. The prices of investment goods will go up and so other assets will become more desirable and will be bid up as well; then others; and others. Prices will rise generally, in fact, making it less attractive to hold depreciating cash balances. People will scramble to exchange their cash for interest-bearing assets, and so interest rates will be bid up once again. Price expectations may even lead to some overshooting as people continue to reduce their cash balances and buy interest-bearing assets and other goods even after prices have begun to stabilize.

The result is that, after the initial fall, interest rates will be bid up again and will settle at a new rate, albeit with some oscillation at first. The new rate will depend upon the scale of the inflation generated by the monetary acceleration. If prices are rising at ten per cent per annum, for instance, a nominal rate of interest less than this would be *negative* in real terms, so we can expect the rate to settle at some figure higher than this, depending on the supply and demand conditions at the time (Figure 6).

This wavering of the interest rate as it settles down to its new value casts gloom on fiscal policy measures, because it tells us that interest rates by themselves are not very good indicators of what is actually going on in an economy. So given that past monetary accelerations or decelerations will have effects on interest rates that will persist for some time and might be working in the opposite direction, it would be folly to plan new monetary measures on the basis of where interest rates happen to be. Fiscal policy cannot use monetary measures as a crutch to help it over the problem of inconvenient movements in interest rates.

The fiscal policy enthusiasts' confusion on this point, says

Figure 6
Full effect of an increase in monetary growth on the nominal interest rate

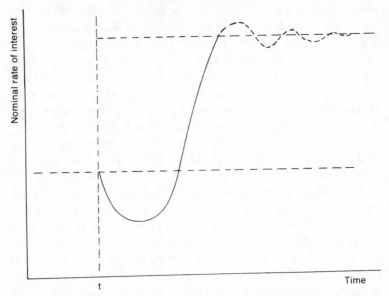

Source: *Monetary Trends in the United States and the United Kingdom*, page 493.

Friedman, is ultimately caused by the failure of traditional Keynesians to bear in mind the real/nominal distinction.[5] The interest rate does not tell us anything if we ignore prices, and high nominal interest rates are more likely to be a sign of *high* rates of monetary acceleration in the past than of constriction in the present. Even if this is recognized, the rate of interest is still a poor guide, because it does not in fact measure the abundance or scarcity of money: it measures the abundance or scarcity of *credit*, which, as we have seen in Chapter 4, is a very different thing. This second oversight can lead to equally fatal fiscal policy blunders when interest rates are taken as a guide to determine when monetary changes are needed.

Real and nominal linkages

If Friedman can complain with gusto that Keynesians make

oversights in their own policy analysis, they are not backward in making the same complaint about him. In particular, they suggest that it has to be admitted that real factors, such as real interest rates and real income, *do* affect the demand function for money. It is therefore wrong of Friedman to oversell his division of economic events into the real and the nominal. Monetary measures do have some effect on real magnitudes, and real phenomena also have an influence on the ultimate effects of monetary disturbances. Friedman's rule-of-thumb division of the economy into real and nominal segments is not watertight. By overlooking this, Friedman has made monetary policy appear more powerful than it really is. In true life, there is always some leakage, possibly a great deal of leakage.

Interest rates again. Interest rates once again provide a favoured battleground for this argument. At one extreme there is the spectre of the liquidity trap which Keynes raised as a theoretical possiblity (although he noted that he knew of no example of it hitherto).[6] But since then, argues Friedman, there have been many opportunities to test whether there is in fact an absolute preference for liquidity at low rates of interest – by courtesy of the deliberate attempts of central banks to peg interest rates at a low level in order to encourage investment. Despite the resistance of a few unreconstructed Keynesians, it has become clear that economists can no longer believe in the existence of the liquidity trap. There is

wide agreement that the conditions of near-absolute liquidity preference, if they occur at all, are very rare, so that this strand of Keynesian analysis has receded to the status of a theoretical curiosity.[7]

At the opposite extreme to this is the theory that the demand for money is completely inelastic with respect to interest rates (that is, that changes in real interest rates have absolutely no effect on the demand for money). Friedman assures us, however, that he does *not* subscribe to this completely watertight separation of nominal effects from real factors. This concession, coupled with the evidence on the liquidity trap, means that the difference between Friedman and the Keynesians is not one that rests on fundamental issues: both sides are agreed that real factors *can* contaminate monetary policy. The question is not *whether* monetary measures can be sidetracked by real events, but the *extent* to which real factors obstruct their progress through to price and income changes.

For his part, Friedman has conceded some of the ground in this dispute over the years. He accepts a progressively greater role for interest rates in determining the demand for money,[8] though his careful wording sometimes masks the extent of the change. His 1959 article on the demand for money[9] suggests strongly that little or no impact from interest rates could be discerned in the demand function for money, but seven years later he was at pains to point out that this failure to find any strong connexion between interest rates and the demand for money was *not* the same as saying that none existed, which would be a misrepresentation of his true position.[10] A statement that appeared a little later seems to find Friedman even more in retreat, but still fighting:

Interest rates clearly play an important role in affecting both the quantity of money people wish to hold ... and in transmitting the influence of monetary changes through the credit market. Yet, as an empirical matter, there is a much looser relation between either the level of interest rates or their rates of change, on the one hand, and rates of change in nominal income, output, and prices, on the other, than between the rates of change in the quantity of money and these same magnitudes.[11]

To defend his view that money is not only important in the determination of nominal income, but powerful enough to brush aside most of the other factors (including interest rates) which get in its way, Friedman notes that in the United States over ninety years, the year-to-year correlation between percentage changes in the quantity of money and percentage changes in nominal income is 0.7, which is high, and that it is also fairly stable. From this it appears that the combined effect of *all* real factors on the link between money and nominal income is minor. Monetary policy is not as easily deflected as the Keynesians might suppose.

EMPIRICAL TESTS OF MONETARY AND FISCAL POLICY

Friedman has argued that those who proclaim the efficacy of fiscal policy have presented no sound evidence for their point of view, but that there is a good deal of evidence to demonstrate the superiority of monetary over fiscal measures.[12]

Some studies

One set of studies which Friedman has quoted approvingly was carried out by the Federal Reserve Bank of St Louis. These studies concentrated on the question of whether monetary or fiscal policy is more powerful, more predictable and faster. A number of commonly accepted measures of the state of fiscal policy were used in the test.

The results, as summarized in a 1968 article by the Bank's researchers,[13] show that fiscal policies do not appear to be larger, more predictable or faster than monetary measures in their effects on economic activity. Far from the superiority of fiscal policy being evident, as most orthodox economists agreed at the time, no influence could in fact be demonstrated: either the traditional measures were inadequate or there was no influence at all.

The results seem to confirm Friedman's notion that fiscal measures have only a small and temporary impact on the economy unless they happen to precipitate monetary changes. When the Bank separated government expenditure policy from tax policy, it was found that expenditure had some effect, but that taxation changes had none or virtually none. An expenditure increase tended to boost income for the two quarterly periods after the change and then to have to have a negative influence for the next two. Friedman's explanation is that the increased expenditure by the government, although it might initially stimulate economic activity, has to be financed somehow: if it is financed by borrowing, interest rates are bid up and investment becomes depressed; if it is financed by creating money, nominal income may be raised but there will be little or no effect on real income.

Wartime inflations. More evidence comes from Friedman's own work comparing inflation in the United States during three wartime periods.[14] The question raised by this study is whether the price movements are better explained by reference to monetary or to fiscal indicators; and in Friedman's words, 'the answer was completely unambiguous'.[15]

As we saw in Chapter 5, Friedman calculated that the annual government deficit was about twice the proportion of national income in the American Civil War that it was during the First World War: yet prices rose by roughly the same amount. During the Second World War, there was a yet larger rise in nominal income, albeit manifested principally in terms of increased output rather than prices, but although the deficit was large, it was no larger than during the civil war, and so there seems to be no consistent relationship between this fiscal magnitude and the scale of subsequent changes in income.

The percentage increase in the money stock, however, gives us a good guide to the subsequent increases in price during the three wartime periods. Moreover, the effect of monetary changes is even clearer if we examine particular years in each period: for example, after both world wars there was a sharp fall in the government deficit, but no accompanying drop in income or prices. The continuous upward trend in prices is, however, explained by the fact that the money stock continued to rise, even after the deficit had been cut, and hence continued to fuel inflation.

Friedman concludes that the quantity theory (and monetary measures) gives a good indication of economic events during the three wartime periods, and is consistent with the evidence, while the Keynesian income-expenditure model (and fiscal indicators) does not. Put simply:

It turns out that you get a very clear, straight-forward interpretation of price behavior in those three wars by looking at monetary magnitudes; you do not get an explanation by looking at fiscal magnitudes.[16]

Broad historical movements. Further evidence comes from the long-term examination of the monetary history of the United States conducted by Friedman in collaboration with Anna Schwartz.[17] The significant point here is that, over nearly a century, fiscal policy has changed greatly. For most of the early decades examined by the study, the government budget was negligible. After the Second World War, however, government expenditure, borrowing and taxation grew to become very significant magnitudes indeed. And yet it was discovered that, despite this huge change in the size and scope of fiscal measures, the steady relationship between monetary and other economic changes was undisturbed. There was no indication that the increasing arsenal of fiscal weapons even scratched the surface of the quantity theory explanation of events.

The Friedman and Meiselman study

In a celebrated 1963 study, Friedman and his colleague David Meiselman probed deeper beneath the surface and tested the Keynesian income-expenditure theory upon which fiscal policy thinking was based, and went on to compare the predictive power of simple monetary and fiscal models. The results, according to Friedman, were once again striking.

Considering economic changes over some six decades, Friedman and Meiselman investigated whether changes in the money stock or changes in public expenditure had a more consistent influence on the movement of income. They deliberately chose the simplest and least cluttered versions of the two theories for comparison, and concluded from the evidence that the simple monetarist model was much more reliable.

A great deal of controversy greeted this result.[18] Some authors showed that the simple Keynesian theory could predict more effectively if the definition of the autonomous expenditure variable was widened, and others argued that the monetarist model was weakened by the practical difficulties of monetary control. But, even so, it became clear that to explain events satisfactorily, no simple Keynesian model would do: it had to be progressively extended, widened, amended and supplemented in order to improve its performance.

The debate on the Friedman and Meiselman study threw

into sharp relief the debate between the two schools of thought. The Keynesians did not shrink from extensive model-building, arguing that increasing refinements may be necessary for a sound explanation of events. The monetarists, however, were seeking a simple and unambiguous model that could be readily tested. But, whatever interpretations are put on the evidence, the study led to general agreement that monetary measures *are* important and systematic in their influence on economic activity.

Conclusion. Friedman may be optimistic in his assertion that there is no evidence to support the view that fiscal measures have much effect on economic activity. Sophisticated models of the economy have been devised which suggest that there is strength in both monetary and fiscal policy, and that fiscal policy is certainly not unimportant. Control of government expenditure and taxation has long been, and remains, an instrument widely accepted and used by many government authorities.

Yet the proponents of fiscal policy have come to rely on models which are perhaps of excessive complexity in order to shore up their case, and this makes prediction far from easy, which, in turn, makes fiscal policy measures of little use. And, as Friedman says, much of the available evidence suggests that fiscal policy has only a temporary and minor influence on income. The empirical work strongly indicates, he continues, that monetary policy is the key variable, and that its influence is little affected by changes in interest rates, government expenditure policies and most other real events. Its influence on nominal income is clear and simple, proceeding through a wide channel of portfolio adjustments to its ultimate effect on prices and output, subject only to the uncertainty of a long and variable lag.

CHAPTER TEN

The Role of Monetary Policy

Every severe contraction has been accompanied by an absolute decline in the stock of money, and the severity of the contraction has been in roughly the same order as the decline in the stock of money.[1]

ECONOMIC policy, whether fiscal, monetary or a combination of the two, has traditionally aimed at high employment, stable prices and rapid growth.[2] There is widespread agreement on the virtue of these goals, but less on the degree to which one should be sacrificed to achieve another, and even less on the question of which policy instruments are best suited to achieve which results.

For a long period, however, a 'high and stable' level of employment was regarded as the main objective, with few dissenting voices. Monetary policy was dragooned into the fight for this goal and, for a few years, did seem to be helping. In the initial period after the establishment of the Federal Reserve System in the United States, for example, many observers commented favourably on the apparent ability of the system to ward off depressions and to check inflations, and there was a growing confidence in the ability of the system to 'fine tune' the economy (although that phrase was not used until later) and in the capacity of monetary measures to exert a strong and significant influence on economic activity.

The Depression years dispelled this confidence, however, albeit for the wrong reasons.[3] It was assumed that the Depression occurred *despite* an expansionary monetary policy, and that this proved monetary policy to be ineffective at checking a depression (although it might remain useful for checking an inflation). Monetary policy appeared to be like a string; it could be used to pull business activity down, but not to push it up. It was many years, of course, before Friedman and Schwartz demonstrated that the Depression between the two world wars was due to a *shortage* of money rather than an expansion in it, but doubts about the effectiveness of monetary policy were long established by then, and Keynes had built up a powerful model giving a non-monetary explanation of depression phases. To Keynes, and to the economic orthodoxy which built upon his work, investment and autonomous spending were the keys. A shortage of investment opportunities, or a tendency for people not to invest, would set in train a depression that could not be stopped by monetary exertions. Government spending could be raised to offset it, however, and tax reductions could undermine the public's thriftiness, so the authorities could spend their way out of a depression.[4] If monetary policy had any value, it was probably in keeping interest rates low, so that investment would proceed apace.

This downgrading of monetary policy received a shock after the Second World War, when 'cheap money' policies could not be maintained as the market pressure on interest rates made it impossible for central banks to continue pegging them down. The additional problem that expenditure changes took a long time to put in motion and seemed to be slow in taking effect led to something of a revival in the fortunes of monetary policy, but still it was used only in conjunction with fiscal measures. In particular, inflationary monetary policy was used to absorb the employment consequences of changes in demand. Since, in the prevailing Keynesian model, a fall in demand precipitates a lowering of wages or employment, and since wages are notoriously sticky downwards, a fall in demand for whatever reason produces unemployment. But inflation could then be used to give the illusion that wages were not falling, even when their real value was being eroded, and so unemployment could be avoided. Thus, monetary policy was seen as being useful to mitigate some of the side-effects of Keynesian demand management policies.

Within another two decades, however, the pendulum had swung decidedly in the direction of monetary policy, which gained considerable influence in the political and academic communities, partly as a result of Friedman's championing of the cause. But acceptance of the importance of monetary policy does not mean that it should be considered as omnipotent. There are, says Friedman, many things which monetary policy *cannot* do, and to be aware of these is just as important as being aware of its abilities. Accordingly, it is wise to consider the limitations of monetary policy before we consider what should be its targets and how it should be practised.

The limitations of monetary policy

There are three goals that have commonly been set for monetary policy, none of which Friedman believes it can achieve. These are the pegging of interest rates, the generation of full employment, and the stabilization of cyclical fluctuations in income.

Pegging interest rates. The failure of postwar cheap money policies was no isolated or unique case, says Friedman, but betrayed the general inability of the economic authorities to peg interest rates (or any prices) above or below their market level for any length of time. Although an expansionary monetary policy may depress interest rates for a short period, it cannot be expected to peg them indefinitely.

To reduce interest rates, monetary authorities purchase securities, thus raising their prices and lowering their yields. But that same process, increases the reserves available to the banks and expands bank credit and thus the total quantity of money by a considerable amount. This more rapid monetary expansion stimulates spending, and therefore incomes (since one man's spending is another man's income). Rising income will increase the demand for mortgages and other loans, which puts an upward pressure on interest rates. Ultimately, if people expect prices to continue rising, lenders will demand higher interest rates to compensate. Although this expectations effect may be slow to appear, it will be equally slow to dissipate after price rises have eased. Hence, the very measure which caused the initial fall in interest rates later serves to bid them up. If they are to be pegged, the authorities may resort to still *more* monetary expansion through open market purchases; but this will simply compound the problem. Such measures can never peg interest rates much below their market level for very long.

Employment policy. Exactly the same is true of employment. Just as there are market rates of interest, there is a 'natural rate' of unemployment, which depends on the real state of the demand for workers, their supply and the institutional imperfections of employment markets.

A monetary expansion will stimulate spending, which might indeed cause retailers and wholesalers to increase their stocks and manufacturers to boost their output and take on more workers. But as the boom works through to prices, people will simply adjust their expectations to the new trend, and the stimulating effect of the monetary expansion will evaporate. Like interest rates, unemployment is a magnitude which cannot be pegged below its market level for any length of time.

Stabilization policy. The attempt to make 'fine tuning' adjustments to the level of business activity and incomes is equally mistaken, according to Friedman. The lag in the effect of monetary policy is long and variable. To reduce cyclical fluctuations in half, it would have to be of the right size, in the right direction and at the right time, to a very high degree of accuracy; but the problems of discerning what policy is required and when, and the length of time it takes for the policy to work through the economic system and show its effects, are great. It is more likely, therefore, that attempted stabilization policy will in fact turn out to be destabilizing; and the more determined it is, the more severe the destabilization is likely to be.

Proper targets for monetary policy

Friedman is adamant that monetary policy cannot be used to peg real magnitudes or to control real factors such as interest rates, levels of employment or real incomes. But he argues that monetary policy can nevertheless have a significant effect on these items, although the effect is not always desirable nor predictable. When it is working smoothly, money is of great benefit to everyone in the economic system; but once it goes awry, it taints and dislocates every activity and every economic relationship. Hence, we must be careful about the targets we set for monetary policy, and about how it is conducted.

Avoiding mistakes. The first target for monetary policy is that we should recognize its considerable power for mischief and avoid mistakes. Small declines in the quantity of money, against the background of a rising money stock, precipitated the catastrophic events of the interwar period, showing how apparently insignificant policy changes can make a substantial impact on economic life. Money affects every part of the economy, and so should be treated with respect.

Stable background. If business activity is to thrive, those who engage in it must be able to make decisions with confidence, in good time and without fear of sudden changes that might interfere with their plans. Accordingly, a fitting target for monetary policy is the construction of a stable background against which business transactions can be made. Specifically, a stable level or growth of prices is preferable to sharp fluctuations that make future planning impossible.

Offsetting other policies. Monetary policy, says Friedman, *does* have a role in offsetting the effects of other policies, although not as employed by Keynesian economists as a device to make fiscal contractions more palatable. For example, if the economy was shifting from wartime to peacetime production, monetary policy could be used to ease the transition by a slightly higher rate of monetary growth than would otherwise be desirable – although experience tells us to be cautious in this exercise.[5]

The conduct of monetary policy

Given this fairly restricted role for monetary policy, important and useful though it is, the next issue to address is how it should be conducted. There are two clear principles which suggest themselves before we consider the appropriate institutional arrangements.

Use controllable magnitudes only. There is something of a tendency for the monetary authorities to suppose that they can control a wide range of magnitudes, whereas this is in fact untrue. Every monetary authority supposes that it can control the stock of money; nearly all suppose that this means they can in turn control the movement of prices; and some presume they can control the exchange rate and that they should try to do so.

To Friedman, exchange rates are inherently uncontrollable because they depend upon the relative states of different economies: the only way of improving the exchange rate is generally sound economic management at home, but the rates cannot be pegged indefinitely except at the expense of frequent crises, shortages, surpluses and dislocation. And, as already mentioned, it would be absurd to focus economic policy on setting a stable background for such a small portion of total trade. If policy has an appropriate main target in this respect, it must be to create stable conditions for domestic transactions, not for foreign ones.

Although prices have a clear and discernible relationship to monetary movements, it is an indirect link, making it impossible to predict at all accurately just what price effects will spring from any particular monetary change. The only thing which monetary policy can hope to control with confidence is the monetary total itself, and this, says Friedman, must be the appropriate magnitude to watch. From there on, we simply have to wait until the smooth growth of the quantity of money has its stabilizing and beneficial effect on the other economic factors that are important to us but not susceptible to direct control.

Avoidance of swings. Another basic principle in monetary policy must be the avoidance of sharp policy swings. The monetary authorities of many important countries, sometimes due to changes in government and sometimes due to a conviction that monetary measures work faster and are more controllable than they really are, allowed monetary policy to fluctuate dramatically throughout the 1960s and 1970s in particular. To Friedman, this is a sure way to damage an economy, because it makes future movements in spending and prices unpredictable and hence reduces the efficiency of any business enterprise.

These, then, are the limits, targets and rules of conduct of monetary policy. Friedman's suggestions about the institutional arrangements appropriate to the efficient conduct of monetary policy are no less confident and highly imaginative.

FRIEDMAN'S PROPOSALS FOR MONETARY REFORM

Although Friedman has absorbed many criticisms and has apparently adjusted his analytical reasoning in the light of some of them, he has clung to a number of prescriptions for monetary reform. Depending on his audience, he has sometimes refined the proposals or suggested less radical alternatives; but every line of his writings on monetary policy is based on the same determination to ensure that such a vital commodity as money is treated with respect and is not used as the discretionary toy of the policymakers. One of his central themes has been the search for a monetary mechanism that is automatic – providing extra liquidity when it is needed, and reducing the rate of monetary growth when inflation threatens.

A radical proposal for automatic adjustment

Early in his career, Friedman began to seek an *automatic* adjustment mechanism which would overcome the problem of the lag and would be more likely to be in the right direction at the right time than discretionary monetary policy. At first he supposed some mixture of automatic and discretionary policy would be best, because even an automatic system might sometimes be too strong or too weak in its effects; but before long, he came to propose a system that left little room for discretion.

The proposal. The first element in Friedman's automatic system, which he put forward as a long-term objective, is the imposition of 100% reserve requirements on the banks, an idea he adopted from his Chicago teacher, Henry Simons.[6] Under such a rule, banks would have to keep the entire value of their customers' deposits in their vaults, and could not lend out the portion that was not needed for routine daily withdrawals. This proposal makes the money supply equal to the monetary base, since there is no opportunity for private money creation by the banks, and so it is easier for the authorities to control. (Of course, the banks would continue to be investors, lending out sums on behalf of their clients, but this activity would be separate from their deposit-management function and so gives them no scope for using idle deposits to create new money.)

As well as losing their discretionary control over reserve requirements, the 100% rule also means that the monetary authorities cannot use variations in the 'rediscount' rate – the rate at which the central bank will buy assets from or extend loans to any commercial bank that wants to augment its reserves and become more liquid – because the commercial banks could never find themselves short of reserves. Friedman welcomes both facts as further helping to reduce the likelihood and ease of discretionary policies. Indeed, he would go further: his long-term reform calls for the abolition of the monetary authorities' powers to deal in government debt through open market operations.

The second step in Friedman's proposal is to set *limits on government expenditure*. A decision must be made in advance as to what proportion of income is to be spent by the government, and what needs there are for government expenditure; and the budget is fixed accordingly. That is, the budget would not be used as an instrument of countercyclical economic policy, but only to finance the range of government services which are genuinely desired.

Transfer payments, such as unemployment compensation, pensions and welfare allowances, should also be set out in advance, according to Friedman, although they will of course fluctuate over the business cycle. When conditions are hard, transfer payments to the unemployed and others are likely to rise in total, but will do so according to a rule set out beforehand rather than by current discretion.

The last strand in Friedman's proposal is a reformed tax system that places primary reliance on *personal income tax*. Exemptions would be minimized, so that the tax yield would fluctuate fairly predictably along with the business cycle. In the boom, more tax would be taken by the government, and government expenditures would amount to less. In the slump, government expenditures would be higher and the tax take would be lower. In other words, the public sector budget would fluctuate automatically over the cycle, and if taxes were collected quickly (such as under a withholding tax system), the right expansion or contraction would occur at the right time.

Operation of the proposal. The proposal is elegant because it greatly increases the speed and precision with which monetary changes are made, and therefore enchances the effect they are likely to have in smoothing business fluctuations. Under this system, government expenditure has to be financed by taxation or by the creation of new money: the government could not borrow by issuing interest-bearing stock to the public. The balance between needs and policies would thus become automatic: in a period of high income, tax receipts will be high and transfer payments will be small, so there will be a government surplus. This surplus means that funds are being diverted out of the stream of income, and total demand is being reduced, resulting in a stabilizing effect on incomes and a reduction in the quantity of money. When incomes are low, there will be a smaller tax yield and large income transfers, producing a government deficit that can be financed only by the creation of new money, which adds to the stream of income and thus has a stabilizing effect.

Abolition of the central bank. This automatic system, of course, implies the abolition of the central banking institutions which at present decide the course of monetary policy. In Friedman's view, the creation of such institutions in the United States in particular has brought down a hail of misfortunes and even

the occasional disaster. Inept policies by discretionary monetary authorities have illustrated his point that conscious interference can rarely if ever hope to stabilize economic fluctuations. Thus he concludes:

> As a matter of long-run reform, I would like to see the Federal
> Reserve System in its present form abolished and replaced by a
> 100 per cent reserve deposit banking system in which there was
> no monetary authority possessing discretionary powers over the
> quantity of money... I am convinced by the evidence... that the
> establishment of the Federal Reserve System was a mistake and
> that the system has failed to promote the objectives for which it
> was established.[7]

Friedman never appears to have been in much doubt that
an 'independent' central bank is in any event a mythical idea.
While it may seem sensible to have an independent central
bank in order to keep monetary control away from politicians,
in practice central bankers have been interventionist on behalf
of the governments of the day. Central banks must by their
nature have close links to the executive powers, and to some
extent the central bankers owe their jobs to the political authorities and so cannot be fully independent. On the other hand,
a truly independent central bank would enjoy a great deal
of power without any responsibility to the public, and Friedman doubts that this would be a desirable state of affairs.
But it is precisely because they are *not* independent that central
bank policies have tended to vacillate so widely, depending
largely on the personalities of the controlling individuals and
the particular needs of the politicians of the day.[8]

Immediate reform proposals

A less radical reform package has also been proposed by Friedman, which starts from the assumption that central banks,
open market operations and fractional reserve banking are
all here to stay – for a while, at least. Its essential elements
are a monetary *rule* for smooth and regular expansion of the
quantity of money, limits to government spending and taxa-

tion, and escalator clauses to index contracts (especially government obligations) against inflation.

A monetary rule. Friedman suggests that legislative action be taken to ensure that monetary policy is conducted according to set targets, without interference from the political authorities.[9] Instead of monetary discretion, we would have a monetary *rule*. Monetary policy could not be destabilizing because it would itself be perfectly stable and would not be used in attempts to interfere with *real* economic events.

This raises the question of what rule is appropriate. A *stable price target* has been suggested, but to Friedman this gives the authorities far too much leeway. Since the effects of monetary changes on prices occur with a long and variable lag, and vary in strength, it would be impossible for the authorities to decide accurately what policy is required today in order to bring future prices to some agreed level. Once again, the unstable link between money and other magnitudes means that it is really only the money stock that the authorities can hope to control accurately and it is this, says Friedman, that is in consequence the most fitting object for a monetary rule.

Friedman therefore suggests that it is desirable to legislate for a fixed rule in terms of the *growth of the stock of money*: the monetary authorities should be instructed to achieve, on average, a specified rate of growth in the stock of money, meaning currency plus all deposits in commercial banks. The specified rate would probably be somewhere between three and five per cent growth per annum to allow for real growth in output.

Friedman has been at pains to point out that this is not a rule which should be immutable if our knowledge improved or if it turned out to be an inadequate guide; but he thinks that over the years it would show its worth. Cyclical movements would not be avoided, but the non-discretionary policy would prevent some of the wildest swings, which were due to cyclical movements being *reinforced* by inept and ill-timed monetary measures.

Government spending. A strong theme running through Friedman's writings on policy is his insistence that government budgets should, on average, be balanced, and that persistent fiscal expansions cannot be sustained. In his early writings, he shows less concern with the matter, and contemplates fiscal measures and even inflation as serious policy options, but he nevertheless concludes that of the policies available,

A good combination... would be a roughly balanced budget together with whatever associated monetary policy would prevent inflation. No policy very far from this combination is likely to be appropriate.[10]

Friedman's concern about this issue has, however, grown considerably, partly because of the increasing share of income taken by the government since he began writing. Of his investigation of monetary trends over a century, Friedman has noted that:

At the beginning of that period, the government budget was negligible. In the period since World War II, the government budget has been mammoth.[11]

And he has never doubted that

the share of activity assigned government is likely to have far more important consequences for other objectives – particularly political freedom and economic efficiency – than for stability.[12]

Friedman's package for economic stability and the elimination of inflation must, therefore, include some long-term reduction of the government's share of activity, principally because of the prodigious economic power which a large budget gives to the political authorities. The larger the government budget, the more leverage fiscal and monetary policies have, and the more chance there is of them being used too strongly; hence the danger that the economy will be jolted massively out of kilter by inappropriate policies. Equally important, Friedman argues that the government tends to be less efficient than the private sector in its use of resources, and that we are 'not getting out money's worth out of it'.[13] This poor use of resources actually makes economic problems even harder to solve, because nobody spends somebody else's money as well, as carefully and as economically as he spends his own. That is why the growth of government has meant less effective use of resources. In addition, government has imposed rules and regulations, intervened here and there, nationalized industries and levied high taxes which have reduced people's incentives to work, to save, to invest. The combination of all this has resulted in slow growth. That is why inflation and slow growth are so very closely related.[14]

Indexation. Another idea which Friedman has pioneered is widespread indexation. This is simply the expression of all amounts in contracts in real rather than nominal quantities: the incorporation of cost of living clauses in wage and other agreements.[15]

The indexation proposal is designed for two purposes, to make inflation less attractive to governments, and to enable individuals to adjust more quickly to inflation when it does occur. To reduce the government's benefits from inflation, Friedman suggests that tax thresholds, corporate taxation and interest on government securities should all be indexed. Thus, individuals would not find themselves being projected into higher and higher tax brackets through fiscal drag (or 'bracket creep'), just because their nominal wages happened to be rising (although their real wages were unchanged). Corporations, too, would be spared this effect. Those who lent to the government would also be protected: no longer would there be an incentive for the government, having borrowed currency of one value, to inflate and then repay its loans in devalued currency.

Friedman suggests that the same principle should be encouraged as far as possible in the private sector. There would then be no need for overbidding in wage negotiations, to allow for future price rises as well as past ones. Borrowing and lending too could take place with more certainty. More generally, expectations would match reality more closely than in a world of high and rapidly changing inflation rates, and nominal changes would have a much smaller effect on real magnitudes and therefore on economic efficiency.

The critics of Friedman's proposals

Friedman has found no shortage of economists willing to attack his proposals. Both his radical package and his more modest suggestions for a monetary rule have come under fire, but the latter proposal has probably drawn more objections because it is closer to what people suppose to be politically feasible.

Political feasibility. Friedman's automatic stabilization package, with its 100% reserve banking idea and other radical policies, has been at times opposed, at times ignored, on the same grounds of 'political impossibility'. However, this is not an argument that Friedman has ever supposed valid. His methodology is that of the positive economist: to say what *can* be done and what consequences will follow, not to judge what is or is not politically feasible. Secondly, some of his other radical ideas have in fact been adopted: few people supposed that exchange controls would be abandoned until they suddenly were. This has led Friedman to disparage the argument of 'political impossibility' from his colleagues. As he says,

economists have not turned out to be good forecasters about what is politically feasible. That is one reason why I have been inclined myself to give little weight to political feasibility – in the sense of the prospect that any proposal will be quickly or readily enacted.[16]

Stable money in practice. A more telling argument against a monetary rule is the one that periods of stability in the growth of the quantity of money have not, in fact, been associated with stability in the price level or employment. During the years 1953–7, for example, the money stock in the United States grew at a fairly smooth rate of two per cent. During 1971–5, it grew at the larger but still fairly consistent rate of seven per cent. Yet both these periods were times of marked instability. The former period saw a contraction, a recovery and another contraction, while the early 1970s showed marked fluctuations in prices and output.[17]

For his part, Friedman urges us to remember that there are many factors which confuse the link between money and prices or output, and that, while smooth monetary growth can be expected to reduce some economic fluctuations, it is unlikely to end them all. All we can hope for is that the instability will be less than if we deliberately attempt to interfere. Secondly, to take the 1971–5 case as an example, monetary policy cannot be expected to produce nirvana: it cannot stop inflation without a recession, and so even a deliberately smooth growth in money will be associated with some fluctuations in business activity as past events work through the system. The monetary rule needs a long trial. Thirdly, to take that case again, it is by no means certain that monetary growth was at all smooth: it may have *averaged* a certain level, but monetary policy in the United States has been plagued by sharp swings in direction, which obviously generate economic instability. Given Friedman's view that it takes months or years for monetary changes to work through into changes in economic activity, the years just before the 1971–5 period are interesting.[18] In 1967–8, M2 rose at 9.4 per cent in the United States – far above Friedman's target – before being brought down to the more acceptable level of 4.0 for six months. Seeing no immediate halt to inflation, however, the authorities stepped hard on the brake and M2 grew at only 0.2 per cent up to February 1970. With the onset of recession, the rate was increased again to 9.2 per cent up to January 1971, and then there was a veritable monetary explosion as M2 grew at 13.8 per cent for six months, followed by another contraction down to 3.9 per cent. In Friedman's view, it is not at all surprising that this should have heralded a period of economic instability.

Friedman also cites in his defence the numerous cases in the past where a more stable monetary policy would clearly have been far preferable to the active, but inept, policies that were actually pursued. The 1929–33 case is the most dramatic, when the monetary authorities allowed a total contraction in the quantity of money of about one third. If they had prevented this contraction, says Friedman, the Great Depression would not have occurred.

Temporary variations. Some economists cite evidence that there is no need for a monetary rule to be quite as restrictive as Friedman has proposed for it to have the desired effects. Work done on computer models, in particular, suggests that a monetary growth which departs from the trend for two or three quarters is acceptable provided that it is compensated for by a subsequent departure in the opposite direction.[19]

Friedman, of course, is doubtful about the use of large-scale models to describe events, and believes that an appeal to the evidence is far more persuasive. Since the effects of a monetary change are spread over a period of time, a temporary departure in one direction followed by a temporary departure in the other will probably cause some of the adverse effects to cancel out. But this seems a risky course for monetary policy. Furthermore, Friedman's view of the evidence of the 1960s and 1970s in particular is clear: there have been strong variations in the direction of monetary policy, and these have in fact produced strong fluctuations in prices, income and general business activity. Plainly, a steady course is better by far than one which permits the authorities too much latitude, which can be abused, and which does not seem to be successful in practice.

Outside shocks. Another complaint against Friedman's monetary rule is that it allows us no flexibility to deal with outside shocks to demand that could have severe repercussions on business activity and incomes. Believers in fiscal measures and in discretionary monetary policy point out that there have been only five or six recessions since 1927, most of them lasting under a year precisely because they could be compensated for by discretionary stabilization policy. There are all kinds of severe shocks that can beset the economy: wars, sudden rises in government expenditure, trade changes, lower agricultural yields, technical changes, populations shifts, and so on. There must, say the critics, be some means of absorbing these.[20]

In Friedman's view, there can in fact be a certain flexibility: he has suggested a two per cent channel for monetary growth, which should be able to cope with population changes and many other factors which impinge on the economic system. Otherwise, it might in fact be best *not* to deviate from the rule at all: a sharp rise in the price of a vital import such as oil, for example, might cause some temporary hardship, but a non-inflationary economy might well be able to adjust faster than an inflationary one. And in extreme cases, such as the recovery from wartime periods, Friedman does admit that some flexibility is desirable. Quite how this mixture of a fixed rule with occasional flexibility can be achieved is not very clear in Friedman's writings, however. Presumably the postwar situation, for example, would have to be covered by legislating a new but temporary rule allowing greater monetary growth than usual.

In any event, Friedman rejects the thesis that the comparative absence of depressions in the United States and other countries since the Second World War is a good indication that countercyclical policy has worked. On the contrary, he says, it is only because these economies have been made recession-proof that this illusion has arisen.[21] Governments, ever fearful of the political and other consequences of recessions, have always tended to inflate at the slightest indication that one might be on the way. Hence there have been no major depressions, which some observers interpret as a sign of economic stability: but there have been major *inflations*, which indicate that this is not the case.

Adjustment to other factors. Critics also argue that it is important to be able to adjust to less dramatic factors, including those which arise from inside the economic system itself, since even some minor and easily corrigible trends can have severe consequences if they are left unattended to. For example, there are in the real world all kinds of market imperfections, which make adjustments of wages, prices, employment and exchange rates slow. A 'fixed throttle' formula would condemn us to long periods of economic slack, or inflation, if the process of adjustment to changing market conditions is slow: plainly, it would be better if the monetary authorities had the power to intervene to offset these rigidities and help the economy back to full employment equilibrium.

Friedman's most elegant argument on this subject is based on an analogy with the commonly accepted rule that free speech should prevail. There are undoubtedly cases when we think it would be better for certain individuals to be silenced, where their views are controversial or dangerous. Often, there is widespread public agreement about the fact. But we restrain ourselves from silencing by force those we disagree with, because we have found that a blanket rule, granting free speech to all, is the best one to adopt in the long term. It may be damaging on occasions, but it is preferable to the awesome discretionary power that would be necessary if it were not adopted. Similarly with monetary policy: although we can see that it might be harmful on particular occasions, we will in general find it better to have one fixed rule and make no use of arbitrary discretion, rather than attempt to interfere and make a judgement about what is the best policy in each case.

Friedman's view on this is perhaps reinforced by his belief that other economic factors cannot do a great deal of damage. Fiscal changes, for example, do not have very much effect anyway, and so it is hardly worth arming ourselves specially against them.[22] A stable monetary background, says Friedman, is likely to produce an economy that is able to adjust quickly and efficiently, because individuals in the marketplace do not have to worry excessively about what government policy will be tomorrow and how it will affect their wages, their receipts or their costs. Consequently, major dislocations and distortions will be that much less likely if a monetary rule is put into effect.

The effects of Friedman's proposals

However the theoretical arguments about the monetary rule may twist and turn, Friedman's advocacy of it has had a powerful effect on the monetary authorities in the United States and some other countries. Britain, Germany and other nations have adopted or are currently adopting monetary targets in an attempt to reduce inflation. Nearly all governments are now aware of the virtues of closer control over the quantity of money, although some have yet to be convinced that a narrow range of monetary growth, as advocated by Friedman, is altogether desirable. Throughout the world, there is far more reliance on and concern with monetary indicators, and there can be no doubt that this is in large measure due to Friedman.

If the adoption of monetary rules becomes more widespread, it will be fascinating indeed to consider the outcome. If more stable monetary growth becomes a reality – at present, even those countries which have professed themselves convinced by monetarism have not been able to exert sufficient control to make the expansion steady[23] – it will be interesting to see whether a greater stability in business activity results.

PART 4: MARKETS AND METHODS

CHAPTER ELEVEN

Friedman the Market Economist

> Wherever we find any large element of individual free-
> dom, some measure of progress in the material com-
> forts at the disposal of ordinary citizens, and wide-
> spread hope of further progress in the future, there
> we also find that economic activitity is organized
> mainly through the free market. Wherever the state
> undertakes to control in detail the economic activities
> of its citizens, wherever, that is, detailed central eco-
> nomic planning reigns, there ordinary citizens are in
> political fetters, have a low standard of living, and
> have little power to control their own destiny.[1]

FRIEDMAN'S quantity theory explains the great power of money,
and the need for it to be controlled. But his empirical observations on the actual conduct of monetary policy in the past
show the extreme dangers of supposing that our overvaunting
reason is sufficient to harness that power and direct it as we
wish. Indeed, attempted stabilization policies have, in Friedman's opinion, caused more harm than good.

This theme, that even the best-intentioned interventions in
the economy have a habit of making matters worse rather
than better, is in fact a more general one in Friedman's
thought. His popular expositions of free-market ideology,
Capitalism and Freedom, *Free to Choose* and *Tyranny of the Status
Quo* (all co-authored by his wife, Rose), chart in great detail
how governments attempt to improve on the free market economy, only to lose its economic and social benefits in the process,
thus generally eroding living standards.

The striking difference between *Capitalism and Freedom* (1962)
and *Free to Choose* (1979) or *Tyranny of the Status Quo* (1983)
is that the later works draw on far more examples of such
misguided intervention. To some extent this is because they
are intended to be more narrative and less theoretical, but

the growth of government itself has greatly increased the material available:

From 1933 to 1983, the population of the United States didn't quite double, but the total number of employees of the federal government alone multiplied almost fivefold.[2]

Much of this growth is concerned with the regulation of industry, where, for instance, Friedman notes that the number of government bureaucrats employed in regulatory agencies in the United States tripled between 1970 and 1979, from 28,000 to 81,000. The *Federal Register*, established in 1936 to record all the regulations, hearings and other matters connected with the regulatory agencies, contained 16,850 pages in 1966, while its 36,487 pages in 1978 were sufficient to fill a bookshelf more than three metres in length.[3] As the public sector industries continued to grow after 1966, so their service became still less oriented to satisfying consumers, and so their trade unions became even more extensive and powerful. As ever-larger sums were prised from taxpayers to support ever-larger numbers of school 'administrators' and the construction of increasingly vast and impersonal schools, the shortcomings of government-run schools became ever more clear.[4] All of these events provided vivid examples of how government ventures may well benefit a small class of bureaucrats and interest groups; but that they have a habit of impoverishing and providing an inferior service to the unidentifiable millions who have no choice but to pay their taxes and accept the standard provided.

It would, indeed, have been difficult to write *Free to Choose* or *Tyranny of the Status Quo* and ignore these practical illustrations of how government interventionism generally backfires. Readers in 1962, with fewer such examples available to them, might have had more faith in the virtues of regulation and government ventures, and *Capitalism and Freedom* appropriately begins with an examination of the threat which large and centralized government poses to individual freedom, rather than to economic efficiency. But in the 1979 work, the starting point is a paean to the remarkable power of the market system, when unfettered, to allocate resources efficiently, to signal and correct any shortages or surpluses, to curb arbitrary social discrimination, to provide variety, to promote experiment and to satisfy diverse tastes while preserving peace and order. Few would have doubted Friedman's faith in the free market before; but *Free to Choose* seems to exhibit an even greater scepticism about the types and number of activities which can usefully be undertaken by government without generating greater harm, often to those they are intended to assist, and *Tyranny of the Status Quo* warns of the almost unstoppable nature of government programmes once they are established.

The power of the market

To Friedman, it is not a matter of theoretical conjecture but an item of empirical fact that the market system has the remarkable power of raising material standards quicker than any other while at the same time promoting choice, diversity, the welfare of the underprivileged *and* a number of other non-economic values which we all regard as just as important as material prosperity.

Allocative power. The system of voluntary exchange has a surprising ability to bring about the co-operation of thousands or millions of individuals in the efficient production of the goods and services which people want to consume. By way of illustration, Friedman quotes the example of an ordinary pencil.[5] No single person knows how to make a pencil: it requires the co-operation of large numbers of people. The loggers who cut the trees need saws, trucks, rope and other gear to fell them and move them, all of which requires the skill of miners, steelmakers, foundrymen, production workers and ropemakers; then the trees have to be milled and planed by yet others; the graphite core has to be mined in countries such as Sri Lanka, and the graphite transported overseas by merchant seamen; similarly, the metal ferrule starts from ore which has to be mined, alloyed, beaten into sheets and stamped into shape; the eraser at the end needs rubber and seed oil, which must be grown, extracted, transported and manufactured; and so on. As Friedman continues the story:

None of the thousands of persons involved in producing the pencil performed his task because he wanted a pencil. Some among them never saw a pencil and would not know what it is for. Each saw his work as a way to get the goods and services he wanted – goods and services we produced in order to get the pencil we wanted. Every time we go to the store and buy a pencil, we are exchanging a little bit of our services for the infinitesimal amount of services that each of the thousands contributed toward producing the pencil.[6]

Transmission of information. The remarkable thing in this example is that the pencil can be produced at all without the need for anyone to co-ordinate the activities of all the people involved from some central point. It does *not* require a government bureau to assess the need for pencils and to issue orders to everyone in the chain, from the retailers through the manufacturers to the miners and the loggers. In the market economy, this is performed simply and effectively by the price mechanism.

It is easy to see in principle how the price mechanism co-ordinates the activities of everyone involved in the production of a product such as a pencil, but it is remarkable that it works so well. If, for some reason, customers want more pencils, retailers will find that they are selling more and will order larger quantities from the manufacturer. The manufacturer, in turn, will have to order more supplies of graphite, wood and metal, and will have to pay higher prices at auctions in order to get the full quantity he needs. The suppliers, in turn, will have to expand their output, but will be willing to pay higher wages in order to attract the new workers they need. And so the entire process adjusts to satisfy the new demand. The miners, the loggers and the suppliers do not have to know that there has been an increase in the demand for pencils, nor do they need to be told by a central planning agency that they must increase their output to satisfy it. It is the marginally higher *prices*, working their way through the entire process, which induce them to do so.

In this way, the self-interest of everyone in the production chain co-ordinates their activities and ensures that consumers are satisfied – not only in their demand for pencils but for all the goods and sevices they need. Furthermore, the market system ensures that these wants are satisfied at the lowest possible cost, because this again will be in the interests of everyone involved in the production process. The manufacturers will be in close touch with suppliers of wood, and will be looking constantly for cheaper sources; sawmills will in turn be seeking better quality and lower-cost timber; logging companies will always be attempting to use their manpower and machinery most cost-effectively so that they stay ahead of the competition. The remarkable thing is that each person needs to be an expert only on his own part of the process: the movement of a very few prices is sufficient to co-ordinate the entire system quickly and efficiently so that it produces the end products at the lowest possible cost.

Removing discrimination. Friedman devotes a great deal of attention to what he sees as a very important aspect of the market economy, its tendency to whittle away arbitrary discrimination between people on the grounds of their race, religion, sex or other characteristics.

There are two main points here. The first is that the price mechanism co-ordinates the activities of many individuals, so that *nobody in the chain knows all the others involved.* Thus, even the efforts of people who hate each other can be efficiently co-ordinated. As Friedman puts it:

No one who buys bread knows whether the wheat from which it is made was grown by a Communist or a Republican, by a constitutionalist or a Fascist, or, for that matter, by a Negro or a white. This illustrates how an impersonal market separates economic activities from political views and protects men from being discrimated against in their economic activities for reasons that are irrelevant to their productivity . . . [7]

The second point is that *an individiual who does discriminate imposes costs upon himself,* because it restricts its choice of sup-

pliers and customers. In consequence, there is a marked disin-
centive against discrimination in the market economy, without
the need for legislative measures.

A businessman or an entrepreneur who expresses preferences in his
business activities that are not related to productive efficiency is
at a disadvantage compared to other individuals who do not. Such
an individual is in effect imposing higher costs on himself than are
other individuals who do not have such preferences. Hence, in a
free market they will tend to drive him out.[8]

Similarly, the individual who objects to working alongside
someone whose skin is a different colour limits his choice of
employers and will generally have to accept a lower return
for his work. In Friedman's view, he should be free to do
so if he chooses: that is simply his 'taste' and he is quite entitled
to pay for its satisfaction, however much others might regard
it as an undesirable preference. But the market economy is
far more likely, in Friedman's view, to end such discrimination
by producing a voluntary and lasting change in attitudes than
any legislated attempt to achieve the same. To him,

It is a striking historical fact that the development of capitalism
has been accompanied by a major reduction in the extent to which
particular religious, racial, or social groups have ... been discrimi-
nated against.[9]

Diversity without disorder. One of the advantages of the free
market is that it allows many different tastes to be satisfied
without the need to reach political consensus on what tastes should
be satisfied by what methods. It can satisfy people with different and even competing preferences without causing social
disorder: it is, in effect, a system of proportional representation.

In the political 'market', on the other hand, practicalities
mean that the available choices are limited and infrequent.
Elections cannot be held every day, and may be years apart.
We vote, not for the particular policies we would like to see
implemented, but for one of the *packages* of different policies
on offer from the competing parties. And when one package

has attracted fifty-one per cent of the votes, a hundred per cent of the population is bound by it,[10] even those who did not like many parts of the package they decided to vote for, and those in the minority who hated every part of it. This must generate tension and bitterness in any society:

The use of political channels, while inevitable, tends to strain the social cohesion essential for a stable society . . . Fundamental differences in basic values can seldom if ever be resolved at the ballot box . . .[11]

The result is an unpleasant mixture of conformity in outcome with fragmentation in attitudes.

The economic marketplace is very different.[12] There, the opportunities for choice are not limited. We can choose individual products rather than be forced to accept some particular assortment of products that includes some we do not want. We can choose every day what we need, and are not restricted to selecting an assortment of commodities every four years or so. If a small minority want to buy particular products, such as cars, they do so at their own expense: the others neither get cars they do not want, nor have to pay for them. The strains on the social fabric are avoided, although diversity flourishes. Someone who wants to buy an exotic necktie is free to do so: there is no need to stage a costly and divisive election campaign or get the majority of the population to agree with his tastes.

The inefficiency of the political 'marketplace', compared with the economic market in which individuals can make daily choices between alternative products and continually select the quantity of each product they desire, has important implications for the role of government. Specifically, it suggests that as many activities as possible should be decided by economic rather than by political mechanisms:

The widespread use of the market reduces the strain on the social fabric by rendering conformity unneccessary with respect to any activities it encompasses. The wider the range of activities covered by the market, the fewer are the issues on which explicitly political decisions are required and hence on which it is necessary to achieve agreement.[13]

The role of government

What, then, are the activities which in Friedman's opinion ought to be left to the political process? As his starting point, Friedman takes the few items that Adam Smith listed over two centuries ago, and he adds only one more to the famous list.[14]

Protection. The first and second duties of government are the *protection of individuals in the society from coercion* emanating from outside or from their fellow citizens. Military and police forces are required for this function, and Friedman regards this provision as mainly a government responsibility, partly because government is usually regarded as the agency that should have a monopoly on the legitimate use of force and partly because the free market does not work well in such areas. Critics may remind Friedman that there is no reason why a country or a local government unit should not purchase its defence and policing services from competing private suppliers; but it remains impossible for different individuals to get different amounts of police or defence protection according to their individual wishes, and so some sort of communal decision is necessary.[15]

A rule-maker and umpire. The second duty goes beyond the mere provision of police forces. Protection of individuals from their fellows requires means *to agree the rules which will govern our dealings with others*, and to interpret, modify or enforce those rules as necessary. There must be some way to resolve disputes. Of course, this can make use of voluntary mechanisms, and Friedman recognizes that, in the United States at least, most disagreements on commercial contracts are resolved by a system of private arbitration; but the court of last resort is provided by the government's judicial system.

To Friedman, a free market economy is a system of voluntary exchange: consequently, it cannot work unless people are able to make agreements with each other in confidence, secure in the knowledge that business contracts will be enforceable and will not be subject to arbitrary changes in the future. The role of government therefore includes facilitating voluntary exchanges by setting and enforcing general rules for such agreements. This may not be an easy task, and even the definition of what constitutes the private property that an individual can exchange is troublesome. Should an inventor have the sole and eternal right to market his invention, for example? Does my title to land deny someone else the right to fly over it in an aircraft, or does this depend on his height or the noise he makes? The complexity of such questions has led to the development of a large body of case law, which makes it easier for people to predict the principles and practicalities which will govern the execution of the agreements they enter into. Friedman believes that the existence of rules of this kind is important if agreements are to be possible at all, although the exact definitions and precise nature of the rules themselves may be less crucial.[16]

Public goods. The third main function of government, according to Adam Smith and to Friedman, is the *provision of goods which the voluntary exchange system is unable to provide,* but which are nonetheless generally desired. An example might be the provision of roads: sometimes these could be financed by tolls, but in many cases the cost of collecting the tolls would be large in comparison with the costs of building and maintaining the roads themselves. Consequently, these would be 'public works' that are generally accepted to be necessary but which it is not in the interests of private individuals to provide.

Another example is the effect of an individual's actions on other people, such as the nuisance caused by a smoky factory chimney. The factory owner might be quite willing to compensate people in the locality for their inconvenience and extra laundry bills, but as a practical matter it is impossible to identify all those affected and the size of the compensation that would be appropriate. Or it might be that an individual makes his garden particularly beautiful, and that passers-by greatly enjoy the sight. However much they might be willing to pay for the privilege, it is not feasible to charge everyone for this enjoyment. So government intervention to prevent nuisances and encourage beneficial actions may be justified in such cases where there is a 'market failure'.

Almost everything we do has some effects on 'third parties', but that is not to say that Adam Smith's idea justifies government action nearly everywhere: for government measures also have third-party effects, and *government failure*, says Friedman, is just as likely to be a problem when the government attempts to provide goods or services but (like the factory owner or the gardener) is unable to identify the gainers or losers and to charge or compensate accordingly. Thus, he concludes, it is essential to examine both the benefits and the costs of proposed government interventions before we can decide whether they are a significant improvement on what the market, with its admitted occasional shortcomings, can achieve.[17]

Responsibilty. The fourth duty of government, which Friedman adds to Adam Smith's original list, is to protect members of the community who cannot be regarded as 'responsible' individuals, principally children and the insane. This does, of course, present philosophical difficulties to those who, like Friedman, believe that personal freedom is vitally important, but who nevertheless believe that it can only apply to responsible individuals. The definitional questions are no less problematic.

While the duty to protect non-responsible individuals ultimately devolves on government, it is quite probable that others will, in fact, take it upon themselves. For example, charitable institutions exist to care for the insane, and we normally expect parents to take responsibility for their children.

These, then, are the functions which Friedman assigns to government. They are plainly limited, and would certainly *not* justify many of the steps commonly taken by central authorities, such as price supports, tariffs, quotas, minimum wages, detailed industrial regulation, compulsory pension schemes, licensing of professions, rent control or the legal protection of monopolies.

The problems of government power

A limited role for government is not desirable simply because the market system is generally more efficient at providing individuals with the assortment of goods they desire, at the lowest prices, than any system of central and political control. Nor is it simply that the taking and enforcement of decisions through the ballot box leads to dissent and factions. To Friedman, *free economic activity is essential to political and personal freedom itself*. Furthermore, when government takes over an economic function, it tends to be operated according to the self-interest of those who provide it rather than for the benefit of those for whom it is supposed to be provided. And when government becomes the source of economic power, influence rests with the few who have most lobbying skill and muscle, rather than with the millions who are affected.

Economic and political freedom. To Friedman, economic and political freedoms are inseparable. An individual who cannot go abroad because of exchange restrictions, who cannot pursue his chosen occupation because of licensing arrangements, who cannot import goods because of quotas, or who cannot sell goods at the price he chooses, is certainly not free. Although these are all 'economic' measures, they are enforced by coercion and therefore constitute a curb on political freedom.

At the best of times, the concentration of coercive powers in the hands of government authorities poses a potential threat to political freedom. By ensuring that economic activity is *not* subject to government control, a market economy eliminates some part of this threat. Indeed, it enables economic power to be a counterweight to political power rather than its invariable reinforcement, because economic power can be widely dispersed. Each individual has economic power, and there can be a large number of wealthy people in an economy, all of them with different views and objectives. Political power, on the other hand, is more difficult to decentralize, and its objectives have to be more unified.

A vivid example of the advantages of decentralized economic power, in contrast to the threat posed by concentrated political authority, is in the area of political argument itself.[18] If economic life, and thus all jobs, are under the control of the political authorities, it would, says Friedman, take an act of considerable self-denial for a socialist government to permit its employees to advocate capitalist policies directly contrary to official doctrine. Political argument is thus stifled by the threat of economic retribution by the authorities.

Even if the authorities proved tolerant, the socialist society would provide few opportunities for activists to finance their movement – to issue pamphlets, to hold meetings, to buy advertising space, and so on. High public officials are unlikely to be sympathetic, and the only hope would be to raise small amounts of money from large numbers of people. In a capitalist society, however, it is necessary only to convince a few wealthy people to get funds to launch an idea, and many radical causes, including Marxism, have been so financed. It may not even be necessary to do more than convince an individual that the cause is potentially profitable – a commercial publisher, for example, cannot afford to publish only those writings he agrees with.

Even if funds *could* be found to promote a cause in the socialist society, there would be further difficulties. The activist supporters of capitalism would have to persuade a government paper factory to sell them paper, a government printing house to print their newspapers and notices, a government agency to rent out meeting halls, and so on. Few are likely to be sympathetic; all are likely to be worried about their own livelihoods if they give aid to this radical cause. In a capitalist society, however, paper manufacturers and printers are just as willing to sell paper or printing services to a Communist Party newspaper as to the *Wall Street Journal,* and suppliers of other services, similarly, cannot afford to discriminate in a competitive market.

To sum up, it is clear that the advocacy of new ideas or unpopular causes is much more difficult and problematic in a socialist society than in a capitalist one, and in consequence there is likely to be far less political discussion and political freedom. As Friedman puts it:

I know of no example in time or place of a society that has been marked by a large measure of political freedom, and that has not also used something comparable to a free market to organize the bulk of economic activity.[19]

Bureaucratic and special interest power. As the number of things controlled by the government increases, more of the detail must be left to the decisions of administrators. Even today in supposedly 'capitalist' countries such as the United States, no single citizen could keep up-to-date will all the issues being discussed by the politicians. It is likewise doubtful, says Friedman, that politicians could actually find the time to read all the rules and laws they are expected to vote on, far less study them. And so the civil service not only administers the decisions that are made, but advises on, and influences, the nature of the decisions that *are* made.

This plainly causes a large number of problems.[20] In the first place, bureaucrats have more power to influence decisions as government becomes larger and more complex, and they obviously have an interest in doing so. Moreover, by issuing regulations, by pressing on quickly with the administration of some laws and moving slowly on others, they can greatly alter the result. The courts, being required to rule on increasingly complex and far-reaching legislation, have been drawn into the legislative and administrative processes and have been unable to remain impartial interpreters of the law. Since the bureaucrats are in charge of spending the money of anonymous taxpayers on equally anonymous beneficiaries, they are little interested in the cost of the services they organize or the quality of service provided. The temptations, and the opportunities, for fraud and corruption increase as the range of government activities increases.

A more subtle problem is the extent to which power in such a society shifts away from the individual and his elected representatives towards the professional administrators and those with the skill and the connexions to influence them. Those who have a grievance, or those who see a way of gaining some advantage from a government measure, seek favourable rulings from bureaucrats, and are naturally prepared to invest time and money in the process. Today, legislators are lobbied for their influence over bureaucrats, rather than the other way round; and government jobs are sought not so much for their own career prospects as for the contacts and inside knowledge which will be useful in a subsequent career in business, trade unionism, and so on.

With so much power over economic life concentrated in the hands of the government and its administrators, it is not surprising that groups should attempt to extract special rulings for their own benefit and should be prepared to spend heavily in their lobbying efforts. The prospects of obtaining not only large government contracts, but also rulings which make business more difficult for competitors – such as quotas on imports, legal restrictions on the entry of new people into professions, special tax allowances or government grants of monopoly power – are all at stake. It is therefore no surprise that even business corporations have been corrupted as government power has grown. To Friedman, it is perplexing but true that today:

Business corporations are not a defense of free enterprise. On the contrary, they are one of the chief sources of danger. The two greatest enemies of free enterprise in the United States, in my opinion, have been on the one hand, my fellow intellectuals, and on the other hand, the business corporations . . .[21]

Government and monopoly power

It is perhaps insufficiently understood that:

Probably the most important source of monopoly power has been government assistance, direct and indirect.[22]

Indeed, it is difficult to think of any monopoly which would continue to exist without a corporate tax structure that encourages giantism or without special government concessions such as restrictions on foreign competition and new entry into the market. Even more important monopolies, however, are those which the government grants to itself.

A free market economy, in fact, tends to work *against* monopoly power: if people are free to accumulate capital, even the largest firm can face equally large competitors, not to mention many hundreds or thousands of small ones. But, even with the heavy regulation and intervention presently under-taken by the governments of supposedly 'capitalist' countries, industrial monopolies are still quite rare, says Friedman – although they tend to be noticed because they are more news-worthy than other companies. In some industries, where large size makes for efficiency because of the economies of scale, it is easy to confuse the large *absolute* size needed for effective competition with the large *relative* size that would imply the presence of monopoly power. Lastly, in sectors other than manufacturing, there is a marked preponderence of small firms working in a highly competitive way, although these are rarely noted when people are criticizing the 'prevalence' of monopo-lies.[23]

Government assistance to monopoly. Where monopoly power does exist, says Friedman, it generally does so with the consent or assistance of government. Tariffs on imports, for example, are an important source of monopoly power, since they insulate domestic producers from the threat of foreign competition. There is also a widespread use of government powers to protect cartel arrangements, usually justified by the alleged need for an 'orderly' or 'regulated' market. Thus, governments support the cartel arrangements of airlines, freight transport, radio and television, oil and gas production, banking, and many other industries. Price controls, occupational licensure arrange-ments, building codes and a host of other government powers all serve to make new entry into markets more difficult and thus work to preserve existing monopoly powers.

A serious problem, in Friedman's view, is the tax on corpor-ations; this encourages corporations to re-invest their surplus instead of distributing it as profits upon which shareholders would have to pay taxes. Hence, firms tend to grow larger than is economically efficient simply because of the tax system. Friedman argues that corporate taxes should therefore be abolished.

Monopolies of labour. Capital, however, is not the only factor of production where monopoly power is fostered by government intervention. Monopolies of labour, where they exist, are also aided by it. The problem is not, of course, very great in the United States, where only about a quarter of the workforce is unionized; but in countries such as the United Kingdom, where there are large public sector industries such as coal mining, public utilities, railways and hospitals, unions tend to be much stronger.[24] The connexion between government involvement and the monopoly power of labour is not accidental.

Friedman points out that about eighty per cent of the total national income of the United States goes to pay wages, salaries and fringe benefits; profits are a mere six per cent. So if the unions achieve wage increases for their members without increases in productivity, these are unlikely to come out of the already small item of profits. Wage increases for one group, says Friedman, come principally from others, and if union power is successful in raising the wages of, say, ten or fifteen per cent of the workforce by ten or fifteen per cent above what would prevail in a free market, it would require the other eighty-five or ninety per cent to suffer a loss of about four per cent. Friedman believes that this has in fact happened, and that *the effect of strong trade unions has been to make most workers worse off* than they otherwise would have been.

Only with the aid of some distorting factor or factors can unions raise wages above the market level for any long period. Violence or the threat of violence is one such factor; another is the collusion between employees and employers to gain a monopoly of the product they jointly produce. But most important is the existence of government regulations which enforce wage rates above the market level. In the United States, the Davis-Bacon Act requires contractors on government projects to pay wages of a certain level, and has been interpreted generously to boost wages in most such cases up to the official union rate. Minimum wage regulations also operate widely in private sector industries, and the effect is the same: some workers in the unionized or the controlled sectors are helped, but other groups, such as teenagers and, in particular, minorities, find themselves priced out of the labour market. Not only will an employer be able to hire fewer people if he is paying higher wages under threat of legal punishment; he will refuse to hire anyone whose experience or skill is not sufficient to make his labour *worth* the required minimum payment. Such restrictive laws undoubtedly generate unemployment, therefore, but this is disguised by the fact that:

the people who are helped are visible – the people whose wages are raised ... The people who are hurt are anonymous and their problem is not clearly connected to its cause ...[25]

Licensure. Another means of restricting the number of individuals who may enter the workforce is to have legally enforced restrictions on entry. This is used particularly in the professions, such as medicine and the law, upon which Friedman and Simon Kuznets conducted a great deal of research.[26] 'Professional' bodies representing physicians, dentists, lawyers, airline pilots and others are in effect highly successful trade unions, according to Friedman, and their success stems from the fact that they have convinced governments of the need to regulate entry into their particular industries. The justification offered is always consumer protection. But consumers themselves never promote such restrictions; only the members of the professions concerned do that. Friedman doubts that such restrictions have done much, if anything, to raise standards: indeed, they have enabled the licensed practitioners to rest on their laurels and have prevented the introduction of new methods into their industries. The main effect has been to raise the price of their services.

Government monopolies. There are some services, such as telephones or domestic gas supply, which it might be difficult or costly for more than one supplier to provide. These 'technical' monopolies present us with a choice: should we have a private monopoly, a regulated private monopoly or a public monopoly?

According to Friedman, in a choice among evils, the private unregulated monopoly is generally to be preferred. This is particularly true when we look at the poor performance which the others have, in practice, delivered. There is a tendency for government monopolies to arise and persist for no good reason: the United States government's monopoly on carrying the mail was conferred because in the nineteenth century it could not compete with the Pony Express! And once a service is established, the government looks after its own – it is rare for government services to be opened up to competition or for government employees to lose their jobs (although it does happen from time to time).

But competition is essential if any industry is not to ossify. If the mail service were opened up to competition, for example, Friedman believes that large numbers of new firms would quickly enter the market, introduce new technology and revolutionize the entire business. But nobody is prepared to lobby for such a change because nobody other than the government is currently in the business: only *after* it is opened up to competition will people begin to look at it and seek out new opportunities inside it. In all government monopolies there is a tendency not to move with the times and not to provide the consumer with the high standards of service which even a glimmer or competition would produce. Asks Friedman:

Why do we have a poor postal service? Poor long-distance train service? Poor schools? Because in each case there is essentially only one place we can get the service.[17]

That is the fault of monopoly power, and monopoly power is almost always due to direct or indirect government intervention.

Consumer protection

It is strange that the very institution which is the cause of so much monopoly power should also set itself up as the guardian of consumer interests by instituting the regulation of industry and various 'consumer protection' measures. Friedman is in no doubt on the matter:

The great danger to the consumer is monopoly – whether private or governmental. His most effective protection is free competition at home and free trade throughout the world.[28]

Free competition, however, is the one thing which industrial regulation seeks to avoid.

For example, the regulations surrounding the introduction of new drugs onto the market are deliberately strict in order to ensure that each new drug is thoroughly tested, and so they deliberately *forbid* free entry to the drugs market. To Friedman, however, there are costs involved in such restrictions as well as the obvious benefits that harmful drugs are less likely to be made available. Excessive restrictions, such as those prevailing in the United States, effectively kill the development of new drugs, making it very costly for manufacturers to bring them to the market. People in the United States die, in numbers beyond tens of thousands per year, because drugs which are in use in other countries are not available there. But these victims are not easy to identify and therefore the exact balance of costs and benefits is rarely considered. The regulation of other products, such as the rules governing consumer products safety, pose similar but more general problems. Again, almost every product has some risks associated with it, and in Friedman's judgement it should be up to the consumer to decide for himself what the balance between cost, risk and practicality should be.

Friedman's free market economy would certainly not leave the consumer unguarded, however. The possibility of very expensive liability suits in the event of a product proving faulty will provide a clear incentive for companies to test their products thoroughly before marketing them. Some companies will also make a marketing point out of the particularly stringent safety tests they impose, or may incorporate optional safety features in their products which those consumers who particularly desire them can opt for. New products tend to be introduced slowly into a market economy, taking time to 'catch on'; but this in itself helps protect the public from major disasters, because faulty products can usually be spotted at an early stage.

The government, for its part, can make major mistakes when attempting to ensure product safety. For example, the United States government required the use of a flame retardant on children's clothing, but had subsequently to ban the chemical when it was discovered to be a potent carcinogen. In an unregulated economy, a few manufacturers would undoubtedly have introduced the retardant as a marketing attraction; but its dangers would have been discovered long before it was in general circulation and before millions of children had been put at risk. To Friedman, a virtue of the free market is that it works in this gradual way, avoiding the all-or-nothing mistakes of government agencies.

Costs of controls. These risks are not the only costs of industrial regulation. Attempts to conserve energy by taxing or rationing oil-based products, for example, impose the obvious burden of higher prices on consumers; but they also impose the administrative cost of enforcement and the inevitable waiting and searching that occurs when a product is in short supply. Furthermore, it is usually poorer people who suffer most. If a factory has to bear the cost of re-equipping to meet pollution controls (or has to close down completely), the employment consequences for ordinary workers living nearby are likely to be serious. Moreover, the existence of regulatory mechanisms encourages lobbying by vested interest groups at the expense of the poorer sectors of society.

We cannot eliminate the risks inherent in every product, nor the third-party effects of problems like pollution, says Friedman. The costs of ending pollution entirely might well be excessive when compared to the gains, and so a simple regulation outlawing all pollution would do more harm than good. The best mechanism is, once again, the price mechanism: the costs and the benefits can be made to balance by the imposition of a tax. A tax on effluent discharge over a certain amount, for example, may not cure the pollution immediately or entirely, but it would put the costs borne by the community directly back onto the polluter. It would also be a powerful incentive for the polluter to seek out new technologies that produce less waste and thereby to reduce his tax bill. In this context, it is useful to remember that pollution is not the product of industrialization: in the advanced countries, the air and water have become cleaner as it has become more possible to produce goods cleanly. It is merely a problem of pricing.

The market as a consumer protection. Friedman believes that the free market is likely to be a far better guardian of consumer interests than any government agency. Competititon allows choice to the consumer, so that he can select products he has confidence in and reject those he feels may be less reliable. Not only will it be possible to choose between products with different safety features, but between products offering different combinations of safety and cost, so that consumers can decide on their preferred combinations, although all will be ultimately protected by the threat of liability actions against manufacturers of poor products. When a government agency enforces particular standards on all manufacturers, however, it raises the cost to everyone, including consumers who disagree with the standards imposed, and it imposes the risk that a major mistake might be made.

Retailers, also, are important in this free market consumer protection system. They are generally good judges of products and naturally wish to preserve their reputation by making sure their customers do not buy substandard products. This is a large part of the 'goodwill' that goes with a business and is a marketable item. Therefore, it is not necessary for every consumer to make himself an expert on every product before he buys it; the retailer's expertise, and that of the wholesaler in turn, will already have judged it for him.

Lastly, of course, information about the relative strengths and weaknesses of different products is a marketable commodity, and this is where consumer groups and a host of newspaper columns and specialist magazines help the potential customer. To Friedman, these provide a ready guide through the wide range of goods produced by the free market and a stimulus on manufacturers to maintain high standards at low cost. There can be no doubt of the advantages of such diversity over the strict regulation of products according to arbitrary standards that are perceived as being desirable by government bureaucrats.

The market and equality[29]

Another source of doubt about the free market economy is its alleged tendency to produce large disparities in income. In the first instance, Friedman argues that this is untrue: there is just as much of a spread of incomes in, say, the Soviet Union as there is in the United States. Secondly, the important kind of equality we should be seeking is equality of opportunity, not equality of outcome, and this is a point on which the capitalist economy triumphs every time.

In capitalism, income is indeed spread, but most income goes to human services rather than to the services of property. Furthermore, inequality is acceptable provided that there is mobility, allowing those who start on the bottom rung of the ladder to work themselves up. There are many other advantages to capitalism: not only does it produce the range of goods the consumer wants, but it tends to replace the toil and drudgery of work with more pleasant methods as new technology is developed. But the entire system would become untenable if, at the end of some arbitrary period, all wealth were to be redistributed and all incomes equalized. It is the incentives of wealth and high incomes which encourage enterprise in a mobile economy.

Friedman argues that any attempt to level incomes to a single standard would itself be fraught with arbitrary contradictions. Every job has not only financial rewards but psychological ones. There is no objective means of assessing the job satisfaction people have, since everyone has different tastes, and thus no means of working out the total benefit of a job to an individual and the size of adjustment needed. Furthermore, some occupations carry large risks of injury or failure. It is hardly likely that people would choose to become actors, or racing drivers, or boxers, if for their pains they received precisely the same income as everyone else. By enforcing income equality, we would be denied the benefits we enjoy from those who presently occupy a multitude of risky jobs. The only means of ensuring complete equality and still filling these jobs would be coercion of the most rigid sort. Anything less than complete equality would require an arbitrary bureaucratic decision from the ruling elite, which is the exact opposite of equality of opportunity.

Friedman is in no doubt that free market capitalism promotes equality of opportunity far more than the rigid and restricted societies of the socialist bloc. Most of the benefits of capitalism have helped the ordinary people rather than the rich. High government spending and high taxation, on the other hand, usually serve to bring forth a new class of privileged individuals, the bureaucrats and unions who administer the government projects. Socialist policies do not end privilege; but a free society prevents it from being institutionalized and makes opportunities for advancement open to all.

But high taxes do not merely produce a new elite of government workers: they encourage evasion and a disrespect for the law. The higher taxes become, the more worthwhile it is to avoid or evade them, and the more sectional interest groups demand tax relief on housing, pensions, health and other 'worthwhile' expenditure that the authorities would wish to encourage. The net effect of a progressive tax is to be quite *arbitrary*, therefore: to Friedman, the best proposal would be to have a flat-rate tax on all incomes above a certain amount, with deductions only for legitimate business expenses. The reduced opportunities for wealthy tax-avoiders, together with the smaller band of government administrators that would be needed, would in Friedman's opinion tend to increase equality rather than reduce it. Effective measures against monopoly power would contribute to the same effect.

Education and welfare services

Education is an important area where increasing reliance on government supply rather than the market has produced falling standards and lower satisfaction with the results.[30] Private schooling was originally universal in the United States and other countries, and worked well. But increasing governmental control, begun with the laudable intention of raising standards, has effectively taken education out of the hands of parents and put it under the control of 'experts' and government administrators. The result has been a marked tendency to giant schools that might suit administrative convenience but not the wishes of parents or students. Costs continue to rise, administrative empires expand, but those who are paying for education – the parents and taxpayers – have less and less control over how schools are organized and run.

The voucher. Friedman recognizes that it is important to ensure that children are properly educated regardless of their parents' circumstances, and that it is necessary for all individuals to have at least a basic standard of education in a society based on voluntary co-operation. The problem, he believes, requires a mixture of public and private elements in its solution.

The proposal he makes is for a voucher to be given to each parent representing a certain value (perhaps the usual cost of providing a basic education to the standards that were thought a desirable minimum). Parents would then be able to 'spend' these vouchers at any recognized school, adding to them with their own money if they desired their children to attend a school that was more expensive. This voucher could, and should, be available for use at any school within the government system as well as private ones.

Friedman believes that this proposal would revolutionize education. The costs of running a private school would probably be much less than those involved in present government institutions, since private schools have an incentive to keep a sharp eye on waste and inefficiency; their educational record would also make them attractive to parents. It is quite possible that the voucher would enable millions of parents to leave the government system and take advantage of the wide choice of private schools available. This in turn would encourage more private schools to open, perhaps specializing in subjects not offered by the government institutions, or perhaps of smaller size, more convenient location or different educational philosophy.

It would be a government function to ensure that the private schools maintain minimum educational standards, and perhaps that a core of certain subjects were taught. Apart from that, parental choice would encourage the better schools and would tend to drive out the less successful ones. Parental choice would be restored in education: it is likely that the most successful schools would give parents a large measure of control over the selection and retention of teachers and other important aspects of the operation of the schools.

For higher education, there is still a case for a government subsidy because of the general benefits which spill over to the whole community from advanced teaching and research, but Friedman suggests that here too a voucher system would ensure funds went to the institutions that were genuinely deserving of such support. For vocational training, where the benefit is almost entirely concentrated on the student rather than the community, Friedman finds no case for subsidy. However, if we wish to make it easier for people to take up vocational training and other higher education, this might be achieved through a loan system: investing institutions could perhaps offer loans to students and take repayments as a set percentage of the student's final earnings. Once again, by putting the purchasing power into the hands of the students or parents themselves instead of relying on government officials to direct the provision of education from central funds, this system would ensure that the best institutions prospered while less successful ones, unable to attract students, were driven out. There would also be a constant pressure to strive for excellence and efficiency which is not present today because of the domination of education by the government.

Other welfare measures. Similar mechanisms, using the allocative power of the market to provide services and to select between them, instead of relying on the decisions of bureaucrats, can be applied to the other important welfare areas of housing, pensions and the relief of poverty.[31]

On *housing*, for example, Friedman argues that government projects have actually worsened conditions for the poor, since communities have had to be broken up before new houses can be built, and because 'problem' families have been concentrated in government housing schemes, leading to a general worsening of the area. Once again, the planning, provision and allocation of housing is dominated by special interests if left to the government, which causes further serious problems.

Welfare, for its part, is a rag-bag of different programmes which the poor people they are designed to help have difficulty in finding their way through. Furthermore, since welfare projects are not financed by, nor directed towards, the people who administer them, inefficiency is bound to reign. Indeed, there is a tendency for welfare provisions to benefit the legislating classes who devise them rather than the genuinely poor.

Pensions provided by the government work on the chain-letter principle, says Friedman. The tax that supports them is regressive, and the benefits they pay are highly arbitrary. More important, it is a compulsory system with no scope for personal choice. It is not necessary to nationalize the pension business to ensure that everyone has provision for old age: all that is required is to make the holding of some kind of pension plan compulsory. Even then, Friedman sees no grounds to force people into such a decision if they choose not to; compulsion has large costs on everyone, but very little gain.

The general solution to all these welfare problems is to recognize that *poverty is caused by a shortage of cash*. It can be cured by giving cash to those who need it, and such a solution means we can dispense with the huge bureaux which provide government-run services for the poor. Friedman suggests a negative income tax, so that all those below a certain income would *receive* money from the tax authorities instead of having to *pay* tax (as those above would have to do). This greatly extends the choice available to those in need: they can use their cash benefits to purchase the *combination* of goods and services which they and their families need, rather than the arbitrary selection of items which legislators think appropriate. They can shop around for the best quality at the lowest price, further stimulating the competitive force of the market. And they have access to precisely the same markets as even the most wealthy individual, so there is no need for them to put up with a second-best service.

Solving the problems of poverty through the market, says Friedman, is likely to be far more effective than the attempts to solve them by the provision of government services: they rarely work. As he remarks:

If a balance be struck, there can be little doubt that the record is dismal. The greater part of the new ventures undertaken by government in the past few decades have failed to achieve their objectives.[32]

And that means that the poor are worse off than they ought to be because they have been forced to depend on government rather than the power of the market; the process is entirely counter-productive.

CONCLUSION

Friedman's general preference for market systems rather than government intervention has a firm practical base. After years of increasing government expenditure on a number of import-ant services, it is now possible to compare the reality of the public sector with the reality of the private, whereas before it was a more theoretical argument. When we look at the record, we face a long list of perverted official programmes: those which have simply failed to deliver the intended services, those which have imposed costs greater than the benefits they brought, and those which have been twisted by the self-interest of the people designing or administering them.

Where there is a large government sector, says Friedman, such problems will always arise. Government is more subject to *concentrated interest groups*, while the market economy changes under the diffuse pressure of *millions of individual consumers*. Government tends to promote *monopolies*, whereas the market breaks them down and thus stimulates new experiment, new products and faster progress. Government substitutes the jud-gement of *officials* for the judgement of those who are supposed to benefit, and even the best-intentioned bureaucrats cannot claim to know an individual's needs as well as the individual himself.

There is a need, then, to limit the scope of government; and Friedman suggests (for the United States at least) a constitutional limit on taxation and spending. But there is a significant change in his attitude between *Free to Choose* and *Tyranny of the Status Quo* – one written before the first Reagan and Thatcher administrations, the other written four or five years later. The practical difficulties faced by those two administrations caused him to give new emphasis to the fact that even under the best of circumstances,

a massive government cannot be reordered and reduced overnight. A government that has been built up over the decades cannot be dismantled in one or two years. The image that comes to mind is of a supertanker. The officer on the bridge must order a turn many miles before the actual turn occurs.[33]

Any attempt to restrain government growth is checked by several 'tyrannies' – the tyranny of the beneficiaries, who club together to oppose budget cuts; the tyranny of the politicians, who are eager to use public money to buy more votes; the tyranny of the bureaucracy, which grows insensibly and protects its own existence by thwarting change. So:

Any measure that affects a *concentrated* group significantly – either favorably or unfavorably – tends to have effects on the individual members of that group that are substantial, occur promptly, and are highly visible. The effects of the same measure on the individual members of a *diffused* group – again, whether favorable or unfavorable – tend to be trivial, longer delayed, and less visible . . . It motivates politicians to make grandiose promises to such special interests before an election . . .[34]

and so makes it harder for the burden on the diffused group of taxpayers to be brought under control.

Friedman's view is undoubtedly correct that

a candidate for head of state who hopes to make a real difference has to do more than get elected; he or she must have a detailed program of action well worked out before the election . . .[35]

Yet we might doubt whether Friedman's own balanced budget proposals would be attractive as an election platform, uniting as it does so many interest groups against it. But the dismal domination of government by special interests demonstrates clearly the importance of getting economic decision-making out of the hands of politicians and into the hands of ordinary people; and as floating exchange rates show, stranger things *have* happened. It is one of Friedman's most engaging characteristics that he has always been, and remains, an optimist.

CHAPTER TWELVE

Methodological Issues

I am so happily blessed with critics that I have been
forced to adopt the general rule of not replying to
them.'

Like all pathbreaking thinkers, Friedman has left in his wake
a stream of new problems as well as solutions to old ones.
His monetary theory and empirical findings have suggested
further questions that have launched many hundreds of
researchers in quest of the answers. His positive methodology
has sparked off a lengthy debate about the nature and purpose
of economic enquiry. And his sweeping prescriptions have
given rise to continuing political argument about whether,
and how, they should be implemented.

Many critics have argued that Friedman tends to paint
on too large a canvas, forgetting the details from which his
macroeconomic picture is made up, and leaving important
gaps that ruin the entire composition. But Friedman's supporters would retort that it does not matter if the details need
to be filled in by others, because the outlines of his theory
have been drawn on such a grand scale, and with such vigour
and precision. Hence, it is not necessarily a criticism of Friedman's febrile mind that his work has generated so many questions, some of which will no doubt be solved in the future,
and some of which are by their very nature almost impossible
to decide definitively. Indeed, it is something of a compliment.

The monetarist economic model

Friedman's major contribution to economics is the establishment of a completely new economic model. He provides a
diagnosis of some of the major ailments that have beset the
economies of the world since the Second World War, and
explains how one particularly important factor, because it per-

meates every economic transaction, is a large part of the cause. He insists that the crucial importance of this factor, the quantity of money, can be demonstrated by empirical tests. Having demonstrated to his satisfaction the relationship between the quantity of money and nominal income, he then explains how policies aimed at controlling this quantity more accurately, and removing the temptations for politicians to dash into inflation, should be effected.

Friedman's professional career has concentrated on the establishment, testing and elaboration of this model. Although he is delightful as an opponent in debate because of his vivid imagery and intellectual adroitness, many of his critics from the old Keynesians to the new 'Austrians' complain that his understanding of the intricacies of their own analysis is superficial and that many of his attacks on them miss the point. But these complaints are often founded on a misapprehension about Friedman's working method, which is not mesmerized by analytical complexity but demands that theories should be simple yet charged with an ability to predict events. It is plain that Friedman *has* established such a body of theory, and his method has been to subject it to rigorous testing and to show its predictive power, rather than to be sidetracked into detailed criticism of other contenders. It is to gain some understanding of this methodological approach that we must now examine it more closely.

FRIEDMAN'S METHODOLOGICAL APPROACH

Any sympathetic evaluation of Friedman's work must proceed from an appreciation of his distinctive view about the nature and purpose of intellectual enquiry. A number of economists, particularly Keynesians but also many members of the Austrian School, begin with a methodology that is so different that it is sometimes impossible for them to communicate with Friedman at all.[2] The difference is not just one about economic facts, nor even of value judgements: it is a difference of view about the entire purpose of economic theorizing.

To Friedman, the hallmark of a good theory in economics is its *predictive power*.[3] We form and use theories to help us anticipate future events and to control them, and it is this capacity to predict and control events which gives a theory its usefulness. For example, Friedman's theory that a substantial change in the quantity of money will eventually precipitate a substantial change in nominal incomes is useful because it tells us much about the cause of inflation and how to prevent it. This theory is one which is worth our debating, discussing, checking and using – it is not an elegant but useless curiosity. Nobody would engage in the process of intellectual enquiry unless it was of practical importance, which forces us to conclude that the development of ideas which help us control and shape the world is what economics is all about, so that predictive power must be the economist's constant target.

This power has to be worked for, however: it comes only from venturing new theories and testing them against events. We put forward new theories encapsulating new attempts at prediction, and then check them to see whether they do in fact predict. By this empirical process we can gradually weed out those theories which do not predict the future and those which predict less reliably than others. We can never *prove* a theory, because unexpected events in the future might make it fail – no matter how much we have come to trust it. The most we can do, says Friedman, is *fail* to *dis*prove it; but that makes the theory worth having until the time when (or if) it does let us down or its predictive power is outshone by another, better theory.

A natural scientist can often test theories very rapidly, because he can alter natural conditions (such as temperature and pressure) in his experiments. Unfortunately for economics, there can be few 'controlled' experiments, partly because an economic situation is never repeated exactly at another time, and partly because ethical and practical difficulties prevent us from manipulating economic factors at will for experimental purposes. This simply means that the testing of economic theories is slow: we have to attempt to gauge the effects of the multitude of complicating factors that we cannot isolate. For example, we may hypothesize that the demand for money is fairly stable: but we would face practical difficulties in attempting to control all interest rates to see if they had any effect on it, and ethical problems in robbing people of their wealth in order to conduct the experiment.

Choosing economic theories

Human beings could think up an infinite variety of successful theories, however, and so we require tests in addition to that of predictive power in order to select the most useful. In any scientific enquiry, we have therefore come to prefer theories that are simple to test, that are consistent with other theories that we accept, that are 'fruitful' in suggesting new lines of enquiry and answers to other problems, and that are applicable under a wide variety of circumstances.

But in this elimination process we must not forget that our overriding purpose is prediction. Some economists make the mistake of judging a theory on the 'realism' of its assumptions rather than on its predictions, says Friedman. Many people are inclined to dismiss economic theories that assume 'pure' competition, or 'perfect' markets, or 'homogeneity' of capital. Yet no economist genuinely expects such perfection in real life: the question is whether, by assuming these things, one can deduce theories that explain events. For example, one fruitful and useful economic theory is that businesses behave *as if* they are seeking to maximize their returns. From this theory we are able to predict with considerable success how businesses will react to a wide range of events, and it is therefore of considerable value – in comparing the likely effects of different economic policies, for instance. The assumptions are very unrealistic: businessmen do not calculate marginal and average costs and revenues and solve the complex simultaneous equations that would be necessary to ensure that returns are always maximized. In fact, they rely on their innate expertise, their 'feel' for market conditions or some trade secrets they might not admit to: but the hypothesis is correct, that they behave *as if* they were return-maximizers.

This hypothesis is simple, useful and fruitful, and consequently we would not wish to discard it. The economist who is seeking 'realism', on the other hand, finds himself drawn into a quagmire of complexity. He would find it quite impossible to interview all businessmen about how they would act in all circumstances, to decide whether their reports were true or false, and to summarize the information received in a useful and digestible form. The task would be endless, and it would in any case be impossible to produce a perfectly realistic picture of business strategy. Friedman would ask if this (possibly improved but never perfect) 'realism' actually produced predictions that were significantly better.

The importance of Friedman's methodology

We can begin to understand now that Friedman's dispute with some other schools of economists is not just that they over-emphasize the importance of 'realistic' assumptions: more fundamentally, they have lost sight of the true purpose of economic enquiry.

The problem with economic theories that take pride in the 'realism' of their assumptions is that each new event has to be somehow incorporated into the theory. If an event occurs that was not predicted, the theory has to be extended to show the special circumstances that made it happen; another unexpected event requires another adjustment; and so on. But this process robs the theory of any predictive power it might once have had, because it adjusts to suit *any* occurrence and becomes merely a description of what has been, rather than a forecast of what we expect to come. For instance, Keynesians did not expect such rapid inflation in response to postwar 'cheap money' policies, and had to revise their orthodoxy to account for it, while the breakdown of the 'Phillips curve' trade-off between inflation and unemployment caused them to seek refuge in new refinements about the 'real' workings of employment markets and wage determination processes. Similarly, Marx's theory of economic stages, in which communist revolution would follow industrialization, was disproved when the first such revolution occurred in the *agricultural* economy of Russia – requiring the application of an overcoat of 'Leninism', which incorporated strong party organization as a major explanatory factor. Revolutions have since occurred, or failed, in countries with various degrees of economic development, and with party structures of various strength; each result is given its own *ad hoc* explanation. Such theories become useless for prediction: if one event occurs, they claim it to be predicted, but if the opposite had occurred, it too would have been predicted by the (suitably amended) theory. It is clear that they are not really *predicting* events at all, simply giving an *interpretation*, possibly a wildly mistaken one, to past events.

We are therefore wise to avoid these attempts to give a complete account of the world if we can instead devise simple theories that give useful predictions (and which could, in principle at least, be disproved by events that did not fit the forecasts). In Friedman's view, it may be interesting to probe beneath the surface to find out the exact machanics of the process that is summarized by the theory, but it is a pointless exercise if it does not help us to improve its power. For example, many economists of the Austrian School would deny the validity of Friedman's macroeconomic approach entirely: to them, individual prices and markets are what counts, and macroeconomic concepts are simply averages and aggregates that actually disguise what is really going on. Friedman seems to accept that individual price changes, market structures and personal motives might indeed be important, but argues that they are so multifarious and inaccessible that we can only see the *pattern* that they form. Only if closer scrutiny of the individual elements will significantly improve our prediction of the macroeconomic pattern they form do we need to work out the details.

This approach may explain why Friedman is reluctant to speculate about the actual mechanisms that cause his macroeconomic variables to show consistent relationships. He believes, for example, that a number of plausible explanations about how monetary changes work their way into prices are possible, but the important thing is that they *do* and that the end result is predictable.

To Friedman, the Keynesians and others have misunderstood the nature of an economic model. A model is a simplified representation of the economy, and is tested in order to make predictions about how the real thing will behave – like a model aircraft in a wind-tunnel. It does not pretend to be a perfect representation, nor to show how the real thing will behave in all circumstances. Just as wind-tunnel models do not always show up *all* real-life problems, the economic model might prove inadequate, in which case we have to construct a new and better one, or to admit that there are some things which our hypothesis is not designed to explain.[4] The Keynesian approach, on the other hand, is to attempt to rebuild the model at each stage until it is just as large and complex as the real thing, by which time it is impossible to understand or test it.

Hence the value which Friedman recognizes of the small-scale economic theory – the hypothesis which is simple and designed to explain a limited set of phenomena, which admits that other factors might interfere, but which is generally adequate to the task of prediction and useful in helping us to cope with events. Indeed, many of the research projects which Friedman's writings have spawned are just this kind of small-scale model building and testing, yielding limited but useful predictions.[5]

If economic enquiry is seen as an evolutionary process, in which new hypotheses are advanced, tested and accepted or rejected on the basis of their performance, then this variety and heterogeneity must provide the basis for rapid progress. This is hardly likely to be a feature of the lumbering search for descriptive 'realism'.

Can economics be value-free?

One question posed by Friedman's work is whether he is correct in his assertion that economics is a science like physics, which can be, and should be, free from judgements of value. Perhaps it is the philosophical intricacy of this problem, and the doubt that it could ever be firmly decided even in principle, which explains its persistence: but it is of course at the core of Friedman's 'positive' approach to economics.

Friedman approaches economic method from the point of view of the mathematician, true to his original training. He sees the purpose of the economist as being like that of the natural scientist, to put forward new theories and hypotheses that allow us to make predictions about what events will occur in the future or to explain simply what occurred in the past. The predictions contained in such a theory or hypothesis are either borne out by events or they are not: and so economics is as much an objective science as any of the natural sciences can claim to be.[6] There is no reason why the course of sound economic enquiry should be twisted as a result of the personal or political opinions of economists; there should be general agreement about economic theory, just as there is about a central body of theory in physics or any other natural science.

To Friedman, most disagreements in economics are disagreements on items that are, fortunately, capable of being decided objectively, although it may take more empirical testing before everyone is convinced one way or the other. Thus, economics will gradually build up an accepted body of theory like any other science, and although the values of those engaged in economics might have some impact on the exact course of their theorizing and empirical testing, the subject matter of economics is still ultimately objective. In Friedman's words:

> The economist's value judgements doubtless influence the subjects he works on and perhaps also at times the conclusions he reaches... Yet this does not alter the fundamental point that, in principle there are no value judgments in economics.[7]

Consequently, economists can indeed strive to build up an objective body of theory, theory which in time will grow sufficiently to settle the major policy questions of today.

The debate over a minimum wage legislation is a case in point. Proponents of minimum wage laws predict that, when implemented, they will contribute to the abolition of poverty. Opponents, like Friedman, argue that they will in fact produce a rise in unemployment and an inefficient employment market, and will therefore tend to increase poverty, not cure it. Testing these theories is a difficult matter, and it may take years or even decades before all the evidence comes in. But, in Friedman's judgement, it *will* eventually come in, in a form which makes the results clear to all, and at that point this disagreement between economists will be resolved and empirical study will turn to further points of disagreement. There is no shortage of such potential disagreements on issues such as the effects of trade unions, the impact of price controls, the strengths and weaknesses of import restrictions, the merits of regulation of industry, the prudence of stabilization policy, and many more. As the evidence on each one is gathered, says Friedman, our ability to predict the future will be further and further improved.

According to Friedman there is, in fact, general agreement on aims: nearly everyone accepts that the goal of economics is the achievement of high and stable employment levels, stable prices and maximum freedom of international trade. There may be some obvious disagreement in values when it comes to issues such as the distribution of income, for example, but even here much of the debate is a matter of objective and testable fact: whether a progressive tax will in fact equalize incomes or be arbitrary in its effects, whether redistribution of incomes will impoverish us all by killing incentives, and so on. Thus, 'the basic differences among economists are empirical, not theoretical'.[8]

But economists *do* disagree. Where they do, says Friedman, this is more likely to arise from simple differences in viewpoint rather than from some irreconcilable argument about values. For example, the *time horizon* of different economists may not be the same: one may feel that the market economy is too slow in its achievement of employment, price and trade goals, and may feel the need to intervene to speed matters up. Such an individual may recognize that the intervention can cause problems later on, but may hope to solve those when the time comes. Politicians in particular are inclined to seek the immediate effects of interventionist policies. Again, the *complexity* of the economic system, and some *uncertainty* about the exact results of economic policies, make disagreements more likely. When faced with doubts about the evidence, economists and politicians tend to fall back on their personal and political values. But as our knowledge in economics increases, the scope for value judgements of this kind must necessarily shrink.

Objections to Friedman's view. If Friedman is correct, it means that economics should be treated as an empirical science like any other, with conclusions that are demonstrable and useful rather than the mere opinion of interested advocates. But there remain questions which make us wonder just how objective economics, or any social science for that matter, can truly be.

The first source of difficulty is the fact that the economist himself has values which he may introduce into the assessment of the facts he observes, giving his work a 'subjective' element. Friedman, for example, argues that the velocity of money has changed only 'moderately' over the decades, and suggests that his belief in the stability of the demand for money is thereby corroborated. Other economists, however, might deny the fact: in their judgements, the variations in velocity that have occurred might be 'great' and might even be interpreted as a 'significant' departure from stability.[9] At other moments, Friedman confines his theory to the *substantial* rises in prices that will follow *substantial* monetary expansions. Yet this again implies a measure of personal judgement in the interpretation of the results, since 'substantial' might mean different things to different economists. If even the champion of positive economics has to resort to such judgements, what hope is there for economics as a 'science'?

The second problem facing the economist is that his economic theories, however objective they may be, carry significant non-economic or political implications. This confusion of facts and values is much less common in the natural sciences, although the problem caused to evolutionary theory by religious preconceptions is a notable example. In economics, however, almost every empirical question has its political overtones. The advocacy of a monetary rule, for instance, is consistent with a political philosophy, like Friedman's, that is generally sceptical about the good that governments can do by intervention in the economy; those with more faith in interventionism generally incline to support the opposite view. Again, some of Friedman's critics might recognize the problems that are caused when education is controlled by the government, but might believe that these are lesser dangers than allowing the wider variation in educational standards that they fear a free market system might produce.

While he understands these points, Friedman still maintains that his own theories, and indeed the mainsteam of economic argument, are free from such value judgements. While his monetary theory may be congenial to the believer in limited government, it results from objective analysis rather than political disposition:

Certainly, the monetary policy I have come to favor – a steady rate of growth in the quantity of money – is highly congenial to my preference for limiting government so far as possible by clearly specified rules ... no value judgements can explain why I have been led to the conclusion that ... inflation is primarily a monetary phenomenon ... no value judgement can explain why I regard the quantity of money rather than the rate of interest or 'money market conditions' as the crucial variable for monetary policy ...[10]

Friedman himself points out a third difficulty, that the subject matter of economics is complicated and that controlled experimentation is impossible. An economic policy cannot be tested under a number of specific conditions, because the economy does not stand still and conditions are never repeated exactly nor conform precisely to what we would wish. According to Friedman, however, this is simply a quantitative difference between economics and the natural sciences, not a difference in kind. In the natural sciences too, it is often difficult to control our experimental conditions precisely. If conditions cannot be controlled, there are more sources of confusion when we assess the outcome of a particular event, which makes the course of economic enquiry slower than some others. But although extraneous or random factors might occasionally confuse our results, this does not mean that we are unable gradually to whittle down those results to extract a sound body of theory.

Conclusion. It is hard for many people to be as confident as Friedman that economics can be divorced or largely distanced from questions of value, and the last point is a source of particular concern. Economic policies are advocated today that failed in the past, solely on the assumption that crucial factors in the past no longer apply. It remains a good question whether economists can ever learn from their mistakes, and thus whether economics can ever graduate to the unimpeachable status of being a science.

This concern about the status of economics is, of course, only a special instance of the debate which has long raged about the status of all social sciences. It may be that Friedman and his critics, being professional economists rather than professional philosophers of science, are not well qualified to dispute the finer points of the argument. But Friedman's own methodological approach does come to his aid. The predictions which his theory makes are broad and testible. Although he embellishes the theory with predictions on more minor matters, his fundamental concern is always in sight: the relationship between changes in monetary aggregates and changes in nominal income. Although this theory has sparked off a long and involved debate about *how* such a link may work and *to what extent* it can be relied on, the simplicity of the original hypothesis is never lost to its author: the theory can be subject to wide testing; arguments about the details do not deny the validity of the overall principle.

This does suggest that progress in economics is not only slow, but limited to rather broad predictions of the pattern of events rather than precise description of each of the multitude of events making up each day's economic activity. But, to Friedman, our ability gradually to learn about this macroeconomic pattern, while limited, is nevertheless extremely valuable.

Macroeconomic predictions

It is also possible to start from the opposite point of view, and object that macroeconomic reasoning is founded on an error, and that the manipulation of macroeconomic concepts – averages, totals and other statistical measures – is not the way to find out what is actually going on in an economy. Each of the individual investment decisions summarized in the Keynesian aggregate of 'investment', for example, depends entirely on the motives of specific individuals, each of which might be different. Any movement of the macroeconomic aggregates occurs only because the millions of individual investors actually *do* something. It is not good enough to say, for example, that a fall in the interest rate leads to more investment. A fall in the interest rate no doubt changes the priorities of the millions of individuals in the economy, but what happens depends on the state of their *motives*; some may invest more, others less, and the Keynesian aggregate describes only the balance of their actions. So it is simply wrong to suggest (or fall into the trap of supposing) that 'the' rate of interest affects 'the' level of investment. To do so misses out the essential element that actually describes what is going on: the motives of individuals which cause them to act in a new way.

According to this theorectical approach, the movement of aggregates and averages is neither here nor there, but is just a convenient way of describing in summary form the actions of millions of individuals. *Individuals* may be influenced by the particular prices they find in the marketplace, the particular rates of interest they can obtain, and the particular investment opportunities they perceive. But the *aggregate* volume of their transactions cannot be said to be dependent upon the *average* level of prices or interest rates. The averages and aggregates are just descriptions that exist only in the minds of statisticians, and are devised after the events themselves.

In defence of Friedman. Although this argument is powerful and increasingly popular, it does not necessarily dispose of the entirety of macroeconomic reasoning. Friedman does not address it squarely and satisfactorily, but his methodological approach provides the answer to it.

It is certainly correct that macroeconomic aggregates are only summary numbers, and that none has any effect on another. Only individual actions respond to individual events. But that is not to deny that, on balance, individuals act in ways which are predictable overall: while we cannot tell what the response of each individual will be, we can nevertheless predict with some assurance what the overall pattern of events will be.

Economics, and social sciences in general, are thus engaged in a process of *pattern prediction*.[11] Patterns are made up of individual elements; the strands of wool in a carpet, the tiles in a mosaic, the brushstrokes on a painting or the individual geese in their flying formation. In each case we can see and understand the overall pattern, although the exact positioning of the individual elements makes no difference. The geese could exchange places without the pattern disappearing. The same pattern can be seen on two carpets, even though different strands of wool go into their manufacture. The pattern of the mosaic would look the same whether the tiles used were ceramic or plastic.

In Friedman's defence, therefore, we can argue that the same can be said in economics. Even though we do not know how the individuals in an economy will react, we can nevertheless gain useful knowledge as long as their resultant action forms some kind of pattern which we can predict. If we can predict, say, the *overall* effect of a particular economic policy, then even though we do not know in detail how each individual will respond, we have still made a valuable contribution to knowledge.

Friedman's method is very much in this vein. Indeed, he shows a marked lack of interest in the behaviour of the particular elements in the overall pattern he sets out to study. He argues, for instance, that a monetary expansion will work through to prices, and although he is prepared to venture some guesses about the exact nature of the transmission process from one to the other, he regards this as a fairly fruitless exercise. If the pattern is predictable, then that is sufficient for him; others can worry about the exact way in which individuals change their portfolios to compensate or the precise movements in the individual prices that are changed, one by one, to produce the overall results. Indeed, the details of the process, like the strands in a carpet, might be so many that it is impossible to enumerate them with any accuracy or describe them in any useful way other than in terms of the pattern that they form. But science seeks usable predictions rather than involved and useless descriptions of specific events.

Shortcomings of aggregation

There are, undoubtedly, many problems raised by the kind of aggregation which the macroeconomist like Friedman has to resort to. Many of these Friedman himself appreciates.

Mixing unlike quantities. An obvious problem of the aggregation which macroeconomists have to resort to is that it lumps together items which should not really be classed together. For this reason, much of Friedman's work has been attacked because of the selection that he has had to make in drawing up his aggregates. The problem about the definition of money, already mentioned, is one such example. The exact definition of the price index is another source of difficulty, even though it is crucial to Friedman's work. As he says:

An enormous number of prices exist for almost any commodity or service. Shall retail or wholesale prices be used? Those in New York or Chicago? As of January or December? Rural or Urban? How are different qualities to be treated? If an average is to be used, how should the average be constructed?[12]

In reply to the critics, Friedman argues that the exact mixture of items summarized in an economic aggregate is not important. What *is* crucial is whether the patterns so established are related in any discernible and predictable way. There may indeed be many different ways of defining the price index, and many different kinds of asset that might or might not be included in the definition of money. But, having discerned the existence of some rough relationship between the two, the positive economist is quite within his rights to attempt to hone down the definitions until the relationship becomes even more clear. Once that is done, we can be more certain in our own minds which items need to be controlled by monetary policy and which are of less influence.

Certainly, some information is likely to be lost when we lump together different kinds of things under the same definition. But, according to Friedman, if the overall aggregates behave in predictable ways, then something of value has been learnt. It is up to the doubters to demonstrate if and why our understanding will be improved by closer examination of the particular items that make up the overall pattern.

Obscuring important items. Another similar criticism is sometimes made of Friedman's work: that it tells us little about various important items that are crucial to most economic or political policy. For example, Friedman does not go into much detail to explain whether an increase in nominal income is likely to be manifested in terms of increased prices or increased output, although for the economist, the politician and the businessman this is vital information. By concentrating on a few large aggregates, it is possible to ignore what is really important.

Again, Friedman rejects the charge. He does consider the division of nominal income into prices and output, but can find no incontrovertible way to predict the outcome. It may be that this is a shortcoming of the theory; but a theory is not intended to explain everything. Friedman's quantity theory is in fact very powerful in its predictions about nominal income changes, but perhaps we must resort to other authors if we are able to predict the exact division of it between prices and output. Certainly, this information may be of very great importance; but that shortcoming does not deny the magnitude of what has been achieved so for.

Crucial differences in effects. The most telling criticism along these lines is that by ignoring *relative* price changes, Friedman has ignored all that is important in the adjustment of a market economy.

Friedman himself has argued the importance of prices: that a rising price for pencils, for example, will cause timber, metal and graphite to be diverted into the production of pencils more than they otherwise would. By such changes in relative prices does the market economy allocate resources in the most efficient manner possible. Yet in his monetary theory Friedman largely ignores the effects of relative prices, although he does (perhaps feebly) admit that they may have an effect. In his words:

> Different activities have different time-speeds of adjustment. Some prices, wages and production schedules are fixed a long time in advance; others can be adjusted promptly. As a result, a slowdown of total spending produces substantial shifts in *relative* prices, which will sooner or later have to be corrected; the correction will in turn cause economic disturbances.[13]

This is, indeed, an important point. If the quantity of money is raised by a given percentage, nobody would suggest that *all* prices are likely to rise by exactly the same proportion. In the first place, prices are more likely to be bid up in *some* markets first, with price rises only working through to others in time, like the ripples spreading over the surface of a pool after a stone has been thrown in. This distortion in relative prices, even if it is temporary, may cause serious misallocations of resources, which can impoverish everyone. New money is not dropped uniformly across the economy from helicopters; it enters at certain points. If the industries first afffected presume that this new money is in fact a swing in *relative* demand towards their own products, they might order new capital, hire new workers and otherwise tool up for the boom. Once it is realized that it is only a general inflationary process rather than a genuine change in demand, the same industries find themselves in possession of stocks, capital and workers that they no longer need. It may not be possible to redeploy those factors as easily or as quickly as the owners would like, and so they incur *real* costs in attempting to adjust.

It is perhaps a pity that Friedman does not absorb more of this brand of thinking into his monetary theory. By tending to presume that markets are capable of costless adjustment (despite occasional *remarks* to the contrary), Friedman does not explain some important phenomena which are in fact perfectly compatible with his thinking. For example, a major cause of the depression which must follow an inflation is this kind of adjustment problem. The industries which do well from inflation, usually those nearest to the government – the nationalized industries and the outdated industries which governments attempt to shore up with direct grants in an attempt to 'save jobs' – are the most seriously affected when the inflation stops. Resources that have been attracted to them over the years (because of the high relative prices the inflation has produced in their sector) suddenly become useless. This is a real waste of resources; monetary policy is certainly not neutral in this respect. Again, those same firms will undoubtedly need to shed some of their workforce when the monetary slowdown makes useless their privileged position of being first in line for every inflationary boost. This is a clear explanation of why inflation should *produce* rather than reduce unemployment, and in its full form is perhaps an easier and more powerful explanation than that given by Friedman, whose discussions of the importance of relative prices are marginal.

There is a second point here which is also important. As we have seen, different people react if different ways. An increase in ther quantity of money, even if it *were* dropped from helicopters, would not lead everyone to behave in exactly the same way. Some might spend their new wealth, others might invest it, and others might store it up. The result will certainly be that the shape of the economy is slightly different after the increase from what it was before. The pattern of activity will have subtly changed, according to the particular motives of the individuals concerned. Hence, it again seems likely that monetary changes will lead to *real* distortions in the economy which might be vitally important but which Friedman's theory glides over.

Of all the objections made to Friedman's method, the question of changes in relative prices is probably the most persuasive. If relative price changes are important, causing real and lasting dislocations in economic activity, then the straightforward quantity theory may actually overlook effects of major importance. Indeed, the real effects which Friedman supposes will be dissipated in time may even be more significant than any change in nominal price averages, although the policy implications will be much the same. However, Friedman's response is characteristically blunt: he will believe in the importance of 'first round' changes in relative prices when the evidence is submitted. The question is an empirical matter, not a theoretical one; and as we have seen, the differences between economists are empirical, not theoretical.

Conclusion

Friedman's greatest asset, and one of the reasons for the popularity of his theories, has been this empirical approach. Not for him the heated but idle speculations on theoretical niceties that can be of interest only to other economists. His work has become popular because it helps in practice to make predictions. Painstaking work on the movements of monetary and other aggregates over a century has convinced both the profession and the public of the fact that monetary movements are linked to prices and output. The failure of the Keynesian orthodoxy has spurred on the economic authorities to search for and adopt a new approach.

Friedman's ability to shatter the icons of consensus is, indeed, particularly important in this respect. The Keynesian orthodoxy, by its nature a model-building and model-refining movement, was never slow in finding a special explanation to fit the circumstances of the moment and so to explain why Keynesian predictions were not in fact borne out by events. Thus the 'cheap money' policies which brought about postwar inflation were defended in principle even though they were discreetly changed in practice. The concurrence of rising inflation and rising unemployment was explained by a 'temporary' outward shift in the Phillips curve. Other shortcomings in the basic model were interpreted as demonstrating the need for more advanced and complex economic models. There is no doubt that this process could have gone on indefinitely, were it not for the fact that a simpler explanation was to hand for all these events, just as the theory that the earth should be regarded as the centre of the solar system was long defended despite the convoluted explanations it required. Yet when faced with a model which explains most or all of the same phenomena more simply (and perhaps yields some new insights), such convoluted theories tend to fall by the wayside. Friedman happened to enter the debate at just the right time to accelerate the replacement of the Keynesian framework by a superior one.

The focus of economic debate, both at the professional level and amongst the general public, has certainly been changed by this intervention. As we have seen, progress in economics is slow: it takes time for a new theoretical stance to be fully adopted and put to the test. But the actual practice of monetary authorities worldwide, whatever their stated views on the subject, has changed: money is now regarded as a far more powerful factor than it was before or could ever have been in the Keynesian framework. That contribution is not insubstantial by any means, and it offers the prospect of permanently controlling the inflation that has become the most important economic problem of the age. The credit for this advance can be laid squarely at the feet of Milton Friedman.

Notes

Chapter 1: Friedman's place in the history of economic thought

1. *The Counter-Revolution in Monetary Theory*, pages 21–2.

2. 'Inflation' here is used as Friedman uses it, to designate a process of continually rising prices, producing a fall in the purchasing power of any unit of money (such as a dollar, pound, yen or peseta). Some economists use the word to signify the debasement of the currency or the expansion of the quantity of money itself, rather than any price rises which may result: but, attractive though this use is, popular language has overtaken it.

3. See E.G. Dolan, *Basic Economics* (Hinsdale, Illinois: Dryden Press, 1977), page 206.

4. John Burton, 'Positively Milton Friedman', in J.R. Shackleton and Gareth Locksley, *Twelve Contemporary Economists* (London: Macmillan, 1981), pages 53–71 (page 54).

5. Harry G. Johnson, *Further Essays in Monetary Economics* (London: George Allen and Unwin, 1972), page 22.

6. Leonard Silk, *The Economists* (New York: Basic Books, 1976), page 44. Several points below derive from this source.

7. 'Discussion of the Inflationary Gap', *American Economic Review*, Vol. 32 (June 1942), pages 314–20.

8. In *Essays in Positive Economics*, pages 251–62; see especially the note on page 253.

9. For example, in *Verdict on Rent Control* (London: Institute of Economic Affairs, 1972), pages 17–32.

10. See, for example, 'Comments on Monetary Policy', in *Essays in Positive Economics*, pages 263–73.

11. See, for example, 'The Effects of a Full-Employment Policy on Economic Stability: A Formal Analysis' and 'A Monetary and Fiscal Framework for Economic Stability', both in *Essays in Positive Economics*, pages 117–32 and 133–56.

12. For Friedman's explanation of the fall of Keynesian economics, see especially *Dollars and Deficits*, pages 10–15; *The Counter-Revolution in Monetary Theory*, pages 15–20; 'Money: Quantity Theory', page 439; and 'The Role of Monetary Policy', page 2.

13. 'Money: Quantity Theory', page 439.

14. Harry G. Johnson, *Essays in Monetary Economics* (London: George Allen and Unwin, 1967), page 31.

15. 'The Quantity Theory of Money – A Restatement', in *Studies in the Quantity Theory of Money*, pages 3–21.

16. Harry G. Johnson, *Essays in Monetary Economics* (London: George Allen and Unwin, 1967), page 33.

17. The relationship between income and the demand for money is traced in 'The Demand for Money: Some Theoretical and Empirical Results', especially pages 333–5.

18. Particularly in *A Tract on Monetary Reform* (New York: Harcourt Brace & Co., 1924).

19. *Dollars and Deficits*, page 13.

20. *The Counter-Revolution in Monetary Theory*, pages 11–12.

21. In his 'The Effects of a Full-Employment Policy on Economic Stability: A Formal Analysis', reprinted in *Essays in Positive Economics*, pages 117–32.

22. Such as his *Newsweek* columns; see Chapter 3 of *An Economist's Protest*.

23. A.W. Phillips, 'The Relationship Between Unemployment and the Rate of Change of Money Wage Rates in the United Kingdom, 1861–1957', *Economica*, Vol. 59 (November 1958), pages 283–99.

24. For example, in *Milton Friedman's Monetary Framework*, and Chapter 10 of *Monetary Trends in the United States and the United Kingdom*.

25. See *Inflation and Unemployment*, Section IV, and *Tyranny of the Status Quo*, page 88.

26. Niels Thygesen, 'The Scientific Contributions of Milton Friedman', *Scandinavian Journal of Economics*, Vol. 79, No. 1 (1977), pages 68–9.

27. 'The Case for Flexible Exchange Rates', in *Essays in Positive Economics*, pages 157–203.

28. *Dollars and Deficits*, page 209.

29. John Burton, 'Positively Milton Friedman', in J.R. Shackleton and Gareth Locksley, *Twelve Contemporary Economists* (London: Macmillan, 1981), pages 53–71 (page 53).

30. For an exposition of Hayek's views on the 'miracle' of the price system, see Eamonn Butler, *Hayek: His Contribution to the Political and Economic Thought of our Time* (London: Temple Smith, 1983; New York: Universe, 1985), especially pages 45–51.

31. For this treatment, see John Burton, 'Positively Milton Friedman', in J.R. Shackleton and Gareth Locksley, *Twelve Contemporary Economists* (London: Macmillan, 1981, pages 53–71), especially pages 65–9.

Chapter 2: Friedman and the quantity theory of money: an overview

1. 'Money: Quantity Theory', page 433.

2. Specifically, in *Milton Friedman's Monetary Framework*, in Chapter 2 of *Monetary Trends in the United States and the United Kingdom*, and Section 1 of *The Counter-Revolution in Monetary Theory*.

3. *Studies in the Quantity Theory of Money*, page 3.

4. For criticism of Friedman's description of the 'Chicago School', see Don Patinkin, 'The Chicago Tradition, The Quantity Theory, and Friedman', *Journal of Money, Credit, and Banking*, Vol. 1, No. 1 (February 1969), pages 46–70. For Friedman's response, see particularly *Milton Friedman's Monetary Framework*, pages 158–9.

5. 'Money: Quantity Theory', page 433.

6. John Locke, *Some Considerations of the Consequences of the Lowering of Interest and Raising the Value of Money* (London: 1692).

7. David Hume, 'Of Money', in *Essays* (Oxford: Oxford University Press, 1963), pages 289–302 (page 289).

8. See Eamonn Butler (ed.), *The Report of the Bullion Committee of 1810* (London: Adam Smith Institute, 1984).

9. Irving Fisher, *The Purchasing Power of Money* (New York: Macmillan, 1911; revised edition, 1920; second revised edition, 1922; modern reprint, New York: Augustus M. Kelley, 1963).

10. The relationship, and the assumptions, are not so straightforward if we separate money into *currency in circulation* and *deposits*, each of which is likely to have a different velocity. A similar breakdown can also be made in the income and cash-balance approaches described later in the text, again at the cost of some complication.

11. *Milton Friedman's Monetary Framework*, page 8.

12. See the remarks by Don Patinkin in *Milton Friedman's Monetary Framework*, page 116.

13. Although the transactions approach generates controversy and doubt on the definition of money, Friedman himself regards a broad definition as correct and compatible with it. In answer to theories which exclude time and savings deposits, he says that conversion before use is in fact a feature 'of some items that all are willing to regard as money. For example, in the United States, $10,000 is the largest denomination of currency. Such a currency note can be used to effectuate few transactions without first being converted into smaller denominations. No issue of principle is involved.' ('Money: Quantity Theory', page 435).

14. 'Money: Quantity Theory', page 438.

15. J.M. Keynes, *A Tract on Monetary Reform* (London: Macmillan, 1923).

16. Milton Friedman, 'The Keynes Centenary: A Monetarist Reflects', *The Economist*, Vol. 287, No. 7292 (4 June, 1983), page 36.

17. See Chapter 1 above, and *Dollars and Deficits*, pages 13–14; *The Counter-Revolution in Monetary Theory*, pages 11–12; and for fuller statements of the monetary events in the depression period, Chapter 7 of *A Monetary History of the United States* and *Free to Choose*, Chapter 3.

18. J.M. Keynes, *The General Theory of Employment, Interest, and Money* (London: Macmillan, 1966).

19. Money: Quantity Theory', page 438. In fact, the rot had set in with the publication of Keynes's *Treatise on Money* six years before, where the importance of the interest rate is seen as dominant, directly affecting

prices through its effects on saving and investment, and money is given a minor part only as one of many influences on interest rates.

20. 'Money: Quantity Theory', page 439.

21. 'The Quantity Theory of Money: A Restatement', in *Studies in the Quantity Theory of Money*, pages 3–21.

22. 'Money: Quantity Theory', page 439.

23. *Monetary Trends in the United States and the United Kingdom*, page 70.

24. *Dollars and Deficits*, pages 105–6.

25. For examples, see *Milton Friedman's Monetary Framework*, pages 1–2 and 46; *Dollars and Deficits*, page 108; *Monetary Trends in the United States and the United Kingdom*, pages 17–19; 'The Demand for Money: Some Theoretical and Empirical Results', pages 329–31; and *The Counter-Revolution in Monetary Theory*, page 22.

26. 'Commodity-Reserve Currency', in *Essays in Positive Economics*, pages 204–50.

27. For an exposition, see *Dollars and Deficits*, pages 108–9.

28. For example, in *Studies in the Quantity Theory of Money*, page 4.

29. See, for example, *Dollars and Deficits*, page 110.

30. This is presented in detail in *A Monetary History of the United States*, and *Monetary Trends in the United States and the United Kingdom*.

31. *A Program for Monetary Stability*, page 87.

32. *Dollars and Deficits*, page 107.

33. See *An Economist's Protest*, page 28, for this example.

34. *An Economist's Protest*, pages 18–19.

35. For a review of the ineffectiveness of price controls over four thousand years, see Robert L. Schuettinger and Eamonn Butler, *Forty Centuries of Wage and Price Controls* (Washington DC: Heritage Foundation, 1979).

36. See 'A Monetary and Fiscal Framework for Economic Stability' in *Essays in Positive Economics*, pages 133–56, and the subsequent *A Program for Monetary Stability*. Another short and useful exposition of Friedman's policy proposals appears in 'The Role of Monetary Policy', and a discussion of them appears in *Monetary Versus Fiscal Policy*. On a popular level, see *Capitalism and Freedom*, pages 51–5.

37. This idea is the central argument in *Monetary Correction*.

38. This proposal was advanced by Henry Simons in *A Positive Program for Laissez Faire* (Chicago: University of Chicago Press, 1934), and in 'Rules versus Authorities in Monetary Policy', *Journal of Political Economy*, Vol. XLIV (February 1936), pages 1–30. See *A Program for Monetary Stability* for Friedman's exposition.

Chapter 3: Velocity and the demand for money

1. *Studies in the Quantity Theory of Money*, page 4.

2. See *Dollars and Deficits*, pages 31–2, showing the international comparisons which can be made if money is so defined; and the use of the definition for the analysis in *Monetary Trends in the United States and the United Kingdom*,

pages 205–6, and *Dollars and Deficits*, Chapter 7.

3. 'Money: Quantity Theory', page 433.

4. See *Dollar and Deficits*, page 196. For other examples of Friedman's description of the process, see 'Money: Quantity Theory', page 434, and *Dollars and Deficits*, pages 33–4 and 109–10.

5. *Dollars and Deficits*, page 110.

6. *Dollars and Deficits*, pages 33–4.

7. Eamonn Butler (ed.), *The Report of the Bullion Committee of 1810* (London: Adam Smith Institute, 1984).

8. Don Patinkin, for example, argues that the leading Chicago scholar from whom Friedman derives so much, Henry Simons, did not even mention the concept of the demand function for money (*Milton Friedman's Monetary Framework*, page 114), and develops this view at length in 'The Chicago Tradition, the Quantity Theory, and Friedman', *Journal of Money, Credit and Banking*, Vol. 1, No. 1 (February 1969), pages 46–70.

9. For example, *A Monetary History of the United States*, and *Monetary Trends in the United States and the United Kingdom*, especially Chapter 6.

10. For example, in his 'Liquidity Preference as Behaviour toward Risk', *Review of Economic Studies*, Vol. 25 (February 1958), pages 65–86.

11. *Monetary Trends in the United States and the United Kingdon*, page 207.

12. Alvin Hansen, *The American Economy* (New York: McGraw Hill, 1957).

13. For Friedman's exposition of this, see *Milton Friedman's Monetary Framework*, pages 11–15, and *Monetary Trends in the United States and the United Kingdom*, pages 37–41; a more technical presentation can be found in *Studies in the Quantity Theory of Money*, pages 4–11, with additional comments up to page 15. Keynesian and post-Keynesian analyses of the demand function are well presented in some detail in D.G. Pierce and D.M. Shaw, *Monetary Economics* (London: Butterworth, 1974), pages 90–119, and the modern quantity theory approach is outlined in the same volume, pages 119–25. A simpler but excellent presentation of the two views can be found in A.D. Bain, *The Control of the Money Supply* (Harmondsworth, England: Penguin, 1970), pages 82–92.

14. *Studies in the Quantity Theory of Money*, page 14.

15. *The Counter-Revolution in Monetary Theory*, page 25.

16. *Studies in the Quantity Theory of Money*, page 15.

17. *Studies in the Quantity Theory of Money*, pages 8–9.

18. *Monetary Trends in the United States and the United Kingdom*, Chapter 4.

19. 'The Demand for Money', page 329.

20. For indications of the empirical work of other authors, see Howard R. Vane and John L. Thompson, *Monetarism: Theory, Evidence & Policy* (London: Martin Robertson, 1979), pages 44–5; and Geoffrey E.J. Dennis, *Monetary Economics* (London and New York: Longman, 1981), pages 169–70.

21. For a discussion of these issues, see *Monetary Trends in the United States and the United Kingdom*, pages 259–80.

22. Geoffrey E.J. Dennis, *Monetary Economics* (London and New York: Longman, 1981), page 170.

23. Indeed, Friedman argues that price changes might in fact be used as a proxy for the yields on physical assets that are hard to measure: see *Monetary Trends in the United States and the United Kingdom*, pages 474–5.

24. *Monetary Trends in the United States and the United Kingdom*, pages 280–87.

25. *Monetary Trends in the United States and the United Kingdom*, page 207.

26. 'The Demand for Money', pages 328–9.

27. *Monetary Trends in the United States and the United Kingdom*, page 215.

28. 'The Demand for Money', page 329.

29. *A Monetary History of the United States*, page 558.

30. 'The Demand for Money', page 329.

Chapter 4: The supply of money

1. 'Comment on Tobin', *Quarterly Journal of Economics*, Vol. 84 (May 1970), pages 318–27.

2. *Dollars and Deficits*, page 138n.

3. A pathbreaking study of this issue was that of Philip Cagan in 'The Demand for Currency Relative to the Total Money Supply', *Journal of Political Economy*, Vol. 66 (August 1958), pages 303–58.

4. For an example of this view, see Murray Rothbard, 'Austrian Definitions of the Supply of Money', in Louis Spadaro (ed.), *New Directions in Austrian Economics* (Fairway, Kansas: Scheed, Andrews and McMeel, 1978), pages 143–56 (page 148).

5. For a discussion of some of the problems, see M.J. Artis and M.K. Lewis, *Monetary Control in the United Kingdom* (Oxford: Philip Allan, 1981), pages 138–42.

6. 'Money and Business Cycles', page 44. It should be noted that in the British context, Friedman's favourite M2 measure would correspond more closely to sterling M3 (£M3).

7. *Monetary Trends in the United States and the United Kingdom*, pages 216–17.

8. *Monetary Statistics of the United States*, pages 91–2.

9. 'Money and Business Cycles', page 45.

10. Milton Friedman and Anna J. Schwartz, 'The Definition of Money: Net Wealth and Neutrality as Criteria', *Journal of Money, Credit, and Banking*, Vol. 1, No. 1 (February 1969), pages 1–14.

11. See 'The Methodology of Positive Economics' in *Essays in Positive Economics*, pages 3–43.

12. J. Tobin, 'Money, Capital, and Other Stores of Value', *American Economic Review*, Vol. 51, No. 2 (May 1961).

13. See J.G. Gurley and E.S. Shaw, *Money in a Theory of Finance* (Washington DC: Brookings Institution, 1960).

14. Or the opposite might happen: when interest rates are low, banks might attempt to maintain or build up their income, and so reduce their cash/deposit ratio to the minimum. The problem for the monetarist is to predict which is likely to occur, and whether it makes much difference to the result.

15. Philip Cagan, 'The Demand for Currency Relative to the Total Money Supply', *Journal of Political Economy*, Vol. 66 (August 1958), pages 303–58.

16. For an overview of the possible influences on the supply of money, with particular reference to the role of non-bank financial institutions, see the textbook by D.G. Pierce and D.M. Shaw, *Monetary Economics* (London: Butterworth, 1974), Chapter 5; and that of Andrew Crockett, *Money: Theory, Policy and Institutions* (London: Thomas Nelson, second edition, 1979), Chapter 10.

17. *Monetary Trends in the United States and the United Kingdom*, page 63 (and *Milton Friedman's Monetary Framework*, page 53).

18. Milton Friedman, 'The Supply of Money and Changes in Prices and Output', in *The Relationship of Prices to Economic Stability and Growth* (Washington DC: US Congress Document No. 23724, 1958), pages 241–56 (page 249); quoted in 'The Lag in Effect of Monetary Policy'.

19. See, for example, J.M. Culbertson, 'Friedman on the Lag in Effect of Monetary Policy', *Journal of Political Economy*, Vol. 68 (December 1960), pages 617–21.

20. 'The Lag in Effect of Monetary Policy', page 450.

21. Milton Friedman, 'Memorandum on Monetary Policy', in *Memoranda on Monetary Policy* (London: HMSO, Treasury and Civil Service Committee, Series 1979–80).

22. The point is Tobin's, but other objections on these grounds are voiced by Walter Heller in *Monetary Versus Fiscal Policy*, pages 20–21.

23. *Monetary Trends in the United States and the United Kingdom*, page 26.

24. For further remarks on this point, see *Monetary Versus Fiscal Policy*, pages 74–6, and *Dollars and Deficits*, page 144.

25. *Dollars and Deficits*, page 144.

26. *Dollars and Deficits*, page 146.

27. See, for example, *Free to Choose*, Chapter 3; *Capitalism and Freedom*, pages 44–51; 'Money and Business Cycles', pages 50–56; and *A Monetary History of the United States*, Chapter 7.

28. For Hayek's view on inflation, see Eamonn Butler, *Hayek: His Contribution to the Political and Economic Thought of our Time* (London: Temple Smith, 1983; New York: Universe, 1985), Chapter 2.

29. *Free to Choose*, page 282.

30. For a discussion of this see G.K. Shaw, *Macro-Economic Policy* (London: Martin Robertson, second edition, 1973), pages 92–4.

31. For a discussion, see Andrew Crockett, *Money: Theory, Policy, and Institutions* (London: Thomas Nelson, second edition, 1979), pages 142–56.

32. As noted in Howard R. Vane and John L. Thompson, *Monetarism: Theory, Evidence, and Policy* (Oxford: Martin Robertson, 1979), pages 60–61.

33. *Monetary Trends in the United States and the United Kingdom*, pages 33–6.

34. For Friedman's comments on this, see especially *Dollars and Deficits*, Chapters 10 and 11; 'Commodity-Reserve Currency' in *Essays in Positive Economics*, pages 204–50; and *Tyranny of the Status Quo*, pages 99–101.

35. *Dollars and Deficits*, page 256.

36. *Dollars and Deficits*, page 227.

37. For a discussion, see Geoffrey E.J. Dennis, *Monetary Economics* (London and New York: Longman, 1981), page 253.

38. See 'The Case for Flexible Exchange Rates', in *Essays in Positive Economics*, pages 157–203.

Chapter 5: The empirical evidence

1. *A Monetary History of the United States*, page 676.

2. A point made by Niels Thygesen, 'The Scientific Contributions of Milton Friedman', *Scandinavian Journal of Economics*, Vol. 79, No. 1 (1977), pages 56–98 (page 71).

3. See Chapter 4.

4. 'The Role of War in American Economic Development: Price, Income and Monetary Changes in Three Wartime Periods', pages 612–13.

5. On fiscal policy, see Chapter 9 below.

6. 'The Role of War in American Economic Development: Price, Income and Monetary Changes in Three Wartime Periods', page 622.

7. 'The Role of War in American Economic Development: Price, Income and Monetary Changes in Three Wartime Periods', page 623.

8. 'Money and Business Cycles', page 51.

9. 'Money: Quantity Theory', pages 443–4.

10. For a review of these depressions, see 'Money and Business Cycles'.

11. A good and lengthy account of this is to be found in *Free To Choose*, Chapter 3. For a more technical account, see *A Monetary History of The United States*, Chapter 7.

12. 'The Monetary Theory and Policy of Henry Simons', page 11.

13. *The Optimum Quantity of Money*, page 97.

14. *Dollars and Deficits*, page 83.

15. *Dollars and Deficits*, pages 141–3.

16. Hans F. Sennholz, 'Chicago Monetary Tradition in the Light of Austrian Theory', in *Toward Liberty* (Menlo Park, California: Institute for Humane Studies, 1971), Vol. 2, pages 347–66.

17. See, for example, Murray Rothbard, *America's Great Depression* (Princeton NJ: Van Nostrand, 1963).

18. *The Counter-Revolution in Monetary Theory*, page 21. For a brief encapsulation of the evidence, see *Tyranny of the Status Quo*, pages 84–8.

19. 'The Demand for Money: Some Theoretical and Empirical Results', page 329.

20. 'Money and Business Cycles', page 56.

21. This concept is elaborated in detail in *A Theory of the Consumption Function*.

22. *Dollars and Deficits*, page 201.

23. Perhaps the plainest is the summary in *A Theory of the Consumption Function*, pages 220–21.

24. *A Theory of the Consumption Function*, page 227. In parenthesis it might be added that a number of interesting empirical results come out of the hypothesis concerning the ratio of permanent consumption to permanent income, Cp/Yp. This ratio is much higher for wage earners than for entrepreneurs, probably reflecting the greater cushion of savings required by those in risky work and the ability of entrepreneurs to get higher returns on savings. Furthermore, if measured income is very variable, it would tend to exaggerate the *apparent* size of entrepreneurs' permanent incomes. For other implications, see *A Theory of the Consumption Function*, pages 226–30.

25. See 'The Demand for Money', pages 330–36.

26. See especially Niels Thygesen, 'The Scientific Contributions of Milton Friedman', *Scandinavian Journal of Economics*, Vol. 79, No. 1 (1977), pages 56–98 (page 78).

27. *Monetary Trends in the United States and the United Kingdom*, page 208.

28. See 'The Demand for Money', pages 348–51.

Chapter 6: The causes and nature of inflation

1. *Monetary Versus Fiscal Policy*, page 46.

2. Sir John Hicks, 'What is Wrong With Monetarism', *Lloyds Bank Review*, No. 118 (October 1975), page 1.

3. For this distinction, see *Dollars and Deficits*, page 28.

4. In addition to an example of the apparent 'cost-push' inflation caused by a sudden demand for shoes in *An Economist's Protest* (page 28), Friedman also quotes another vivid example from Armen A. Alchian and William R. Allen, *University Economics* (Belmont, California: Wadsworth Publishing Co., 1964), pages 105–6, illustrating the demand/costs confusion:

Pretend that for some reason people's desire for meat increases.... Housewives reveal an increased demand by buying more meat than formerly at the current prices in the meat markets.... The increased demand takes its toll of inventories.... The butcher will buy more meat than usual the next day in order to restore his inventory from its abnormally low level.... Just as butchers use inventories, so packers... also rely on inventories.... Assume that the first day's change in demand was within that inventory limit and therefore was met without a price increase.

Packers restore inventories by instructing their cattle buyers... to buy more cattle than usual. But with all the packers restoring their inventories in this manner, the number of cattle available for sale each day are inadequate to meet the increased total demand *at the old price*....

The buyers will begin to raise their offers... until the price rises to the point where the packers will not want to buy more meat ... than is available from the cattlemen....

The packers experience *a rise in costs*... [so] the packers must charge a higher price to butchers if they are to continue as profitable meat packers.... The butchers, in turn, post higher prices to the housewives.

When housewives complain about the higher price, the butcher in all inno-cence, honesty, and correctness says that it isn't his fault. The cost of meat has gone up. . . . And the packers can honestly say the same thing.

5. *Monetary Correction*, page 10.

6. *Free to Choose*, page 264.

7. 'Money: Quantity Theory', page 434.

8. *Milton Friedman's Monetary Framework*, pages 16–21.

9. *Milton Friedman's Monetary Framework*, page 50.

10. 'The Role of Monetary Policy', page 11.

11. *Monetary Versus Fiscal Policy*, page 47.

12. *Unemployment Versus Inflation?*, page 12.

13. *Dollars and Deficits*, page 24.

14. *Dollars and Deficits*, page 98.

15. *A Monetary History of the United States*, page 583.

16. *Monetary Trends in the United States and the United Kingdom*, Chapter 9.

17. *Dollars and Deficits*, pages 151–2.

18. *Dollars and Deficits*, pages 158–9.

19. A question put by Frank Hahn, *Money and Inflation* (Oxford: Basil Blackwell, 1982), pages 73–4.

20. See, for example, *Milton Friedman's Monetary Framework*.

21. Cf. John Stuart Mill, in *Westminster Review*, No. 41 (June 1844), page 589: 'The issues of a *Government* paper, even when not permanent, will raise prices; because Governments usually issue their paper in purchases for con-sumption. If issued to pay off a portion of the national debt, we believe they would have no effect.'

22. 'Money and Business Cycles', page 60.

23. 'Money and Business Cycles', page 61.

24. *Monetary Trends in the United States and the United Kingdom*, page 30.

25. See F.A. Hayek, *Monetary Theory and the Trade Cycle* (New York: Augustus M. Kelley, reprinted edition, 1976); see also Eamonn Butler, *Hayek: His Contribution to the Political and Economic Thought of our Time* (London: Maurice Temple Smith, 1983; New York: Universe, 1985), pages 58–65.

26. *Monetary Trends in the United States and the United Kingdom*, pages 26–36.

27. *Monetary Trends in the United States and the United Kingdom*, page 31.

28. *Dollars and Deficits*, pages 34–5.

29. *Monetary Correction*, page 17.

30. *Essays in Positive Economics*, page 254.

31. *Monetary Correction*, page 13.

32. J.M. Keynes, *A Tract on Monetary Reform* (London: Macmillan, 1923), page 51.

33. David Hume, 'Of Money', in *Essays* (Oxford: Oxford University Press, 1963), pages 289–302 (page 294).

Chapter 7: Inflation and unemployment

1. *Dollars and Deficits*, page 159.

2. *Unemployment Versus Inflation?*, page 13; for the view of inflation as a 'drug' that requires increasing doses to stimulate, see *Tyranny of the Status Quo,* page 88.

3. *Unemployment Versus Inflation?*, page 17.

4. 'The Role of Monetary Policy', page 8.

5. For comments on the evidence, see Howard R. Vane and John L. Thompson, *Monetarism* (Oxford: Martin Robertson, 1979), pages 92–3.

6. *Inflation and Unemployment,* page 16.

7. *Inflation and Unemployment,* page 24.

8. See *Unemployment Versus Inflation?*, pages 25–8, for a discussion.

9. *Unemployment Versus Inflation?*, pages 27–8.

10. For a critique of monetarist expectations theory from a Keynesian viewpoint, see Frank Hahn, *Money and Inflation* (Oxford: Blackwell, 1982).

11. For example, *Inflation and Unemployment.*

12. For Friedman's presentation of the empirical results, see *Inflation and Unemployment,* pages 18–23.

13. For an outline of some of the studies conducted so far, see Howard R. Vane and John L. Thompson, *Monetarism* (Oxford: Martin Robertson, 1979), page 89.

14. *Monetary Trends in the United States and the United Kingdom,* page 622.

15. F.A. Hayek, *A Tiger by the Tail* (London: Institute of Economic Affairs, 1972), addresses itself at length to this problem. For a condensed outline, see Eamonn Butler, *Hayek: His Contribution to the Political and Economic Thought of our Time* (London: Temple Smith, 1983; New York: Universe, 1985), Chapter 2.

16. *Inflation and Unemployment,* page 30.

17. *Monetary Correction,* Section 4.

18. *Dollars and Deficits,* pages 113–15. For a discussion at length on the inappropriate and ineffective nature of price controls, see Robert L. Schuettinger and Eamonn F. Butler, *Forty Centuries of Wage and Price Controls* (Washington DC: Heritage Foundation, 1979).

19. *Dollars and Deficits,* page 30.

20. *Unemployment Versus Inflation?*, page 30.

21. *Unemployment Versus Inflation?*, page 24.

22. *The Optimum Quantity of Money,* page 105.

23. *Dollars and Deficits,* page 215.

24. *Tyranny of the Status Quo,* page 88.

Chapter 8: The lag and business cycles

1. 'The Lag in Effect of Monetary Policy', page 466.

2. Ralph G. Hawtrey, *The Gold Standard in Theory and Practice* (London: Longman, 1939).

3. For example, see F.A. Hayek, *Monetary Theory and the Trade Cycle* (New York: Augustus M. Kelley, reprint 1975).

4. This appeared as 'Money and Business Cycles' and in their other joint works.

5. 'Money and Business Cycles', pages 32–8.

6. 'The Lag in Effect of Monetary Policy', page 457.

7. 'Money and Business Cycles', page 36.

8. For Friedman's view see 'The Lag in Effect of Monetary Policy', pages 457–9.

9. This is described briefly in 'The Lag in Effect of Monetary Policy', pages 459–61.

10. For this argument, see J.M. Culbertson, 'Friedman on the Lag in Effect of Monetary Policy', *Journal of Political Economy*, Vol. 68 (December 1960), pages 617–21.

11. 'The Lag in Effect of Monetary Policy', pages 451–5.

12. See, for example, James Tobin and Craig Swan, 'Money and Permanent Income: Some Empirical Tests', *American Economic Review Proceedings*, Vol. 59 (May 1969).

13. Outlined in 'The Lag in Effect of Monetary Policy', pages 461–3.

14. *A Program for Monetary Stability*, page 87.

15. 'The Lag in Effect of Monetary Policy', page 464.

16. This analogy is from Walter Heller in *Monetary Versus Fiscal Policy*, page 24.

17. 'Money and Business Cycles', page 55.

18. See *Essays in Positive Economics*, pages 146–8, for an early statement, and *Milton Friedman's Monetary Framework*, pages 140–41, for a later one.

19. This analysis appears in 'The Effects of a Full-Employment Policy on Economic Stability', *Essays in Positive Economics*, pages 117–32.

20. *Essays in Positive Economics*, pages 144–7.

Chapter 9: Keynesian versus monetarist economic policy

1. 'Interest Rates and the Demand for Money', page 72.

2. See, for example, *Monetary Versus Fiscal Policy*, pages 53–6, for this view.

3. For a detailed discussion of the mechanism, see *Milton Friedman's Monetary Framework*, pages 149–51.

4. *Monetary Versus Fiscal Policy*, pages 53–8.

5. *Unemployment Versus Inflation?*, page 17.

6. J.M. Keynes, *The General Theory of Employment, Interest, and Money* (London: Macmillan, 1936), page 207.

7. 'Interest Rates and the Demand for Money', page 71.

8. For an outline of this point, see Niels Thygesen, 'The Scientific Contributions of Milton Friedman', *Scandinavian Journal of Economics*, Vol. 79 (1977), pages 56–98 (pages 64ff).

9. 'The Demand for Money: Some Theoretical and Empirical Results'.

10. See 'Interest Rates and the Demand for Money', page 72 and 72n.

11. *Dollars and Deficits*, pages 135–6.

12. This is quoted briefly in *Monetary Versus Fiscal Policy*, pages 58–9.

13. See Leonall C. Anderson and Herry L. Jordan, 'Monetary and Fiscal Actions: A Test of their Relative Importance in Economic Stabilization', in *Review* (Federal Reserve Bank of St. Louis: November 1968), pages 11–23.

14. 'The Role of War in American Economic Development: Price, Income, and Monetary Changes in Three Wartime Periods', *American Economic Review* (May 1952), pages 612–25, reprinted in *The Optimum Quantity of Money and Other Essays*.

15. *Monetary Versus Fiscal Policy*, page 59.

16. *Monetary Versus Fiscal Policy*, page 59.

17. *A Monetary History of the United States*.

18. See Niels Thygesen, 'The Scientific Contributions of Milton Friedman', *Scandinavian Journal of Economics*, Vol. 79 (1977), pages 56–97 (pages 70–72).

Chapter 10: The role of monetary policy

1. 'Money: Quantity Theory', pages 443–4.

2. 'The Role of Monetary Policy', page 1.

3. For the explanation of the true movements in monetary magnitudes in the depression years, see *A Monetary History of the United States*, Chapter 7; and more popularly, *Free to Choose*, Chapter 3, and more briefly, *Capitalism and Freedom*, Chapter 3.

4. For Friedman's description of Keynes's rationalization, see 'The Role of Monetary Policy', pages 1–2. Most of the succeeding discussion is derived from the same article.

5. For these arguments, see 'The Role of Monetary Policy', pages 11–14.

6. Henry C. Simons, *Economic Policy for a Free Society* (Chicago: University of Chicago Press, 1948), contains the essential proposals. For Friedman's interpretation of Simon's views, see 'The Monetary Theory of Henry Simons'. For Friedman's outline of the 100% reserve banking proposal, see 'A Monetary and Fiscal Framework for Economic Stability', in *Essays in Positive Economics*, pages 133–56.

7. 'Comments on Monetary Policy', page 188.

8. For this criticism, see *Dollars and Deficits*, pages 173–94.

9. For a full explanation of the proposal, see *A Program for Monetary Stability*.

10. *Essays in Positive Economics*, pages 264–5.

11. *Monetary Versus Fiscal Policy*, page 59.

12. *Essays in Positive Economics*, page 141.

13. *Monetary Versus Fiscal Policy*, page 74.

14. 'A Monetarist View', pages 10–11.

15. For a full exposition, see *Monetary Correction*.

16. *Dollars and Deficits*, page 3.

17. This particular example is from Franco Modigliani, 'The Monetarist Controversy or, Should we Forsake Stabilization Policies?', *American Economic Review*, Vol. 69 (1977), pages 1–9.

18. The following points are from 'Have Monetary Policies Failed?', pages 12–13.

19. Niels Thygesen, 'The Scientific Contributions of Milton Friedman', *Scandinavian Journal of Economics*, Vol. 79, No. 1 (1977), pages 56–98, summarizes this and other objections to the monetary rule idea.

20. For an unreconstructed Keynesian view on this ground, see Sir John Hicks, 'What is Wrong with Monetarism', *Lloyds Bank Review*, No. 118 (October 1975), pages 1–13 (especially pages 8–9).

21. *Dollars and Deficits*, pages 72–90, outlines Friedman's views on this.

22. For an instance, see *Monetary Versus Fiscal Policy*, pages 57–8.

23. See, for example, Friedman's criticism of Britain's Thatcher Administration in 'A Monetarist View'.

Chapter 11: Friedman the market economist

1. *Free to Choose*, pages 54–5.

2. *Tyranny of the Status Quo*, page 47.

3. *Free to Choose*, pages 190–91.

4. *Free to Choose*, pages 155–6; *Tyranny of the Status Quo*, pages 143–4 and 153–4.

5. The example was devised by Leonard Read; Friedman quotes it in *Free to Choose*, pages 11–12.

6. *Free to Choose*, pages 12–13.

7. *Capitalism and Freedom*, page 21.

8. *Capitalism and Freedom*, pages 109–10.

9. *Capitalism and Freedom*, page 108.

10. *An Economist's Protest*, page 206.

11. *Capitalism and Freedom*, pages 23–4.

12. See *Free to Choose*, pages 65–6.

13. *Capitalism and Freedom*, page 24.

14. Adam Smith, *The Wealth of Nations*, ed. George Stigler (Chicago: University of Chicago Press, 1976 Book V, Chapter I); see also *Free to Choose*, pages 28–33; and *Capitalism and Freedom*, pages 25–34.

15. *Capitalism and Freedom*, page 23.

16. *Capitalism and Freedom*, page 27.

17. *Free to Choose*, pages 32–3.

18. *Capitalism and Freedom*, pages 16–18.

19. *Capitalism and Freedom*, page 9.

20. For these, see *Free to Choose*, pages 294–8 and 116–19, and *Tyranny of the Status Quo*, pages 47–51.

21. 'The Future of Capitalism', in *Tax Limitation, Inflation, and the Role of Government*, pages 1–13 (page 11).

22. *Capitalism and Freedom*, page 129.

23. For these points, see *Capitalism and Freedom*, Chapter 8.

24. *Free to Choose*, page 233.

25. *Capitalism and Freedom*, page 181.

26. See *Income from Independent Professional Practice*.

27. *Free to Choose*, page 246.

28. *Free to Choose*, page 226.

29. For the arguments in this section, see *Capitalism and Freedom*, Chapter 10; *Free to Choose*, Capter 5; and *Tyranny of the Status Quo*, pages 62–7.

30. On education, see *Free to Choose*, Chapter 6; *Capitalism and Freedom*, Chapter 6; and *Tyranny of the Status Quo*, Chapter 8.

31. On welfare, see *Free to Choose*, Chapter 4, and *Capitalism and Freedom*, Chapters 11 and 12.

32. *Capitalism and Freedom*, page 199.

33. *Tyranny of the Status Quo*, page 42.

34. *Tyranny of the Status Quo*, page 6.

35. *Tyranny of the Status Quo*, page 3.

Chapter 12: Methodological issues

1. 'Comment on Tobin', *Quarterly Journal of Economics*, Vol. 84 (May 1970) pages 319–27 (page 326).

2. A notable case is the debate between Tobin and Friedman in *Milton Friedman's Monetary Framework;* see especially pages 145–6.

3. The principal source for Friedman's views on method is 'The Methodology of Positive Economics', in *Essays in Positive Economics*, pages 3–43.

4. This explanation derives from the pattern of Friedman's work over the years, rather than any clear statement from him about it. For a theoretical exposition of this 'model-building' approach to scientific method, see Madsen Pirie, *Trial & Error & The Idea of Progress* (La Salle, Illinois: Open Court, 1978).

5. An important outline of Freidman's work which proceeds from a sympathetic understanding of his methodological approach and therefore gives a good estimate of Friedman's influence on subsequent economic research is Niels Thygesen, 'The Scientific Contributions of Milton Friedman', *Scandinavian Journal of Economics*, Vol. 79, No. 1 (1977), pages 56–98.

6. 'The Methodology of Positive Economics', in *Essays in Positive Economics*, pages 3–43 (page 4).

7. 'Value Judgments in Economics', in Sidney Hook (ed.), *Human Values and Economic Policy* (New York: New York University Press, 1967), pages 85–93 (page 86).

8. *Milton Friedman's Monetary Framework*, page 61.

9. *Monetary Versus Fiscal Policy*, page 22.

10. *Dollars and Deficits*, pages 8–10.

11. This viewpoint was devised by F.A.Hayek in *Studies in Philosophy, Politics and Economics* (London: Routledge, 1967; and Chicago: University of Chicago Press, 1967), Chapter 2, 'The Theory of Complex Phenomena'.

For discussion, see Eamonn Butler, *Hayek: His Contribution to the Political and Economic Thought of our Time* (London: Maurice Temple Smith, 1983; New York: Universe, 1985), pages 132–50.

12. *Price Theory*, pages 29–30.

13. *Monetary Correction*, page 16.

Select Bibliography

FRIEDMAN'S PRINCIPAL BOOKS AND MONOGRAPHS

(With Carl Shoup and Ruth P. Mack) *Taxing to Prevent Inflation* (New York: Columbia University Press, 1943).

(With Simon Kuznets) *Income from Independent Professional Practice* (New York: National Bureau of Economic Research, 1945).

(With George J. Stigler) *Roofs or Ceilings? The Current Housing Problem* (Irvington-on-Hudson, NY: Foundation for Economic Education, 1946).

Essays in Positive Economics (Chicago: University of Chicago Press, 1953).

(Editor) *Studies in the Quantity Theory of Money* (Chicago: University of Chicago Press, 1956).

A Theory of the Consumption Function (Princeton: Princeton University Press, National Bureau of Economic Research, General Series Number 63, 1957).

A Program for Monetary Stability (New York: Fordham University Press, 1959).

(With Rose Friedman) *Capitalism and Freedom* (Chicago: University of Chicago Press, 1962).

Price Theory (Chicago: Aldine, 1966; revised edition, 1972).

(With Anna J. Schwartz) *A Monetary History of the United States, 1867-1960* (Princeton: Princeton University Press, National Bureau of Economic Research Studies in Business Cycles, Number 12, 1963).

Dollars and Deficits: Inflation, Monetary Policy and the Balance of Payments (Englewood Cliffs, NJ: Prentice-Hall, 1968).

The Optimum Quantity of Money and Other Essays (Chicago: Aldine, 1969).

(With Walter W. Heller) *Monetary Versus Fiscal Policy* (New York: W.W. Norton & Co, 1969).

(With Anna J. Schwartz) *Monetary Statistics of the United States* (New York: Columbia University Press, National Bureau of Economic Research Studies in Business Cycles, Number 20, 1970).

The Counter-Revolution in Monetary Theory (London: Institute of Economic Affairs, 1970).

An Economist's Protest (Glen Ridge, NJ: Thomas Horton, 1972), second edition also published, with additions, as *There's No Such Thing as a Free Lunch* (La Salle, Il: Open Court, 1975).

Milton Friedman's Monetary Framework: A Debate with his Critics (edited by Robert J. Gordon; Chicago: University of Chicago Press, 1974).

Monetary Correction (London: Institute of Economic Affairs, 1974).
Unemployment Versus Inflation? (London: Institute of Economic Affairs, 1975).
From Galbraith to Economic Freedom (London: Institute of Economic Affairs, 1977).
Inflation and Unemployment (London: Institute of Economic Affairs, 1977).
Tax Limitation, Inflation, and the Role of Government (Dallas, TX: The Fisher Institute, 1978).
(With Rose Friedman) *Free to Choose* (New York: Harcourt Brace Jovanovich, 1980; London: Secker & Warburg, 1980).
Focus on Milton Friedman (Vancouver BC: The Fraser Institute, 1982).
(With Anna J. Schwartz) *Monetary Trends in the United States and the United Kingdom* (Chicago: University of Chicago Press, National Bureau of Economic Research Monograph, 1982).
(With Rose Friedman) *Tyranny of the Status Quo* (New York: Harcourt Brace Jovanovich, 1984; London: Secker & Warburg, 1984).

FRIEDMAN'S PRINCIPAL ARTICLES REFERRED TO IN THE TEXT

(A number of these articles also appear in *The Optimum Quantity of Money* but have been itemized separately because that volume is not in print at the time of writing).
'The Role of War in American Economic Development: Price, Income and Monetary Changes in Three Wartime Periods', *American Economic Review, Papers and Proceedings*, Vol. 42 (May 1952), pages 612-25.
'The Demand for Money: Some Theoretical and Empirical Results', *Journal of Political Economy*, Vol. 67 (August 1959), pages 327-51.
'The Lag in Effect of Monetary Policy', *Journal of Political Economy*, Vol. 69 (October 1961), pages 447-66.
(With David Meiselman) 'The Relative Stability of Monetary Velocity and the Investment Multiplier in the United States, 1897-1958', in *Stabilization Policies*, a series of studies prepared for the Commission on Money and Credit (Englewood Cliffs NJ: Prentice-Hall, 1963).
(With Anna Schwartz) 'Money and Business Cycles', *Review of Economics and Statistics*, Vol. 45, Part 2, Supplement (February 1963), pages 32-64.
'Interest Rates and the Demand for Money', *Journal of Law and Economics*, Vol. 9 (October 1966), pages 71-85.
'Value Judgments in Economics', in *Human Values and Economic Policy*, edited by Sidney Hook (New York: New York University Press, 1967), pages 85-93.
'The Monetary Theory and Policy of Henry Simons', *Journal of Law and Economics*, Vol. 10 (October 1967), pages 1-13.
'The Role of Monetary Policy', *American Economic Review*, Vol. 58 (March 1968), pages 1-17.

'Money: Quantity Theory', in *International Encyclopaedia of the Social Sciences* (New York: Macmillan and Free Press, 1968), pages 432-47.

'Have Monetary Policies Failed?', *American Economic Review, Papers and Proceedings*, Vol. 62 (May 1972), pages 11-18.

'Memorandum on Monetary Policy', in Treasury and Civil Service Committee, *Memoranda on Monetary Policy* (London: HMSO, Series 1979-80).

'A Monetarist View', in *Money Talks*, edited by Alan Horrox and Gillian McCredie (London: Methuen, 1983), pages 1-17.

'The Keynes Centenary: A Monetarist Reflects', *The Economist*, Vol. 287, No. 7292 (4 June 1983), pages 35-7.

OTHER IMPORTANT WORKS MENTIONED IN THE TEXT

David Hume, 'Of Money', in *Hume's Essays* (Oxford: Oxford University Press, 1963; first published, 1752).

The Report of the Bullion Committee of 1810, edited with an introduction by Eamonn Butler (London: Adam Smith Institute, 1984).

Irving Fisher, *The Purchasing Power of Money* (New York: Macmillan, 1911; revised edition, 1920; second revised edition, 1922; modern reprint, New York: Augustus M. Kelley, 1963).

John Maynard Keynes, *A Tract on Monetary Reform* (London: Macmillan, 1923).

John Maynard Keynes, *A Treatise on Money* (London: Macmillan, 1930).

John Maynard Keynes, *The General Theory of Employment, Interest, and Money* (London: Macmillan, 1936).

Don Patinkin, 'The Chicago Tradition, the Quantity Theory, and Friedman', *Journal of Money, Credit, and Banking*, Vol. 1, No. 1 (February 1969), pages 46-70.

Niels Thygesen, 'The Scientific Contributions of Milton Friedman', *Scandinavian Journal of Economics*, Vol. 79, No. 1 (1977), pages 56-98.

John Burton, 'Positively Milton Friedman', in J.R. Shackleton and Gareth Locksley, *Twelve Contemporary Economists* (London: Macmillan, 1981).

Index

Anderson, L.C., 259
Artis, M.J., 252
Austrian School, 81, 102, 126–8, 131,
    142, 149, 228, 232

Bain, A.D., 251
Banking sector
  reserve ratios, 68–77, 92, 96, 252
    100% rule, 50, 96, 182, 184, 188,
      259
  and money supply, 30, 50, 55, 74–7,
    81–2, 96, 97–100, 126
  non-bank institutions, 70, 81–2, 253
Base money, *see* Monetary base
Bonds, *see* Financial markets
Benefit ratio, 139
Borrowing, *see* Deficit
Bracket creep, *see* Fiscal drag
Brunner, Karl, 125
Bullion Committee, 25–6, 55, 251, 265
Burns, Arthur, 6
Burton, John, 21, 247, 248, 265
Butler, Eamonn, 248, 249, 250, 251, 253,
    256, 257, 262, 265

Cagan, Philip, 77, 97, 252, 253
Cambridge version, *see* Quantity theory
Central banks, 169, 183–4, *see also*
    Monetary authorities
Chicago School, 3, 7, 25, 35, 55, 249–50,
    251
Cheap money, *see* Easy money
Consumer protection, 8, 214–18
Consumption function, *see* Permanent
    income hypothesis
Credit, and money, 78–9, 168–9
Crockett, A., 253
Culbertson, J.M., 253, 258
Cycles
  business cycles, 76, 143, 150–3, 155,
    182–3
  in interest rates, 166–8
  and lags, 149–60
  and money, 66, 74, 93, 103–9, 150–2
  in prices and output, 121–2

Davis-Bacon Act, 212
Deficits
  public sector, 9, 46, 81, 95, 125–6,
    146, 163–6, 172, 183
  trade, *see* Exchange rates
Demand for money, 53–66, 169–70, 248,
    251
  demand function, 12–14, 55–64, 168–
    70
    income and, 15, 56–7, 62, 64, 169,
      248
    interest rates and, 46–7, 55, 61–2,
      93, 161, 168–70
    prices and, 55, 58, 62–4
  Keynes's view, *see* Keynes
  quantity theory and, 12, 30, 38, 55
  stability of, 12–15, 31–4, 37–8, 49, 53–
    6, 59–66, 73, 81–3, 105–9, 236
  see also Velocity
Deposits
  demand and time deposits, 68, 70–1,
    125
Deposit ratios, *see* Banking sector
  and velocity, 81–2
Depressions, 34, 48, 94, 97–102, 191
  Keynes's view, 16–17, 31–3, 175–6
  monetary nature, 100–1, 175
Director, Aaron, 7
Discrimination, 201–2
Dolan, E.G., 247

Easy money, 4, 11–12, 34, 169, 176, 231
Education, 22, 198, 219–21
Employment
  full employment, 18–19, 32, 146–8,
    175
  see also Unemployment
Equality, 218–9
Equities, *see* Financial markets
Eurocurrency, 70–1, 82
Exchange rates, 20–1, 84–90
  and monetary policy, 50, 83–4, 147,
    180
Expectations
  in demand for money, 58, 61, 63–4

and inflation, 31, 42, 93, 119–23, 140–2, 167
and unemployment, 18–20, 135–6

Federal Register, 198
Federal Reserve, 16, 69, 82, 98–101, 175, 183–4
St. Louis studies, 171–2, 259
Financial markets, 14, 60, 124, 154
Fine tuning, see Stabilization policy
Fiscal drag, 50, 130, 187
Fiscal policy, 9, 46, 81, 95, 156–9, 161–76
see also Taxation
Fisher, Irving, 26, 118, 120, 134
Free market, see market economy
Friedman, Milton
  biographical details, 3–24
    American Economic Association, 5, 17–18, 142
    conversion to monetarism, 10–11
    free-market thought, 7, 22–3, 201–25
    influence, 3–6, 5, 18, 20–1, 23, 90, 188, 192–3, 225, 246
    National Bureau of Economic Research, 7–8
    Nobel Prize, 5–6, 18
  methodology, 7, 24, 72–3, 123–4, 227–46, 261–2
    definition of money, 71–3
    macroeconomics, 238–45
    prediction, 73, 142–3, 228–33, 238–45
    values, 10, 228, 233–8
  works cited
    Capitalism and Freedom, 4, 8, 21, 22, 197–8, 250, 259, 260, 261, 263
    The Counter-Revolution in Monetary Theory, 247, 248, 249, 250, 251, 254, 263
    'The Demand for Money: Some Theoretical and Empirical Results', 248, 251, 252, 254, 255, 258, 264
    'Discussion of the Inflationary Gap', 247
    Dollars and Deficits, 17, 247, 248, 249, 250, 251, 252, 253, 254, 255, 256, 257, 259, 260, 261, 263
    An Economist's Protest, 21, 250, 260, 263

Essays in Positive Economics, 11, 247, 248, 250, 252, 253, 254, 256, 258, 259, 261, 263
Focus on Milton Friedman, 264
Free to Choose, 4, 6, 8, 21, 197–8, 224, 249, 253, 254, 256, 259, 260, 261, 264
From Galbraith to Economic Freedom, 264
'Have Monetary Policies Failed?', 260, 265
Income from Independent Professional Practice, 8, 262, 263
Inflation and Unemployment, 18, 248, 257, 264
'Interest Rates and the Demand for Money', 258, 264
'The Keynes Centenary: A Monetarist Reflects', 249, 265
'The Lag in Effect of Monetary Policy', 253, 257, 264
Milton Friedman's Monetary Framework, 21, 127, 248, 249, 250, 251, 256, 258, 261, 263
Memorandum on Monetary Policy, 253, 264
'A Monetarist View', 259, 260, 265
Monetary Correction, 256, 257, 259, 262
Monetary Versus Fiscal Policy, 250, 253, 255, 256, 258, 259, 260, 261, 263
A Monetary History of the United States, 16, 21, 76, 91, 249, 250, 251, 252, 253, 254, 256, 259, 263
Monetary Statistics of the United States, 21, 91, 252, 263
'The Monetary Theory and Policy of Henry Simons', 259, 264
Monetary Trends in the United States and the United Kingdom, 21, 91, 127, 248, 250, 251, 252, 253, 255, 256, 257
'Money and Business Cycles', 252, 254, 256, 258, 260, 264
'Money: Quantity Theory', 247, 248, 249, 250, 251, 254, 256, 259, 265
Newsweek, 3, 21, 248
The Optimum Quantity of Money and Other Essays, 17, 254, 257, 259, 263
Price Theory, 21, 262, 263

A Program for Monetary Stability, 250, 263

'The Quantity Theory of Money: A Restatement', 12, 248, 250

'The Relative Stability of Monetary Velocity and the Investment Multiplier in the United States, 1897–1958', 264

'The Role of Monetary Policy', 247, 256, 257, 259, 264

'The Role of War in American Economic Development: Price, Income and Monetary Changes in Three Wartime Periods', 254, 259, 264

Roofs or Ceilings?, 10, 263

Studies in the Quantity Theory of money, 34, 248, 249, 250, 251, 263

Taxing to Prevent Inflation, 8–9, 263

Tax Limitation, Inflation and the Role of Government, 260, 264

A Theory of the Consumption Function, 14, 105, 254, 255, 263

There's No Such Thing as a Free Lunch, 21, 263

Tyranny of the Status Quo, 21, 197–9, 224, 248, 253, 257, 260, 261, 264

Unemployment Versus Inflation?, 18, 256, 257, 258, 264

'Value Judgments in Economics', 261, 264

Friedman, Rose, 8, 197, 263, 264

Full employment, *see* Employment

Germany, 11, 31, 48, 96, 144, 192

Gold, 20, 68, 83–90, 96, 101, 150

Government
and interest groups, 223–5
and monopolies, 210–14
role and limits, 5, 22, 24, 182–7, 198–9, 205–9
see also Deficits; Monetary authorities

Gurley, J.G., 74, 252

Hahn, Frank, 256, 257

Hansen, Alvin, 56, 64, 251

Hawtrey, Ralph, 149–50, 257

Hayek, F.A., 21, 127, 144, 149–50, 248, 253, 256, 257, 261

Heller, Walter, 253, 258, 263

Hicks, Sir John, 255, 260

High-powered money, *see* Monetary base

Housing, 9–10, 221

Hume, David, 25, 55, 131, 249, 256, 265

Income
distribution, 129–30, 218–19
division between output and prices, *see* Output
and monetary factors, 15, 32, 36–7, 56, 62, 64, 93, 95, 100, 103–4, 116, 149, 153, 169, 170, 190
and wealth, 56–7, 64

Income version, *see* Quantity theory

Indexation, 50, 186–7
see also Price indexes

Inflation
cost-push, 44–5, 113–5, 255–6
definition, 247
demand-pull, 44–5, 113–5, 153–4
a 'drug', 147, 256–7
effects, 41, 122–4, 129–31, 147
ending, 80–1, 122–3, 129
export of, 88–9
monetary nature, 4, 35, 39–40, 43–5, 114–5, 145, 237
temporary stimulus, 39, 131, 178
a 'tax', 130
unemployment and, 18–20, 42–4, 131, 133–48, 231, 244

Interest rates
demand for money and, 46–7, 55, 61–2, 93, 161, 168–70
Keynesian view, 14, 32–3, 46–7, 55, 60, 166–9, 249–50
money supply and, 46–7, 75, 78–9, 166–8, 252
prices and, 94, 168
policy implications, 36, 47, 50, 166–8, 177–8, 237, 252

Johnson, Harry G., 12, 13, 146, 147

Jordan, H., 259

Jones, Homer, 6

Keynes, John Maynard (later Lord), 8–12, 23, 29–31, 55, 116, 131, 259
The General Theory of Employment, Interest and Money, 12, 14, 31, 56, 98, 265
money, views on, 16–17, 31–4, 56, 59, 109, 175–6
liquidity trap, 31–2, 63, 69
A Tract on Monetary Reform, 30, 248, 249, 256, 265
A Treatise on Money, 249, 265

Keynesian economics, 11, 23, 125, 179,
    245–6, 247, 260
  demand expenditures, 11, 16, 31, 35,
    163–4, 176
  demand for money, 31–2, 55, 108, 251
    and interest rates, 14, 32, 46–7, 55,
      166–8, 249–50
    and income, 14–15, 55
  inflationary gap, 9, 18
  liquidity trap, 12–13, 32, 60, 63–4,
    169
  methodology, 15, 227, 232–3, 239
  multiplier, 163, 166
  Phillips curve, 18, 42, 133–7, 141–4,
    147, 231, 245, 248
  prices and output, 18, 116–7, 128
  portfolio approach, 13–14, 57–9, 74,
    153–4, 174
  testing of, 16–17, 34, 91, 95–6, 100–1,
    171–4
Knight, Frank, 7
Kuznets, Simon, 7, 263

Lag, in effect of monetary policy, 40–1,
    149–60, 174, 178, 185
Lewis, M.K., 252
Liquidity trap, 12–13, 32, 60, 63–4, 169
Locke, John, 25, 249

Mack, Ruth P., 263
Mail service, 214
Market economy, 197–225
  allocative efficiency, 5, 198–201
  consumer protection in, 214–18
  discrimination reduced, 201–2
  education, 22, 219–22
  equality in, 218–19
  government in, 204–14
  housing policy, 9, 221–2
  welfare, 22–4, 222–3
Market failure, 205
  and government failure, 206
Marshall, Alfred, 29
Marxism, 208, 231–2
Meiselman, David, 15, 91, 151, 173–4,
    264
Meltzer, Allan H., 125
Mill, John Stuart, 256
Mitchell, Wesley, 7
Modigliani, Franco, 260
Monetarism, 5, 24, 35–6, 45, 116, 192
Monetary authorities
  and money supply, 68, 73, 77, 83,
    182, 185, 190

  motives and practice, 4, 18, 39–40,
    124, 187, 246
  ultimate source of inflation and
    depression, 46, 54, 80, 145
  see also Federal Reserve
Monetary base
  controls, 75, 77–8, 79–83
  high-powered money, 69–70, 75, 77,
    92, 96–7
Monetary policy
  employment and, 147 see also
    Unemployment
  expansionary, see Easy money
  Friedman's preferred, 175–93 see also
    Monetary rule
  importance of, 3, 103, 143, 161–2,
    179–81, 197
  interest rates and, 36, 47, 51, 166–8,
    177–8, 237, 252
  lags in, see Lag
  limitations, 177–9
  methods of control, 124–6
    base controls, 75, 77–8, 79–83
    credit controls, 78–9, 168
    discount rate, 80, 182
    open market operations, 79–80,
      153, 177
    reserve requirements, 80, 182
    suasion, 80
  stabilization policy and, 17–18, 157–
    60, 179–81
  see also Deficits; Money supply
Monetary rule, 11, 47–8, 160, 184–5,
    190–2, 236
Money, nature of, 13–14, 29–30, 34, 42,
    56–7, 58–60, 64, 72, 93, 103, 108
Money supply, 67–90
  banks and, see Banking sector
  controls, see Monetary policy
  creation, 54 see also Banking sector;
    Monetary policy
  cyclical variations in, 150–2
  definition of, 67–73, 92
    Friedman's definition, 62, 71–3,
      249, 250, 252
  demand deposits, see Deposits
  endogenous or exogenous nature, 30,
    73–7, 81–2, 151–2
  income and, 32, 36–8, 64, 75
  inflation and, 3, 4, 15, 75 see also
    Inflation
  interest rates and, 46–7, 75, 78–9,
    166–8, 151

output and, 19, 119–23 *see also* Output
time deposits, *see* Deposits
Monopolies, 210–3, 219, 223
Multiplier
  Keynesian, 163, 166
  money, 109, 166

National Bureau of Economic Research,
  7–8
  reference cycles, 150–3, 155
Natural rate hypothesis, *see*
  Unemployment
Negative income tax, 22, 222–3

Occupational licensure, 8, 207, 210–14
Open market operations, 79–80, 153,
  177
Output
  and monetary stimulus, 19–20, 43,
    113, 128
  and prices, 33, 39–42, 53, 61, 116–29

Patinkin, Don, 249, 251, 265
Permanent income hypothesis, 14–15,
  66, 104–9, 153–4
Phillips curve, 18, 42, 133–7, 141–4, 147,
  231, 245, 248
  see also Inflation; Unemployment
Pierce, D.G., 251, 253
Pirie, Madsen, 261
Pigou, A.C., 29
Pollution, 216–7
Portfolio analysis, 13–14, 57, 58–9, 74,
  153–4, 174
Prices
  allocative function, 22, 200–1, 245–6
  demand for money and, 55, 58, 62–4,
    85
  interest rates and, 94, 168 *see also*
    Demand for money
  of money and credit, 78–9, 168–9
  output and, 39–42, 53, 61, 116–29
  relative, 75, 114, 119, 124–9, 242–5
  supply of money and, 74–5, 84, 93,
    114–5, 172, 180, 193
  taxation and, 95
Price controls, 47–8, 144–5, 180, 206,
  211, 250
Price indexes, 36–7, 144, 241
Professions, entry into, 8, 207, 210–14
Pseudo gold standards, 86–7
Public works, 162, 205–6

Quantity theory
  Cambridge version, 29–31, 34
  early, 25–6
  empirical testing, 15–17, 61–6, 76–7,
    91–109, 151–2, 171–4
  Friedman's restatement, 3–6, 12, 15,
    34–8, 149
    a theory of demand, 12, 38, 53, 55–
      6, 61
  income version, 27–9, 31, 92
  Keynes's attack, 11, 31, 55
  transactions version, 26–7
    Fisher equation, 26–7

Ratios
  currency/deposit ratios, 74–5, 92, 98–
    100, 151
  reserve ratios, 50, 74–5, 82–3, 92 *see
    also* Banking sector
Real/nominal distinction, 36–9, 41–2,
  54, 67, 92, 113, 117–18, 124,
  147–8, 168–70, 243–5
Robertson, D.H., 29
Roosevelt, F.D., 48
Rothbard, Murray, 102, 252, 254

St. Louis studies, 171–3, 259
Schuettinger, Robert L., 250
Schulz, Henry, 7
Schwartz, Anna, 16–17, 55, 71, 91–2,
  150, 155–7, 173, 176, 252, 263, 264
Sennholz, Hans, 102, 153
Shaw, D.M., 251, 253
Shaw, E.S., 74, 252
Shaw, G.K., 253
Shoup, Carl, 263
Silk, Leonard, 247
Simons, Henry, 7, 182, 250, 251, 259
Smith, Adam, 23, 204–6, 260
Stabilization policy
  error of, 17–18, 89, 160, 161–4, 184,
    190–2, 197, 235
  Friedman's automatic system, 181–4
  lags and, 11, 49–50, 157–66, 161–4,
    178
Stagflation, 19, 35, 134
Stigler, George, 9, 260, 263
Swan, C., 258

Taxation, 8, 22–3, 46, 75, 156–7, 159,
  219, 222–4
  see also Fiscal policy; Negative income
    tax
Thompson, J.L., 251, 253, 257

Thygesen, Neils, 248, 254, 255, 258, 259, 260, 261, 265
Time deposits, *see* Deposits
Tobin, James, 55, 74, 125, 151, 252, 258, 261
Transactions version, *see* Quantity theory
Transmission mechanism
  Keynesian, 60, 116–7, 156 *see also* Financial markets
  monetarist, 38–9, 54, 59–60, 117–23, 153–5

Unemployment
  compensation, 138, 182–3
  inflation and, 18–20, 42–4, 131, 133–48, 231, 244
  natural rate hypothesis, 19, 43, 136–8, 143–8, 178
  Phillips curve, 18–19, 42, 133–8
Unions, 145–6, 210, 212–4
United Kingdom, 40, 68, 83, 90–2, 99, 101, 139, 143, 212
United States
  benefit ratio in, 139
  depressions in, 16–17, 31, 48, 97–102, 175–6, 191–2
  Federal Reserve System, 16, 69, 82, 97–100, 101–4, 175, 183–4
  gold price, 20, 86, 90, 101

  government bureaucracy in, 198, 204, 209–10, 215
  inflations in, 95–6, 172
  monetary factors in, 40, 68, 83, 91–2, 94–3, 143, 191–2, 198
  unions, 212–4

Values in economic theory, 10, 227, 233–8
Vane, H. R., 251, 253
Velocity, 26, 28–9, 53–66, 249
  cycles and, 65–8, 103–4
  definition, 53
  deposit ratios and, 81–2
  reinforcing effect, 56, 93, 103
  tests of, 65–6
  see also Demand for money
Voucher, in education, 22, 220–1

Wages, 6, 43–4, 47–8, 130–1, 138–41, 176, 212–3, 234–5
Wartime inflations, 76, 94–6, 151, 172–3
Wealth
  demand function and, 57–8, 62, 64
  distribution, 129–30, 218–9
  human and non-human, 57–8, 64
  income and, 56–7, 64
Welfare policy, 22–4, 162, 182–3, 222–3
  see also Negative income tax